Summary of Contents

D1131603

Preface xix

1. Setting Up Shop 1

2. Your First Web Pages 19

3. Adding Some Style 71

4. Shaping Up Using CSS 117

5. Picture This! Using Images on Your Web Site 177

6. Tables: Tools for Organizing Data 223

7. Forms: Interacting with Your Audience 249

8. Launching Your Web Site 307

9. Adding a Blog to Your Web Site 339

10. Pimp My Site: Cool Stuff You Can Add for Free 377

11. Where to Now? What You Could Learn Next 407

Index 425

BUILD YOUR OWN WEB SITE THE RIGHT WAY USING HTML & CSS

BY IAN LLOYD
2ND EDITION

Build Your Own Web Site The Right Way Using HTML & CSS

by Ian Lloyd

Copyright © 2008 SitePoint Pty. Ltd.

Managing Editor: Chris Wyness **Editor**: Kelly Steele
Technical Editor: Andrew Tetlaw **Index Editor**: Fred Brown
Technical Editor: Julian Carroll **Cover Design**: Alex Walker
Technical Director: Kevin Yank **Cover Image**: Lucas Chan
Printing History:

First Edition: April 2006
Second Edition: November 2008

Notice of Rights

Notice of Liability

The author and publisher have made every effort to ensure the accuracy of the information herein. However, the information contained in this book is sold without warranty, either express or implied. Neither the authors and SitePoint Pty. Ltd., nor its dealers or distributors will be held liable for any damages to be caused either directly or indirectly by the instructions contained in this book, or by the software or hardware products described herein.

Trademark Notice

Rather than indicating every occurrence of a trademarked name as such, this book uses the names only in an editorial fashion and to the benefit of the trademark owner with no intention of infringement of the trademark.

Published by SitePoint Pty. Ltd.

48 Cambridge Street
Collingwood VIC Australia 3066
Web: www.sitepoint.com
Email: business@sitepoint.com

ISBN 978-0-9804552-7-4
Printed and bound in the United States of America

About the Author

Ian Lloyd is a senior web designer/developer who works full time for a major financial services organisation in the UK on their various web sites. He is the author or co-author of a number of web development books, including SitePoint's Ultimate HTML Reference. He has also contributed articles to industry-leading sites such as A List Apart, Vitamin and .Net magazine. Ian has spoken at several high profile web conferences—including South By Southwest (SXSW) in Austin, Texas and @media in London— on his area of expertise, web accessibility, and is responsible for the respected online accessibility resource Accessify (http://accessify.com/).

Ian lives in Swindon, UK, a town that is known only for two things:

- the famous "magic roundabout"—a mega roundabout that comprises five individual but joined roundabouts

- for being that place from the television show *The Office* (thus making it second in dullness only to Slough)

That said, Ian does his best to get out of Swindon in his treasured air-cooled VW camper van (http://vwkombi.com/) whenever the opportunity (or notoriously grim British weather) allows.

Ian is married to Manda, who doesn't share the Volkswagen fascination to quite the same level but enjoys the weekend trips it affords. He takes too many photos, most of them of his dog 'Fraggle' (a mischievous Cairn Terrier), and is still waiting on that elusive lottery win which will allow them all to head off on travels around the world again.

About The Technical Editors

Andrew Tetlaw has been tinkering with web sites as a web developer since 1997. Before that, he worked as a high school English teacher, an English teacher in Japan, a window cleaner, a car washer, a kitchen hand, and a furniture salesman. He is dedicated to making the world a better place through the technical editing of SitePoint books and kits. He is also a busy father of five, enjoys coffee, and often neglects his blog at http://tetlaw.id.au/.

Julian Carroll has been designing for the Web since 1996. He manages the SitePoint Solutions (http://www.sitepoint.com.au/) team, and is a keen sampler of wine. Prior to his career as a web designer, he played bass in a rock 'n' roll band.

About SitePoint

SitePoint specializes in publishing fun, practical and easy-to-understand content for web professionals. Visit http://www.sitepoint.com/ to access our books, newsletters, articles and community forums.

For Manda, my "better half". This book would not have been possible without your continued support. All my love, Lloydi.

Table of Contents

Preface xix

   What is a Browser? xxi

   Who Should Read This Book? xxiii

   What You'll Learn from This Book xxiii

   How You'll Learn to Build Your Web Site xxiv

      HTML, Markup, CSS... Welcome to Your First Bits of Jargon! xxiv

      Building the Example Site xxvi

      What You Can Expect from the Example Web Site xxvi

   What This Book Won't Tell You xxvi

   What's in This Book? xxvii

   The Book's Web Site xxix

      The Code Archive xxix

      Updates and Errata xxix

   The SitePoint Forums xxx

   The SitePoint Newsletters xxx

   Your Feedback xxxi

   Acknowledgements xxxi

   Conventions Used in This Book xxxii

Chapter 1   **Setting Up Shop** 1

   The Basic Tools You Need 2

      Windows Basic Tools 3

      Mac OS X Basic Tools 5

   Beyond the Basic Tools 6

      Windows Tools 7

      Mac OS X Tools 8

   Not Just Text, Text, Text 9

Windows Tools 11

Mac OS X Tools 12

Creating a Spot for Your Web Site 14

Windows 14

Mac OS X 16

Getting Help 17

Summary 18

Chapter 2   **Your First Web Pages** 19

Nice to Meet You, XHTML 19

Anatomy of a Web Page 19

Viewing the Source 20

Basic Requirements of a Web Page 22

The Doctype 23

The `html` Element 24

The `head` Element 26

The `title` Element 27

`meta` Elements 28

Other `head` Elements 30

The `body` Element 30

The Most Basic Web Page in the World 31

Headings and Document Hierarchy 33

Paragraphs 34

For People Who Love Lists 34

Commenting Your HTML 36

Symbols 39

Diving into Our Web Site 40

The Homepage: the Starting Point for All Web Sites 41

Splitting Up the Page 57

Linking Between Our New Pages 62

The `blockquote` (Who Said That?) 66

The `cite` Element 68

`strong` and `em` 68

Taking a Break 69

Summary 70

Chapter 3   Adding Some Style 71

What is CSS? 72

Inline Styles 72

Adding Inline Styles 73

The `span` Element 74

Embedded Styles 76

Jargon Break 77

Why Embedded Styles Are Better than Inline Styles 77

External Style Sheets 78

Why External Style Sheets Are Better than Embedded Styles 78

Creating an External CSS File 79

Linking CSS to a Web Page 80

Starting to Build Our Style Sheet 81

Stylish Headings 84

A Mixture of New Styles 86

A New Look in a Flash! 88

A Beginner's Palette of Styling Options 91

Recap: the Style Story so Far 93

Looking at Elements in Context 97

Contextual Selectors 100

Grouping Styles 101

Which Rule Wins? 103

Recapping Our Progress 104

Styling Links 104

Class Selectors 109

Styling Partial Text Using span 113

Summary 115

Chapter 4   Shaping Up Using CSS 117

Block-level Elements vs Inline Elements 118

Block-level Elements 118

Inline Elements 120

Inline Begets Inline 121

Inline Elements Can Never Contain Block-level Elements 122

Recap: Block-level and Inline Elements 123

Styling Inline and Block-level Elements 123

Sizing Up the Blocks 124

Setting a Width 124

Setting a Height 125

Adding Borders to Block-level Elements 128

Example Borders 129

Styling Individual Sides of an Element 133

Shorthand Border Styles 134

Border Styles You Can Use 135

Recap: What Have We Learned? 136

Shaping and Sizing Our Diving Site 136

Adding Padding 142

Introducing Padding to the Project Site 144

Margins 145

The Box Model 146

Positioning Elements Anywhere You Like! 148

Showing the Structure 148

Absolute Positioning 151

What We've Achieved: Full CSS Layout 162

Other Layout Options 162

    More Absolute Positioning 162

    Relative Positioning 164

    Floated Positioning 168

Styling Lists 174

Summary 176

Chapter 5 Picture This! Using Images on Your Web Site 177

Inline Images 178

    Anatomy of the Image Element 178

    Web Accessibility 180

GIF vs JPG vs PNG 183

Transparency 184

    PNG: King of Transparency 185

Adding an Image Gallery to the Site 187

    Updating the Navigation 187

    Adding the New Gallery Page 188

    Adding the First Image 189

    Formatting the Picture using CSS 191

    Captioning the Picture 193

Basic Image Editing 198

    Image Cropping 198

    Special Effects 203

    Resizing Large Images 204

    Other Software 206

Filling up the Gallery 206

Sourcing Images for Your Web Site 209

Background Images in CSS 210

    Repeated Patterns 210

Non-repeating Images 214

Shorthand Backgrounds 216

Fixed Heights and Widths 216

Setting a Background for Our Navigation 218

Summary 222

Chapter 6   Tables: Tools for Organizing Data

Chapter 6   **Tables: Tools for Organizing Data** 223

What is a Table? 224

Anatomy of a Table 228

Styling the Table 230

Borders, Spacing, and Alignment 230

Making Your Tables Accessible 233

Linearization 233

summary 234

Captioning your Table 234

Recap 235

Adding an Events Table 235

Stylish Table Cells 241

Advanced Tables 242

Merging Table Cells 242

Advanced Accessibility 244

Summary 246

Chapter 7   Forms: Interacting with Your Audience

Chapter 7   **Forms: Interacting with Your Audience** 249

Anatomy of a Form 250

A Simple Form 251

The Building Blocks of a Form 252

The `form` Element 252

The `fieldset` and `legend` Elements 254

The `label` Element 255

The `input` Element 255

The `select` Element 262

The `textarea` Element 264

Submit Buttons 265

The Default Control Appearance 266

Building a Contact Page 268

Editing the Contact Us Page 269

Adding a `form` and a `fieldset` Element 270

Styling `fieldset` and `legend` with CSS 272

Adding Text Input Controls 274

Tidying up `label` Elements with CSS 278

Adding a `select` Element 280

Adding a `textarea` Element 282

Adding Radio Buttons and Checkboxes 284

Completing the Form: a Submit Button 286

What Have We Achieved? 289

Processing the Form 289

Signing Up for Form Processing 290

Inserting the Form Code 293

Feedback by Email 303

Summary 305

Chapter 8   Launching Your Web Site 307

The Client–Server Model 307

Web Hosting Jargon 309

Hosting Your Web Site—Finding Server Space 309

Free Hosting—with a Catch! 310

Free Hosting—with a Domain Name at Cost 311

What is Web Forwarding? 311

The Downsides of Web Forwarding 312

Paying for Web Hosting 314

Hosting Essentials 314

FTP Access to Your Server 314

Adequate Storage Space 315

A Reasonable Bandwidth Allowance 317

Hosting Nice-to-haves 318

Email Accounts 318

Server Side Includes (SSIs) 319

Support for Scripting Languages and Databases 319

Pre-flight Check—How Do Your Pages Look in Different Browsers? . . . 321

Uploading Files to Your Server 321

FTP Settings 322

Uploading with FileZilla for Windows 322

Uploading with Cyberduck—Mac OS X 327

Other Uploading Tools 329

Recap—Where's Your Site At? 330

Checking Links 330

Validating Your Web Pages 331

Promoting Your Web Site 335

Submit Your Web Site to Search Engines 336

Tell Your Friends and Colleagues 337

Craft an Email Signature with Your Web Site Details 337

Post on a Related Forum 337

Link Exchange 338

Summary 338

Chapter 9   **Adding a Blog to Your Web Site** ... 339

Where to Set up a Blog 340

Signing up for Blogger 343

How Blogger Creates a Web Page 352

Customizing Your Blogger Template 354

    Merging the Blogger Code with Your Existing Web Page 358

Tidying up the Blogger Template 364

    Blog Comments 364

    Validating Your Blog 369

Managing Your Blogger Posts 372

Encouraging Others to Contribute to Your Blog 374

Summary 376

Chapter 10   **Pimp My Site: Cool Stuff You Can Add for Free** 377

Getting the Low-down on Your Visitors 378

    Choosing a Statistics Service 379

    Registering a Google Account 380

    Adding the Statistics Code to Your Web Pages 386

A Search Tool for Your Site 390

Searching by Genre 393

Adding a Blogroll to Your Web Site 399

    Signing up for a Blogroll 399

    Integrating the Blogroll with Your Web Site 402

Discussion Forums 404

Summary 405

Chapter 11   Where to Now? What You Could Learn Next 407

   Improving Your XHTML 408

      The Official Documentation 409

      Other Useful XHTML Resources 410

   Advancing Your CSS Knowledge 412

      The Official Documentation 413

      The Ultimate CSS Reference 414

      HTML Dog 415

      CSS Discussion Lists 415

      Other CSS Resources 416

      The CSS Discuss List's Companion Site 418

   Learning JavaScript 419

   Learning Server-side Programming 421

      Scripting Languages in Brief 422

   Learning PHP 423

      Where Can You Learn PHP? 424

   Summary 424

Index 425

Preface

Congratulations on buying this book. Oh, wait a minute—perhaps you haven't yet. Perhaps you've just picked up the book in your local bookshop, and are trying to decide whether it's right for you. Why should this be the book that makes it into your shopping basket? The answer can be found in the title of the book. It's all about getting it right the first time and not learning bad habits—bad habits that you have to unlearn at a later date—for the purpose of a quick result.

Let's take a step back for a moment, and look at another skill that many people learn at some point in their lives: learning to drive. Apologies if that particular experience is also new to you, but stick with me. For many people, their first driving lessons can be very confusing; they have to figure out which pedals to press, in what order, and manage to drive off without hitting anything. Meanwhile, other more experienced people just jump into their cars, start the engine, and drive from A to B without really thinking about what they're doing. These drivers may have picked up a few bad habits along the way, but if they learned with a proper driving instructor, the chances are they were taught properly from the beginning—following a strict set of rules to ensure they stayed safe.

The driving instructor tells you to check your mirrors diligently, observe speed limits, and avoid cutting corners (literally as well as metaphorically!). Imagine, though, if the instructor told you not to worry about the speed limit signs, to *put your foot down* because the road is clear, or told you that the one-way sign "wasn't all that important at that time of night." It'd be a miracle if you passed your driving test, and the chances are that those bad habits would stay with you (so long as you could manage to keep your license).

Learning to build web pages can be a bit like that.

I've been designing and building web sites for around ten years now, but I can clearly remember the joy of creating my first site. Admittedly, in hindsight, it was a pretty nasty-looking web site, but it achieved the goal at the time—I had published a web site, and I was able to create it with the bare minimum of tools. It gave me an enormous sense of achievement, and made me want to learn more and create even better web sites.

At the time, there was a limited amount of books available that seemed to provide what I wanted, but I lapped up everything I could find, learning some tricks from books, and gaining other ideas from visiting web sites. But then I discovered that I'd been doing it all wrong. The books I had learned from had given me what later turned out to be poor advice; the web sites I'd visited had been built by people learning from the same sources and hence, making use of similar, bad techniques. So, what had gone wrong?

In the early days of the web, when people first started properly to embrace the technology, to publish homepages, and to develop online corporate presences for their companies, they all realized fairly quickly that the medium was limited. Necessity is the mother of invention, though. So, web developers began to coax tricks and displays out of their web pages that were never intended by the technologies they used; the browsers helped them along the way by adding features that offered even more opportunities for this kind of behavior.

Numerous books have been written on the topics of web design and programming, as have many free tutorials that you can read on the web. Many of them were written during those heady years, and were based on what seemed like best practices back then; however, their authors were constrained by browsers that often rendered the same well-designed pages in vastly different ways. This meant that the tutorials' authors needed to resort to *abusing* various features of those browsers, such as using data tables to lay out pages. This certainly encouraged many people to build their first web pages, but it ensured that bad habits were ingrained at an early stage, and many people are still using these bad practices years later.

Web developers the world over have learned bad habits (myself included) and must now try to unlearn them all. There's no longer a need for these practices—they often produce pages that are inflexible, slow to download, and difficult to maintain—but like the badly taught driver who insists on flouting the rules because it's worked for him so far, many developers find these outdated habits difficult to break.

I saw the light many years ago, and have tried to educate as many people as possible since. But for the eager beginner, those same old books are still peddling the same bad old ideas. This just *has* to stop. And it stops here and now.

You're not going to learn any bad habits in this book. Not one.

In this book, you'll learn the right way to build a web site. If there's a wrong way to do things—a way that cuts corners to save time but encourages bad techniques—we won't even tell you about it. Not even as a "by the way, you might try this…" You won't need to avert your eyes—we'll take care of that for you!

What is a Browser?

If you use Microsoft Windows XP or Vista, the browser is probably what you know as the "little blue e on the desktop" (shown in Figure 1), but is commonly called Internet Explorer. The majority of people don't stray beyond using this program for the purposes of viewing web pages—for many, Internet Explorer *is* the Internet.

Internet Explorer 6 icon

Internet Explorer 7 & 8 icon

Figure 1. Internet Explorer—the "little blue e on the desktop"

Internet Explorer (or **IE**, as we'll refer to it from now on) is the most commonly used browser, largely because Microsoft included it as part of the Windows operating system as far back as Windows 95. (This was later to come back and haunt Microsoft: it became the catalyst for a massive anti-trust trial, which ruled that the company had stifled competition by bundling IE with the operating system to the exclusion of all others.)

However, there are other browsers that you can use instead of IE. Still riding a wave of popularity is Firefox,[1] an alternative browser with a number of attractive features that aren't available in IE (at the time of writing), and handles the features of some web pages better than IE can. Firefox is also available for Windows, Mac OS X, and Linux operating systems; IE, however, is only available for Windows operating systems. The screen shots you'll see in this book were taken using Firefox on Windows XP, unless stated otherwise. Because of the cross-platform nature of Firefox and the excellent standards support, I recommend that you download a copy of Firefox for the purposes of working through the exercises in this book.

---

[1] http://www.mozilla.com/firefox/

Alternatively, you might like to try another browser that supports web standards (we'll cover this soon) well. For Windows users, Opera's web browser[2] offers excellent standards support and its own unique set of features (it also has a very loyal following) and, like Firefox, it can be freely downloaded. Mac users can also use the Opera browser, the Firefox-like Camino[3], or simply stick with the Apple browser that is installed by default, Safari[4], which again offers excellent support for web standards. A selection of Mac browser icons appears in Figure 2.

Finally, there's one more browser that you may want to try out—or perhaps you're already putting it through its paces—and that browser is Chrome,[5] courtesy of Google. As I sit writing and updating this chapter, Chrome is the newest, freshest browser available; it's even has that "new browser smell." Okay, so it's not quite the same as a new car smell! But the point is that this browser is literally just *days* old as I write, and currently only available for Windows XP/Vista. By the time you read this, there may also be versions available for Mac OS X and Linux (Google has promised they're on the way), and initial reviews of the browser seem very good too.

Figure 2. There are numerous browsers that you can try for free, as shown by the Mac dock in the image below

Happy with the browser you're currently using? Well, if you're a Windows user and don't want to try a different browser just yet, you can still use IE—as indeed the majority of people using the web still do. In fact, you can be sure that everything you read here will work in all recent browsers, whatever your choice, without any real hiccups.

---

[2] http://www.opera.com/download/
[3] http://caminobrowser.org/
[4] http://apple.com/safari/
[5] http://www.google.com/chrome/

Who Should Read This Book?

Does this sound like you?

- an absolute beginner—at least as far as creating web pages go
- confident with using a computer, but not necessarily a *power user*
- someone who uses the Web a lot, enjoys other people's web sites, and would like to create your own for one of your hobbies, or for a community you belong to
- quickly put off by the techno-babble that computer people tend to speak when you try to discuss a technical problem
- perhaps a little daunted about learning this new skill, but still keen to learn (with some friendly hand-holding)

If any of the above descriptions strikes a chord with you, then this is the book to put in your shopping cart. We'll ease you in gently, and have you building web pages like a pro in no time!

There's no need to worry if you feel the terminology that your 15-year-old nephew keeps spouting is beyond you when you ask him about building web sites. I've assumed no prior knowledge of any of these terms, and I'll be guiding you all the way through the process of creating a web site from scratch. By the end of this book, you'll know how to build the site, obtain some hosting, promote the site, and keep it running once it's live.

The best part is this: what you learn in this book, you'll never have to unlearn. You'll be learning how to build sites the right way from the get-go.

What You'll Learn from This Book

By the time you finish reading this book and trying out the exercises contained within, you'll be able to build a complete web site—the right way—without incurring any costs for expensive software or web hosting.

Using an example web site, I'll guide you through the process of developing web pages from scratch. From these humble beginnings, great things will evolve! By the end of the book, you'll be able to create a web site that includes the following features:

- easy-to-use navigation
- a professional-looking site header
- a regularly updated news/events section
- a *Contact Us* page
- tables—the presentation of data in neatly organized grids
- attractive web page forms
- a simple image gallery
- a search engine that covers your site, as well as related sites
- simple statistics that you can use, for example, to see who's using your site, how they found your site, and so on

You'll also learn how to manage your web site effectively, without it becoming a chore or too technical. I'll show you how you can:

- establish your own dot-com (or dot-net, dot-org, or the like) web address
- find a place to host your web site
- upload your files to your web site
- gain feedback from visitors while avoiding spam emails

How You'll Learn to Build Your Web Site

This book will take you through each new topic using a step-by-step approach. It provides a mixture of examples and practical exercises that will soon have you feeling confident enough to try a little **HTML** for yourself.

HTML, Markup, CSS... Welcome to Your First Bits of Jargon!

From here on in, you're going to see these phrases more and more. But what do they mean?

HTML

HTML stands for HyperText Markup Language. It's the primary language that's used to create web pages, so you'll come to know it very well through the course of this book. We'll be using XHTML syntax in the example web site, an updated version of HTML (the difference between HTML and XHTML is explained in the SitePoint HTML Reference[6]).

Markup

Imagine, if you will, that you're a newspaper editor. You've been passed a news story, but the text—from the heading through to the conclusion—is all the same size, and the headings, paragraphs, quotes, and other features of the text are not clearly indicated. It's just one big block of text. For starters, you'd probably want to emphasize the headline, maybe by displaying it in bold or italic text (or in caps with an exclamation mark if you were working for a tabloid). As an editor, you'd probably grab a pen and start scribbling annotations on the printout: an *h* here to signify a heading, a *p* here, there, and everywhere to show where paragraphs start and end, and a *q* to denote quotations.

This is essentially what markup is—a set of simple tags that suggest the structure of a document: this section is a heading, paragraph, quote, and so on. We'll cover the various tags that HTML uses in detail a little later.

 Markup isn't Computer Code

Markup is not the same as *code*. Often, people incorrectly refer to markup as code, but code goes beyond the basic abilities of markup. With code, you can create programs, and make your web page more dynamic, while markup simply deals with the page's structure. So, if you want to impress your friends and relatives, refer to it as markup rather than code. See, we told you we'd teach you good habits!

CSS

CSS stands for Cascading Style Sheets. We'll be using a combination of XHTML and CSS to create web sites. CSS is a language that lets you control how your web pages look, but we'll go over that in more detail later. For now, it's important that you know what the abbreviation stands for.

Web Standards

Web Standards advocate best practices for building web sites. Whilst the term Web Standards may be used to describe a range of philosophies and specifica-

---

[6] http://reference.sitepoint.com/html/html-vs-xhtml

tions, most frequently we are referring to the recommendations published by the World Wide Web Consortium (**W3C**).

At a practical level, compliance (or adherence) to web standards, refers to the development of web pages that validate according to the W3C recommendations, like those for HTML, XHTML or CSS, or to the guidelines for accessibility.

Building the Example Site

All examples presented in this book are backed up with a sample of the markup you need to write, and a screen shot that shows how the results should look.

Each example is complete: nothing's missing. You'll see the picture build gradually, so you won't be left trying to guess how the example web site arrived at the point it's at. The files we'll use in all the examples are provided in a separate code archive (described in more detail in a moment).

What You Can Expect from the Example Web Site

- a fun web site project that will be built up through the chapters
- a complete web site that demonstrates all the features you're likely to need in your own web site
- all the XHTML and CSS used to build the site in a single download

You can pick up the project at any point, so mistakes you might have made in a previous chapter's exercises won't come back to haunt you!

What This Book Won't Tell You

While it might be tempting to cram everything into one book and claim that the reader will learn everything in 24 hours, the truth is that this isn't necessarily the right approach for everyone.

This book won't try to force-feed you everything there is to know about creating web pages; instead, it focuses on the most useful aspects that you'll find yourself using over and over again.

This book does *not* cover:

- JavaScript

- server-based programming/scripting languages, for example, ASP, PHP, Ruby
- advanced CSS techniques
- search engine optimization techniques

By the time you've finished this book and have had a chance to tackle your own web site, you might want to take the next steps to increasing your site-building knowledge. I'll make recommendations where appropriate throughout the book, and suggest other resources that you might like to check out.

So, this is where the introductory bits end and the process of learning begins—learning how to build web sites the *right* way. So step this way, ladies and gentlemen …

What's in This Book?

Chapter 1: *Setting Up Shop*

In this chapter, we'll make sure that you have all the tools you're going to need to build your web site. I'll explain where you can access the right tools—all of them for free! By the chapter's end, you'll be ready to get cracking on your first web site.

Chapter 2: *Your First Web Pages*

Here, we'll learn what makes a web page. We'll explore XHTML, understand the basic requirements of every web page, and investigate the common elements that you'll see on many web pages. Then, you'll start to create pages yourself. In fact, by the end of this chapter, you'll have the beginnings of your first web site.

Chapter 3: *Adding Some Style*

Now we'll start to add a bit of polish to the web pages we created in Chapter 2. You'll learn what CSS is, and why it's a good technology, before putting it into action for yourself. As the chapter progresses, you'll see the project web site start to take shape as we apply background and foreground colors, change the appearance of text, and make web links look different according to whether they've been visited or not.

Chapter 4: *Shaping Up with CSS*

This chapter builds on Chapter 3's introduction to the color and text-styling abilities of CSS to reveal what CSS can do for border styles and page layouts in general. First, we'll review the full range of border effects that you can apply to elements such as headings and paragraphs. We'll experiment with dotted borders, and big, bold borders, as well as some slightly more subtle effects. In the second half of the chapter, we'll learn how it's possible to use CSS to position the elements of a web page—including blocks of navigation—anywhere on the screen.

Chapter 5: *Picture this! Using Images on Your Web Site*

As the chapter title suggests, this one's all about images. We'll discover the difference between inline images and background images, and look into the issue of making images accessible for blind or visually impaired web surfers. We'll also learn how to adjust pictures to suit your web site using the software that we downloaded in Chapter 1. Then we put all this knowledge together in a practical sense to create a photo gallery for the project site.

Chapter 6: *Tables: Tools for Organizing Data*

Here, we'll learn when tables should be used and, perhaps more importantly, when they should *not* be used. Once the basics are out of the way, I'll show how you can breathe life into an otherwise dull-looking table—again, using CSS—to make it more visually appealing.

Chapter 7: *Forms: Interacting with Your Audience*

In Chapter 7, we learn all about forms—what they're used for, what's required to build a form, and what you can do with the data you collect through your form. I'll teach you what the different form elements—such as text inputs, checkboxes, and so on—do, and show you how to use CSS to make a form look more attractive. Finally—and other books may not explain this—I'll show you how you can use a free web service to have the data that's entered into your form emailed to you.

Chapter 8: *Launching Your Web Site*

It's all well and good to build a web site for fun, but you need a way for people to see it—that's what this chapter is all about. We'll learn about hosting plans, discuss the pros and cons of using free services, and look at the tools you'll need in order to transfer your files from your computer at home to a web server for the world to see.

Chapter 9: *Adding a Blog to Your Web Site*

Blogging's one of the best ways to keep your web site's content fresh and ever-changing. In this chapter, you'll learn what a blog is (that's always a good start), and how you can set one up for yourself. We'll also spend some time making sure it looks consistent with the rest of your web site.

Chapter 10: *Pimp My Site: Cool Stuff You Can Add for Free*

You've heard of the MTV reality program *Pimp My Ride*, right? No? Well, every week, these guys take an everyday car and transform it—with some well-placed and carefully executed cosmetic touches—into a real head-turner of a vehicle. And that's the aim of this chapter for your web site! You'll discover that there are all kinds of tools, plugins, and add-ons that you can build into your web site to make it even more useful for you and your visitors. Among the tools on offer we'll find site search facilities, statistics programs, and online discussion forums.

Chapter 11: *Where to Now? What You Can Learn Next*

In this final chapter, we summarize the skills that you've learned in this book, then consider your options for expanding on these. I'll recommend web sites that I feel can take you to that next level, and books that really should be on your bookshelf—or rather, open on your desk next to your computer! I want to ensure you continue to learn the good stuff once you've put this book down.

The Book's Web Site

Located at http://www.sitepoint.com/books/html2/, the web site supporting this book will give you access to the following facilities:

The Code Archive

As you progress through the text, you'll note a number of references to the code archive. This is a downloadable ZIP archive that contains complete code for all the examples presented in the book. It also includes a copy of the Bubble Under web site, which we use as an example throughout the book.

Updates and Errata

No book is perfect, and I expect that watchful readers will be able to spot at least one or two mistakes before the end of this one. The Errata page, at http://www.sitepoint.com/books/html2/errata.php on the book's web site, will always have the latest information about known typographical and code errors, and necessary updates for new browser releases and versions of web standards.

The SitePoint Forums

If you'd like to communicate with me or anyone else on the SitePoint publishing team about this book, you should join the SitePoint Forums.[7] In fact, you should join that community even if you *don't* want to talk to us, because there are a lot of fun and experienced web designers and developers hanging out there. It's a good way to learn new stuff, have your questions answered (unless you really enjoy waiting on a corporate tech support line), and just have fun.

The SitePoint Newsletters

In addition to books like this one, SitePoint offers free email newsletters.

The weekly *SitePoint Tech Times* covers the latest news, product releases, trends, tips, and techniques for all technical aspects of web development. The long-running *SitePoint Tribune* is a weekly digest of the business and moneymaking aspects of the Web. Whether you're a freelance developer looking for tips to score that dream contract, or a marketing major striving to keep abreast of major search engine changes, this is the newsletter for you. *The SitePoint Design View* is a monthly compilation of the best in web design. From new CSS layout methods to subtle Photoshop techniques, SitePoint's chief designer shares his years of experience in its pages. *The SitePoint Community Crier* is the newsletter of the SitePoint Forums, where over 150,000 web professionals and enthusiasts keep abreast of all SitePoint community matters. Finally, *The SitePoint Market Watch* comes out twice a month with a focus on purchasing and selling web real estate.

Browse the archives or sign up to any of SitePoint's free newsletters at http://www.sitepoint.com/newsletter/.

---

[7] http://www.sitepoint.com/forums/

Your Feedback

If you can't find your answer through the forums, or you wish to contact me for any other reason, the best place to write is books@sitepoint.com. We have a well-staffed email support system set up to track your inquiries, and if our support staff are unable to answer your question, they send it straight to me. Suggestions for improvement, as well as any mistakes you may find are especially welcome.

Acknowledgements

While writing a book sometimes seems like a solitary process, the truth is that there are a lot of people who indirectly guide—or have guided—the hands that type the words on these pages. None of this would have been possible had I not been pointed in the direction of influential and persuasive web sites like webmonkey.com[8], whose CSS tutorial first made me see the light, and individuals such as Jeffrey Zeldman, Molly Holzschlag, and Eric Meyer, whose pioneering work has benefited me (and many others) greatly. However, if I were to list the names of all the people who have inspired me in any way, shape, or form in the last few years, this section would end up looking more like an index! You folks know who you are, keep up the good work!

I would like to acknowledge the work undertaken by the Web Standards Project (of which I am also a member, albeit a pretty inactive one for the last couple of years), and give a little shout-out to my fellow *Britpackers*—wear those Union Jack pants with pride, folks!

Thanks to all those at SitePoint who have helped me in the crafting of this book, particularly to Simon Mackie, my main point of contact and sounding board, and my expert reviewer for the first edition, Marc Garrett—your comments were always on target. Thanks to Matthew Magain, Andrew Tetlaw, and Julian Carroll, who tech edited the book—I hope I didn't leave you much to correct or find fault with! And then of course there's Georgina Laidlaw and Kelly Steele, who ensured that any peculiarly British turns of phrases were removed, despite my best efforts to sneak a few in.

---

[8] http://www.webmonkey.com/

Finally, thanks to Manda for putting up with me when deadlines loomed and I all but shut myself off from civilization to have the chapters in on time. Social life? Oh that! I remember … At those times it seemed like it would never end, but finally we can both see the fruits of my labor.

Conventions Used in This Book

You'll notice that we've used certain typographic and layout styles throughout this book to signify different types of information. Look out for the following:

Markup Samples

Any markup—be that HTML or CSS—will be displayed using a fixed-width font, like so:

webpage.html (excerpt)

```
<h1>A perfect summer's day</h1>
<p>It was a lovely day for a walk in the park. The birds were
    singing and the kids were all back at school.</p>
```

If the code may be found in the book's code archive, the name of the file will appear at the top of the program listing, like this:

example.css

```
.footer {
  background-color: #CCC;
  border-top: 1px solid #333;
}
```

If only part of the file is displayed, this is indicated by the word *excerpt*:

example.css (excerpt)

```
  border-top: 1px solid #333;
```

If additional code is to be inserted into an existing example, the new code will be displayed in bold:

```
.footer {
  background-color: #CCC;
  border-top: 1px solid #333;
  padding: 5px;
}
```

Also, where existing code is required for context, rather than repeat all the code, a vertical ellipsis will be displayed:

```
.footer {
  ⋮
  margin: 5px;
}
```

Some lines of code are intended to be entered on one line, but we've had to wrap them because of page constraints. A ➥ indicates a line break that exists for formatting purposes only, and should be ignored:

```
URL.open("http://www.sitepoint.com/blogs/2007/05/28/user-style-she
➥ets-come-of-age/");
```

Menus

When you need to select an option from a menu, it'll be written as **File** > **Save**; this means "select the **Save** option from the **File** menu."

Tips, Notes, and Warnings

Hey, You!

Tips will give you helpful little pointers.

Ahem, Excuse Me ...

Notes are useful asides that are related—but not critical—to the topic at hand. Think of them as extra tidbits of information.

Make Sure You Always ...

... pay attention to these important points.

 Watch Out!

Warnings will highlight any gotchas that are likely to trip you up along the way.

Setting Up Shop

Before you dive in and start to build your web site, we need to take a little time to get your computer set up and ready for the work that lies ahead. That's what this chapter is all about: ensuring that you have all the tools you need installed and are ready to go.

If you were to look at the hundreds of computing books for sale in your local bookstore, you could be forgiven for thinking that you'd need to invest in a lot of different programs to build a web site. However, the reality is that most of the tools you need are probably sitting there on your computer, tucked away somewhere you wouldn't think to look for them. And if ever you don't have the tool for the job, there's almost certain to be one or more free programs available that can handle the task.

We've made the assumption that you already have an Internet connection, most likely broadband (or similar). Don't worry if you have a slower connection: it won't affect any of the tasks we'll undertake in this book. It will, however, mean that some of the suggested downloads or uploads may take longer to complete, but you probably knew that already.

Planning, Schmanning

At this point, it might be tempting to look at your motives for building a web site. Do you have a project plan? What objectives do you have for the site?

While you probably have some objectives, and some idea of how long you want to spend creating your site, we're going to gloss over the nitty-gritty of project planning to some extent. This is not to say that project planning isn't an important aspect to consider, but we're going to assume that because you've picked up a book entitled *Build Your Own Web Site The Right Way*, you probably want to just get right into the building part.

As this is your first web site and it will be a fairly simple one, we can overlook some of the more detailed aspects of site planning. Later, once you've learned—and moved beyond—the basics of building a site, you may feel ready to tackle a larger, more technically challenging site. When that time comes, proper planning will be a far more important aspect of the job. But now, let's gear up to build our first, simple site.

The Basic Tools You Need

As I mentioned earlier, many of the tools you'll need to build your first web site are already on your computer. So, what tools *do* you need?

- The primary—and most basic—tool that you'll need is a **text editor**; a program that allows you to edit plain text files. You'll use this to write your web pages.

- Once you've written a web page, you can see how it looks in a **web browser**—that's the application you use to view web sites.

- Finally, when you're happy with your new web page, you can put it on the Internet using an **FTP client**—a utility that allows you to transfer files across the Internet using the File Transfer Protocol. Using FTP may seem a little complicated at first, but thankfully you won't need to do it too often. We'll discuss FTP clients in detail in Chapter 8.

You've already got most of these programs on your computer, so let's go and find them.

Windows Basic Tools

In the following section—and indeed the rest of this book—where we refer to the Windows operating system, that's really a shorthand way of saying Windows *Vista* (in all its confusing varieties). Any instructions and screen shots will be with Vista in mind. However, we are not going to shut out all you Windows XP users—and there are many people out there who use XP in preference to Vista, much to Microsoft's displeasure—so where instructions provided for Vista are not the same for XP, we'll cover the differences for you.

Your Text Editor: Notepad

The first tool we'll consider is the text editor. Windows comes with a very simple text editor called Notepad. Many professional web designers who use complicated software packages first started out many years ago using Notepad; indeed, many professionals who have expensive pieces of software that should be time-savers still resort to using Notepad for many tasks. Why? Well, because it's so simple, little can go wrong. It also loads much more quickly than fully-featured web development programs. Bells and whistles are definitely not featured.

You can find Notepad in the **Start** menu: go to **Start** > **All Programs** > **Accessories**.

Shortcut to Notepad

To save yourself navigating to this location each time you want to open Notepad, create a shortcut on your desktop. With the **Start** menu open to display Notepad's location, hold down the **Ctrl** key, click and hold down the mouse button, then drag the Notepad icon to your desktop. When you release the mouse button, a shortcut to the application will appear on your desktop, as in Figure 1.1.

Notepad

Figure 1.1. Creating a shortcut to Notepad

Notepad is the most basic of applications, as you can see from Figure 1.2.

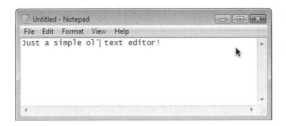

Figure 1.2. Notepad: a contender for the world's plainest program?

Your Web Browser: Internet Explorer

Once you've created a web page using Notepad, you'll need a way to view the results of your handiwork. You'll remember that in the preface to this book, we mentioned Internet Explorer (IE). Well, that's your viewer. As Figure 1.3 shows, Internet Explorer sits right there in the **Start** menu, also in the **Programs** folder (accessed via **All Programs** from the **Start** menu), in the **Quick Launch** area (bottom left of the Start menu, near the Windows logo), and a shortcut may also lurk on your desktop.

Figure 1.3. Internet Explorer: there's no hiding this browser!

Mac OS X Basic Tools

Like Windows, the Mac operating system (specifically OS X; we won't be looking at previous versions of the Mac OS) has a number of tools that you can use straight out of the box. These tools are virtually equivalent to the Windows programs mentioned above.

Your Text Editor: TextEdit

While Windows has Notepad, the Mac has TextEdit, which can be found in the **Applications** folder, as Figure 1.4 illustrates.

Figure 1.4. TextEdit comes as part of Mac OS X's default installation

Unlike Notepad, TextEdit works as a rich text editor by default, which means we can work with fonts, make text bold and italic, and so on. However, we want to work with TextEdit as a plain text editor, so you'll need to adjust some of TextEdit's preferences. Start TextEdit, then select **TextEdit > Preferences** from the menu to bring up the **Preferences** screen. Select **Plain text** within **New Document Attributes**, then close the **Preferences** screen. The next time you create a new file in TextEdit, it will be a plain text document.

Your Web Browser: Safari

The default browser for Mac users is Safari. You can usually find Safari in the **dock** (the dock is the bar of icons at the bottom of your screen), but you can also access it through the Applications folder, as Figure 1.5 illustrates.

Figure 1.5. Safari is available via Mac's Applications folder

 Stick It in the Dock

Just as you can drag shortcuts to programs onto the Windows desktop, you can add programs to the dock in Mac OS X. To add a program to the dock, just drag its icon from the Applications folder onto the dock, and presto! The application is now easily accessible whenever you need it.

If you are using a slightly older Mac, you may also have a copy of Internet Explorer installed. Our advice for Internet Explorer for Mac? Send it to Trash. The Mac version of IE was abandoned by Microsoft many years ago, so it's considerably outdated and is rarely supported or used in the wider world; no new Macs come with this application preinstalled. It also bears no real resemblance to its Windows counterpart, for those more comfortable using IE.

Beyond the Basic Tools

You can certainly make a good start using the tools mentioned above. However, once you're dealing with a handful of web pages and other resources, you may want to go beyond these basic tools. We'll show you how to use some slightly more advanced applications later in the book.

Countless other text editors and web browsers are available for download, and many of them are free. Obviously, we don't have time to describe each and every one of them, so I've settled on a few options that have worked for me in the past, and which you might like to download and have at your disposal. And remember, they're all free!

Windows Tools

NoteTab

NoteTab's tabbed interface lets you have many different files open simultaneously without cluttering up your screen, as Figure 1.6 illustrates. Files that you've opened are remembered even after you close the program and open it again later, which is very useful when you're working on a batch of files over many days. You can download the free NoteTab, or its Light version, from http://www.notetab.com/.

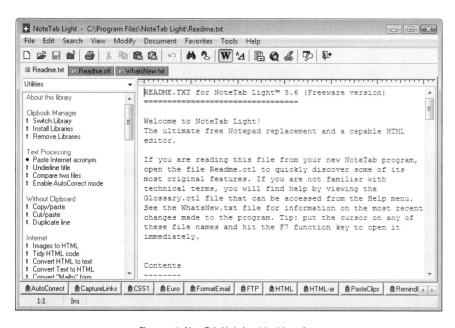

Figure 1.6. NoteTab Light's tabbed interface

Firefox

As mentioned in the Preface, Firefox is a very popular alternative to Internet Explorer and, as we proceed through this book, it will be our browser of choice for a number of reasons. As with NoteTab, Firefox offers a tabbed interface that helps keep your computer free from window clutter. You can download Firefox from http://www.mozilla.com/firefox/; the browser is depicted in Figure 1.7.

Figure 1.7. Firefox—this creature is worth hunting down

Mac OS X Tools

It is true that there are fewer free programs available for the Mac operating system than there are for Windows. However, there are a few programs that you might like to consider as you move beyond the basics.

TextWrangler

TextWrangler is a free, simple text editor made by BareBones Software. As with NoteTab for Windows, TextWrangler can tidy up your workspace by allowing several text files to be open for editing at the same time (the documents are listed in a pull-out *drawer* to one side of the interface, rather than in tabs). You can download TextWrangler, shown in Figure 1.8, from the BareBones Software web site.[1]

---

[1] http://www.barebones.com/products/textwrangler/

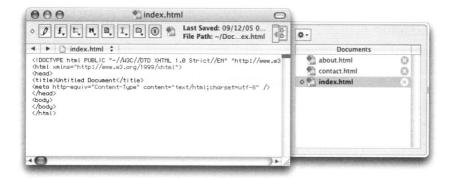

Figure 1.8. TextWrangler, a free text editor from BareBones Software

Firefox

Firefox is popular not just among Windows users, but also with Mac users, many of whom prefer to use it instead of Safari (often because of the extra features—known as **add-ons**—that can be bolted on to the browser). A web page viewed in Firefox should display the same regardless of whether the browser is installed on a PC running Windows XP or Vista, on a Mac running OS X, or on Linux, a free, open source operating system (generally favored by highly technical people who like to tinker with their computers a lot). The predictability of Firefox is a welcome change from the bad old days of endless browser competition, and is one very good reason why we will mainly use Firefox in the examples included in this book.

Not Just Text, Text, Text

You can build an entire web site using just the tools mentioned above, but it won't be the sexiest site on the Web. The missing element here is images: so far, the programs we've mentioned are used to manipulate plain text or view web pages. If your web site is going to be visually appealing, you'll need to be able to create and manipulate images, either from scratch using photos you've taken, or using images that you have the legal right to use on your web site.

Unfortunately, when it comes to image editing software, that old saying, "You get what you pay for," applies. A professional image editing program, like Photoshop or Fireworks, costs hundreds of dollars. While these programs offer some excellent capabilities, we can't really recommend that you go out and pay for them unless you're sure that they're right for you. If you already have a copy of one of these, or a similar image editing program, by all means use it and experiment with it. Programs like Paint Shop Pro or Photoshop Elements (a cut-down version of Photoshop) are more reasonably priced. However, for the purposes of this book, we'll look only at tools that are free to download and offer enough functionality to give you an idea of what's possible.

Keep an eye open for free image editors that are included on disks attached to the covers of Internet, computing, and design magazines. Software vendors often give away older versions of their software in the hope that users might be tempted to upgrade to a new version at a later date. Look out for Paint Shop Pro, or any image editor that supports **layers**—a way to construct an image by stacking 2 or more layers, one on top of the other. While we'll keep our image editing fairly simple throughout this book, it's certainly worth keeping an eye open for free (and full-featured) image editing software, as these offers will not always be available.

 Taking the Big Boys for a Spin

The most commonly used image editing packages are available for trial download. They are large downloads (hundreds of megabytes) and may need to be left to download overnight, even on a broadband connection.

These trial versions are typically available for 30 days' use; after that time you can decide whether you want to pay for the full software or stop using the program. However, those 30 days might just be enough time for you to use the software while you work through this book.

Adobe Photoshop	A trial of the latest version of Photoshop is available for download.[2] If you'd rather try the lighter Photoshop Elements, trial versions are available for Windows[3] and Mac.[4]
Adobe Fireworks	You can download a trial version of Fireworks from the Adobe web site.[5]
Paint Shop Pro	Paint Shop Pro is available for Windows only. To download a trial version, visit the Paint Shop Pro site,[6] and click the **Free Trial** link.

[2] http://www.adobe.com/products/photoshop/
[3] http://www.adobe.com/products/photoshopelwin/
[4] http://www.adobe.com/products/photoshopelmac/
[5] http://www.adobe.com/products/fireworks/
[6] http://www.corel.com/paintshoppro/

Windows Tools

A standard Windows install has not always been blessed with image editing software. Certainly this was the case with Windows XP (although if you bought the computer as a bundle with PC, scanner, or digital camera all together, you might be lucky and find some image editing software included in the deal; scout around in your **Start > All Programs** menu to see what you can uncover).

In Windows Vista, the Photo Gallery application has seen some big improvements over its previous XP incarnation and now includes some basic, but still useful, image manipulation tools, including cropping, color, and contrast adjustment. The Photo Gallery application can be found directly in the **Start** menu.

Figure 1.9. Vista's Photo Gallery application

Picasa

If you're using Vista, the tools offered in Photo Gallery may do everything that you need; if you're using XP, you'll almost certainly need to use an extra application. With that in mind, you might like to try out an excellent image management tool that Google offers for free download. The program is called Picasa, and it's extremely well equipped to handle most of the tasks that you're likely to encounter as you manage imagery for your web site. Download a copy from the Picasa web site,[7] and soon enough you'll be using this program to crop, rotate, add special effects to, and catalog the images stored on your computer. Figure 1.10 gives you an idea of the program's interface.

Figure 1.10. Picasa: Google's free, fully-featured photo and image editing and management tool

Mac OS X Tools

The Mac has a reputation for being favored by designers and creative types, and the platform makes many tools available to the budding artist. However, they usually come at a price, and often that price is higher than those of the Windows equivalents. So, what free software can we use on the Mac, assuming that we want something more permanent than a 30-day trial version of Photoshop or Fireworks?

GraphicConverter

GraphicConverter has much greater capabilities than its name suggests. It's been bundled with new Macs at times, and is also available for download[8] (you'll be

---

[7] http://picasa.google.com/download/

[8] http://www.graphicconverter.net/

encouraged to pay a modest registration fee for the software, but you can try it out for free). Although this is primarily a tool for converting graphic files, it can also be used for simple editing tasks. Using GraphicConverter, which is illustrated in Figure 1.11, you'll be able to crop, resize, rotate, and add text to any image.

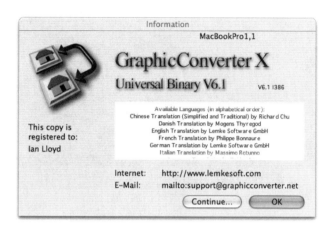

Figure 1.11. GraphicConverter does a lot more than simply convert graphics

iPhoto

Also included with Mac OS X is a program that probably needs no introduction to the experienced Mac user: iPhoto. This excellent program is not intended to be a fully featured image editor; it's really designed for managing and viewing large numbers of photos stored on a computer. It's great for organizing photo albums, but iPhoto also has some very useful editing facilities that take it beyond a mere cataloging tool.

iPhoto, seen in Figure 1.12, can be found in the Applications folder or in the dock.

Figure 1.12. Using the image adjustment tools in iPhoto 6

Creating a Spot for Your Web Site

So far, we've looked at some of the tools that you'll need to create your web site. We've looked at programs that are readily available, and where you can find them on your computer. And for cases in which the free tools that came with your computer are not up to the job, we've suggested other programs that you can download and use. The next task we must tick off our to-do list before we go any further is to create a space for your web site on the hard drive.

Windows

The easiest and most logical place to keep your web site files is in a dedicated folder within the **Documents** folder (or the **My Documents** folder in Windows XP). The **Documents** folder can be found inside your user folder. "But what's this user folder?" I hear you cry. And a fair point too, because it won't be labeled **User** but rather it will be labeled according to the user name that you provided when you first set up Windows. In Windows Vista you'll find the user folders of all local computer account holders under **C:\Users** (in Windows XP it's under **C:\Documents and Settings**) and will have a folder name matching your user name. More conveniently though, you'll find it on your computer's desktop as shown in Figure 1.13.

Figure 1.13. The user folder—in this case the user is "Administrator"—contains the Documents folder (highlighted)

Don't worry if your user folder is not on the desktop: it's easy to get it to appear there (see the tip below for details on how to add this for Vista and XP). Double-click to open your user folder, then double-click on **Documents**, then finally create a new folder called **Web** by selecting **File** > **New** > **Folder**.

Displaying the Users Folder in Vista and the My Documents Folder in Windows XP

Can't find your user folder on your Vista desktop? Missing your **My Documents** folder in XP? In an effort to clean up your desktop, you may have removed the icon by accident—it's easily done. This is how you can return the folder to your desktop:

▪ From the **Start Menu**, select **Control Panel**.

▪ Select **Appearance and Personalization** (or **Appearance and Themes** in XP).

▪ Vista users: choose **Personalization** and listed in the top left, under the title **Tasks** is the option to **Change Desktop Icons**. A new dialogue box will appear: check the option entitled **User's Files** in the section **Desktop Icons**, then press **OK**. You may now also close the **Appearance and Personalization** window.

XP users: select **Change the desktop background** from the list of options, then click the **Customize Desktop...** button at the bottom. Check the **My Documents** option in the dialogue box that appears, then click **OK**. Close the **Appearance and Themes** window also by pressing **OK**.

Your user folder/**My Documents** folder should now be back on the desktop, as shown in Figure 1.14.

Computer

My Computer

Control Panel

My Network Places

Administrator

My Documents

Figure 1.14. Administrator's user folder and **My Documents** folder displayed on the desktop in Windows Vista and Windows XP, respectively

Mac OS X

In Mac OS X, there's already a handy place for you to store your web site files: the **Sites** folder shown in Figure 1.15. Open your home directory (from Finder, select **Go** > **Home**), and there it is.

It's easy to add the **Sites** folder to your sidebar (seen in Figure 1.16) for quick access: just drag the folder to the sidebar in the same way you add items to the dock.

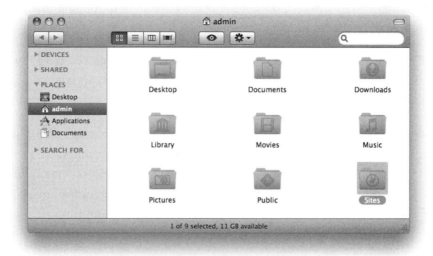

Figure 1.15. The **Sites** folder displayed in the Mac OS X home directory

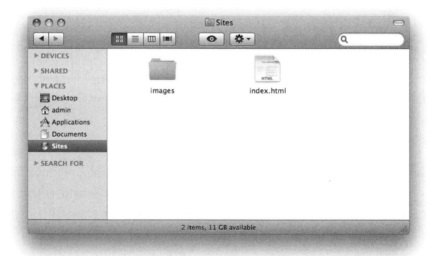

Figure 1.16. The **Sites** folder placed in the sidebar

Getting Help

Books may be a wonderful way to learn: you're sitting there with a computer running, perhaps a cup of coffee keeping your mind ticking over, and a bookmark signifying your progress to date. Great. But what if you don't understand something in the book? What do you do next? Shouting at the book won't help, though there may be some therapeutic value to it!

Hopefully, you won't find yourself with too many questions as you work through this book, but if you're the curious type—or a quick learner—you might want to go beyond what we're going to teach you here.

Whether you're getting stuck or want to learn more, your first stop should be the SitePoint Forums.[9] It will only take a few moments to register, and once you've done so you can log in and ask questions in a range of different forums. Whether you have questions about writing content for your web site, you need marketing tips, or you're facing a few tricky graphic design issues, the hundreds of experts who contribute to and moderate these pages every day will be happy to help out.

Register at SitePoint's forums today; then, when we recommend further reading or research, you'll be good to go. Oh, and did we mention that all this friendly, helpful advice is free of charge? We thought that might encourage you!

Summary

Believe it or not, we've now got everything we need to build our own web site—and all without spending a cent! Not only do we have the basic tools—our text editor (Notepad or TextEdit) and our web browser (Internet Explorer or Safari)—but we've also looked at some alternatives to these.

We've reviewed some simple and freely available image editing programs that can help us spruce up our sites: Picasa for Windows, and GraphicConverter and iPhoto for Mac. Finally, we mentioned some more capable—and more expensive—options, such as Photoshop and Paint Shop Pro.

Now we've got the tools, let's learn how to use them!

---

[9] http://www.sitepoint.com/forums/

Your First Web Pages

A wise man once said that a journey of a thousand miles begins with a single step. In this chapter, you'll take that first metaphorical step on your journey towards web site enlightenment: you'll create your first web page. By the end of the chapter, you'll have duplicated that first page to form the beginnings of a multi-page web site.

Nice to Meet You, XHTML

In the preface to this book, we touched briefly on what XHTML is. In this chapter, we'll learn the basics of XHTML, periodically previewing our progress in a browser, and steadily building up our knowledge of various XHTML **elements** (elements are the basic building blocks of XHTML). Elements tell the web browser what a particular item in the page is: a paragraph, a heading, a quotation, and so on. These elements contain all the information that the browser requires, as we'll soon see.

Anatomy of a Web Page

In the preface, we said that learning XHTML was like taking a driving lesson. To take that analogy a step further, imagine a web page as being the car in which you're learning to drive. There are some things that are essential to the process of driving; others are mere fashion items.

To drive the car you need to have wheels (including the steering wheel), and a place to sit. The car must also have some kind of chassis to which the bodywork can be bolted. An engine is required to power the car, as is bodywork to which your (nonessential, but spiffy) trim can be attached. Anything less, and all you have is a collection of attractive—but useless!—spare parts.

Like the car, your web page also needs to have a chassis: a basic structure upon which everything else can be built. But what does this hypothetical chassis look like? The best way to find out is to roll up our sleeves, figuratively speaking, then take a closer look at what's going on underneath the cosmetic features.

Viewing the Source

One of the great things about learning to build web pages is that we all have the ability to view the source code of other people's web pages. You can learn a lot by simply taking a peek at how someone else's web page was built ... but how do you do that?

Although every browser uses slightly different terminology, the variations in the ways different browsers let us view web page code are so small that the process doesn't need to be spelled out for every browser. Here's the technique you'd use to view a web page's source in IE:

■ Bring up a page in your browser, for example the Web Standards Project's homepage.[1] The Web Standards Project (WaSP) is a group that promotes the benefits of building your web site correctly, so you can be pretty confident that they've got it right.

■ Position your cursor somewhere on the page (other than over an image), and right-click (**Ctrl**-click on a Mac). You should be presented with a context menu similar to those shown in Figure 2.1.

---

[1] http://webstandards.org/

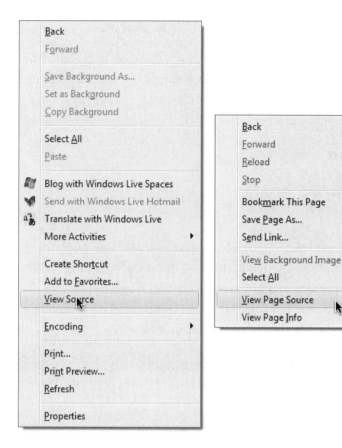

Figure 2.1. Selecting the View Source command after right-clicking on a web page (as seen in Internet Explorer and Firefox, respectively)

■ Select **View Source**, (or **View Page Source** for Firefox) and a new window will appear, displaying all of the page's underlying markup.

At this point, we're not going to analyze the markup that you're looking at, but this is one of those tricks that's really useful to know from the beginning.

 Careful Who You Trust!

Most web pages don't use best-practice techniques, so avoid looking at a page's source unless the web site in question is mentioned in this book as being a good example.

Basic Requirements of a Web Page

As we've already discussed, in any web page there are some basic must-have items. You would have seen all of these if you scanned through the markup that appeared when you tried to *view source* a moment ago:

- a doctype
- an `<html>` tag
- a `<head>` tag
- a `<title>` tag
- a `<body>` tag

These requirements make up the basic skeleton of a web page. It's the chassis of your car with some unpainted bodywork, but no wheels or seats. A car enthusiast would call it a *project*—a solid foundation that needs a little extra work to turn it in to something usable. The same goes for a web page. Here's what these requirements look like when they're combined in a basic web page:

```
<!DOCTYPE html PUBLIC "-//W3C//DTD XHTML 1.0 Strict//EN"
    "http://www.w3.org/TR/xhtml1/DTD/xhtml1-strict.dtd">
<html xmlns="http://www.w3.org/1999/xhtml">
  <head>
    <title>Untitled Document</title>
    <meta http-equiv="Content-Type"
        content="text/html; charset=utf-8"/>
  </head>
  <body>
  </body>
</html>
```

Those of you with eagle eyes may have also spotted the `<meta>` tag in the markup above. I know I haven't mentioned this yet; we'll get to it soon enough. For now be content with the knowledge that, although the `<meta>` tag is not part of the skeletal requirements of a web page, it serves many useful purposes, especially the provision of supporting information about the web page.

The markup above is the most basic web page you'll see here. It contains practically no content of any value (at least, as far as someone who looks at it in a browser is concerned), but it's crucial that you understand what this markup means. Let's delve a little deeper.

The Doctype

```
<!DOCTYPE html PUBLIC "-//W3C//DTD XHTML 1.0 Strict//EN"
    "http://www.w3.org/TR/xhtml1/DTD/xhtml1-strict.dtd">
```

This is known as the **doctype**[2] (short for Document Type Definition). It *must* be the first item on a web page, appearing even before any spacing or carriage returns.

Have you ever taken a document you wrote in Microsoft Word 2007 on one computer, and tried to open it on another computer that only had Word 2000 on it? Frustratingly, without some preemptive massaging when the file is saved in the first place, this doesn't work quite as expected. It fails because Word 2007 includes features that Bill Gates and his team hadn't even dreamed of in 2000, and so Microsoft needed to create a new version of its file format to cater for these new features. Just as Microsoft has many different versions of Word, so too are there different versions of HTML, most recently XHTML and HTML 5. Mercifully, the different versions of HTML have been designed so that it doesn't suffer the same incompatibility gremlins as Word, but it's still important to identify the version of HTML that you're using. This is where the doctype comes in. The doctype's job is to specify which version of HTML the browser should expect to see. The browser uses this information to decide how it should render items on the screen.

The doctype above states that we're using XHTML 1.0 Strict, and includes a **URL** to which the browser can refer: this URL points to the **W3C**'s specification for XHTML 1.0 Strict. Got all that? Okay, let's take a jargon break! There are way too many abbreviations for this paragraph.

HTML5—The New Kid on the Block

Note that at the time of writing, the HTML5 specification is not yet finalized and browser support for it is also incomplete (understandable, given the moving goalposts). For this reason, we'll not be covering HTML5 in this book. You should, however, be aware of its existence at the very least.

---

[2] http://reference.sitepoint.com/html/doctypes/

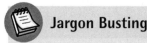

Jargon Busting

URL

> URL stands for Uniform Resource Locator. It's what some (admittedly more geeky) people refer to when they talk about a web site's address. URL is definitely a useful term to know, though, because it's becoming more and more common.

W3C

> W3C is an abbreviation of the name World Wide Web Consortium, a group of smart people spread across the globe who, collectively, come up with proposals for the ways in which computing and markup languages used on the Web should be written. The W3C defines the rules, suggests usage, then publishes the agreed documentation for reference by interested parties, be they web site creators like yourself (once you're done with this book, that is), or software developers who are building the programs that need to understand these languages (such as browsers or authoring software).

> The W3C documents are the starting point, and indeed everything in this book is based on the original documents. But you won't want to look at any W3C documents for a long time yet. They're just plain scary for us mere mortals without Computer Science degrees. Just stick with this book for the time being and I'll guide you through.

The `html` Element

So, the doctype has told the browser to expect a certain version of HTML. What comes next? Some HTML!

An XHTML document is built using elements. Remember, elements are the bricks that create the structures that hold a web page together. But what exactly *is* an element? What does an element look like, and what is its purpose?

- An XHTML element starts and ends with **tags**—the **opening tag** and the **closing tag**.[3]

---

[3] Like any good rule, there are exceptions to this: empty elements, such as `meta`, use special empty tags. We'll take a look at empty tags soon.

- A tag consists of an opening angled bracket (<), some text, and a closing bracket (>).

- Inside a tag, there is a **tag name**; there may also be one or more **attributes**.

Let's take a look at the first element in the page: the html[4] element. Figure 2.2 shows what we have.

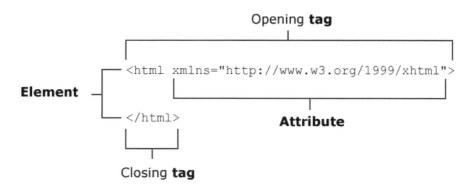

Figure 2.2. Components of a typical XHTML element

Figure 2.2 depicts the opening tag, which marks the start of the element:

```
<html xmlns="http://www.w3.org/1999/xhtml">
```

Below this we see the closing tag, which marks its end (and occurs right at the end of the document):

```
</html>
```

Here's that line again, with the tag name in bold:

```
<html xmlns="http://www.w3.org/1999/xhtml">
```

And there is one **attribute** in the opening tag:

```
<html xmlns="http://www.w3.org/1999/xhtml">
```

---

[4] http://reference.sitepoint.com/html/html/

What's an Attribute?

HTML elements can have a range of different attributes; the available attributes vary depending on which element you're dealing with. Each attribute is made up of a **name** and a **value**, and these are always written as `name="value"`. Some attributes are optional while others are compulsory, but together they give the browser important information that the element wouldn't offer otherwise. For example, the image element (which we'll learn about soon) has a compulsory "image source" attribute, the value of which gives the filename of the image. Attributes appear only in the opening tag of any given element. We'll see more attributes crop up as we work our way through this project, and, at least initially, I'll be making sure to point them out so that you're familiar with them.

Back to the purpose of the `html` element. This is the outermost "container" of our web page; everything else (apart from the `doctype`) is kept within that outer container. Let's peel off that outer layer and take a peek at the contents inside.

There are two major sections inside the `html` element: the `head` and the `body`. It's not going to be difficult to remember the order in which those items should appear, unless you happen to enjoy doing headstands.

The **head** Element

The head[5] element contains information *about* the page, but no information that will be displayed on the page itself. For example, it contains the `title`[6] element, which tells the browser what to display in its **title bar** (the title bar is the very top part of the browser window—the part with minimize, maximize and close buttons):

```
<head>
  <title>Untitled Document</title>
  <meta http-equiv="Content-Type"
      content="text/html; charset=utf-8"/>
</head>
```

---

[5] http://reference.sitepoint.com/html/head/
[6] http://reference.sitepoint.com/html/title/

The `title` Element

The opening `<title>` and closing `</title>` tags are wrapped around the words "Untitled Document" in the markup above. Note that the `<title>` signifies the start, while the closing `</title>` signifies the end of the title. That's how closing tags work: they have forward slashes just after the first < angle bracket.

The Untitled Document title is typical of what HTML authoring software provides as a starting point when you choose to create a new web page; it's up to you to change those words. As Figure 2.3 shows, it really pays to put something meaningful as a title, and not just for the sake of those people who visit our web page.

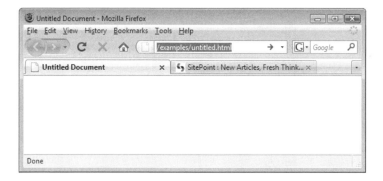

Figure 2.3. "Untitled Document"—not a very helpful title

The content of the `title` element is also used for a number of other purposes:

- It's the name that appears in the **Windows Taskbar**—that strip along the bottom of your Windows desktop that show all the currently open windows—for any open document, as shown in Figure 2.4. It also appears in the dock on a Mac, as Figure 2.5 illustrates. When you have a few windows open, you'll appreciate those people who have made an effort to enter a descriptive `title`!

Figure 2.4. The `title` appearing in the Windows Taskbar

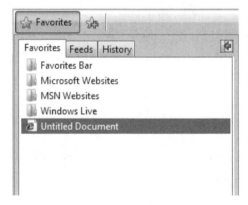

Figure 2.5. The `title` displaying in the Mac dock

■ If users decide to add the page to their bookmarks (or favorites), the `title` will be used to name the bookmark, as Figure 2.6 illustrates.

Figure 2.6. An untitled document saved to IE's favorites

■ Your `title` element is used heavily by search engines to ascertain what your page contains, and what information about it should be displayed in the search results. Just for fun, and to see how many people forget to type in a useful `title`, try searching for the phrase **Untitled Document** in the search engine of your choice.

meta Elements

Inside the `head` element in our simple example, we can see a `meta` element, which is shown in bold below:

```
<head>
  <title>Untitled Document</title>
  <meta http-equiv="Content-Type"
      content="text/html; charset=utf-8"/>
</head>
```

`meta` elements can be used in a web page for many different reasons. Some are used to provide additional information that's not displayed on screen to the browser or to search engines; for instance, the name of the page's author or a copyright notice might be included in `meta` elements. In the example above, the `meta` tag tells the browser which **character set** to use (specifically, UTF-8, which includes the characters needed for web pages in just about any written language).

There are many different uses for `meta` elements, but most of them will make no discernible difference to the way your page looks, and as such, won't be of much interest to you (at least at this stage).

Self-closing Elements

The `meta` element is an example of a **self-closing element** (or an **empty element**). Unlike `title`, the `meta` element needn't contain anything, so we could write it as follows:

```
<meta http-equiv="Content-Type"
    content="text/html; charset=utf-8"></meta>
```

XHTML contains a number of empty elements, and the boffins who put together XHTML decided that writing all those closing tags would get annoying pretty quickly, so they decided to use self-closing tags: tags that end with `/>`. So our `meta` example becomes:

```
<meta http-equiv="Content-Type"
    content="text/html; charset=utf-8"/>
```

The Memory Game: Remembering Difficult Markup

If you're thinking that the doctype and `meta` elements are difficult to remember, and you're wondering how on earth people commit them to memory, don't worry, most people don't. Even the most hardened and world-weary coders would have difficulty remembering these elements exactly, so most do the same thing—they copy from a source they know to be correct (most likely from their last project or piece of work). You'll probably do the same as you work with project files for this book.

Fully-fledged web development programs, such as Dreamweaver, will normally take care of these difficult parts of coding. But if you are using a humble text editor and need some help, you need only remember that there is a completely searchable HTML reference,[7] accessible at any time at SitePoint.com.

Other head Elements

Other items, such as CSS markup and JavaScript code, can appear in the `head` element, but we'll discuss these as we need them.

The body Element

Finally, we get to the place where it all happens. The `body`[8] element of the page contains almost everything that you see on the screen: headings, paragraphs, images, any navigation that's required, and footers that sit at the bottom of the web page:

```
<!DOCTYPE html PUBLIC "-//W3C//DTD XHTML 1.0 Strict//EN"
    "http://www.w3.org/TR/xhtml1/DTD/xhtml1-strict.dtd">
<html xmlns="http://www.w3.org/1999/xhtml">
  <head>
    <title>Untitled Document</title>
    <meta http-equiv="Content-Type"
        content="text/html; charset=utf-8"/>
  </head>
  <body>
  </body>
</html>
```

---

[7] http://reference.sitepoint.com/html/
[8] http://reference.sitepoint.com/html/body/

The Most Basic Web Page in the World

Actually, that heading's a bit of a misnomer: we've already shown you the most basic page—the one without any content. However, to start to appreciate how everything fits together, you really need to see a simple page with some actual content on it. Let's have a go at it, shall we?

Open your text editor and type the following into a new, empty document (or grab the file from the code archive if you don't feel like typing it out):

```
basic.html
<!DOCTYPE html PUBLIC "-//W3C//DTD XHTML 1.0 Strict//EN"
    "http://www.w3.org/TR/xhtml1/DTD/xhtml1-strict.dtd">
<html xmlns="http://www.w3.org/1999/xhtml">
  <head>
    <title>The Most Basic Web Page in the World</title>
    <meta http-equiv="Content-Type"
        content="text/html; charset=utf-8"/>
  </head>
  <body>
    <h1>The Most Basic Web Page in the World</h1>
    <p>This is a very simple web page to get you started.
        Hopefully you will get to see how the markup that drives
        the page relates to the end result that you can see on
        screen.</p>
    <p>This is another paragraph, by the way. Just to show how it
        works.</p>
  </body>
</html>
```

Once you've typed it out, save it as **basic.html**.

If you're using Notepad:

1. Select **File** > **Save As...** from the menu and find the **Web** folder you created inside your **Documents** folder.

2. Enter the filename as `basic.html`.

3. Select **UTF-8** from the **Encoding** drop-down list.

4. Click **Save**.

If you're using TextEdit on a Mac, first make sure that you're in plain text mode, then:

1. Select **File** > **Save As...** from the menu.

2. Find the **Sites** folder, enter the filename as `basic.html`.

3. Select **Unicode (UTF-8)** from the **Plain Text Encoding** drop-down list.

4. Click **Save**.

5. TextEdit will warn you that you're saving a plain text file with an extension other than **.txt**, and offer to append **.txt** to the end of your filename. We want to save this file with an **.html** extension, so click the **Don't Append** button, and your file will be saved.

The Importance of UTF-8

If you neglect to select UTF-8 when saving your files, it's likely that you won't notice much of a difference. However, when someone else tries to view your web site (say, a Korean friend of yours), they'll probably end up with a screen of gobbledygook. Why? Because their computer is set up to read Korean text, and yours is set up to create English text. UTF-8 can handle just about any language there is (including some quite obscure ones) and most computers can read it, so UTF-8 is always a safe bet.

Next, using Windows Explorer or Finder, locate the file that you just saved, and double-click to open it in your browser. Figure 2.7 shows how the page displays.

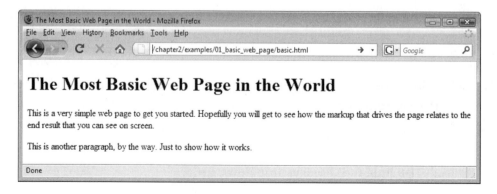

Figure 2.7. Displaying a basic page

Analyzing the Web Page

We've introduced two new elements to our simple page: a heading element, and a couple of paragraph elements, denoted by the <h1>[9] tag and <p>[10] tags, respectively. Do you see how the markup you've typed out relates to what you can see in the browser? Figure 2.8 shows a direct comparison of the document displays.

Figure 2.8. Comparing the source markup with the view presented in the browser

The opening <h1> and closing </h1> tags are wrapped around the words "The Most Basic Web Page in the World," making that the main heading for the page. In the same way, the p elements contain the text in the two paragraphs.

 A Case of Keeping Low

The tags are all lowercase. All of our attribute names will be in lowercase, too. Many older HTML documents include tags and attributes in uppercase, but this isn't allowed in XHTML.

Headings and Document Hierarchy

In the example above, we use an h1 element to show a major heading. If we wanted to include a subheading beneath this heading, we would use the h2 element. A subheading under an h2 would use an h3 element, and so on, until we get to h6.

---

[9] http://reference.sitepoint.com/html/h1/
[10] http://reference.sitepoint.com/html/p/

The lower the heading level, the lesser its importance and the smaller the font size (unless you have re-styled the headings with CSS, but more of that in Chapter 3).

With headings, an important and commonsense practice is to ensure that they do not jump out of sequence. In other words, you should start from level one, and work your way down through the levels in numerical order. You can jump back up from a lower-level heading to a higher one, provided that the content under the higher-level heading to which you've jumped does not refer to concepts that are addressed under the lower-level heading. It may be useful to visualize your headings as a list:

- First Major Heading
  - First Subheading
  - Second Subheading
    - A Sub-subheading
- Another Major Heading
  - Another Subheading

Here's the XHTML view of the example shown above:

```
<h1>First Major Heading</h1>
<h2>First Subheading</h2>
<h2>Second Subheading</h2>
<h3>A Sub-subheading</h3>
<h1>Another Major Heading</h1>
<h2>Another Subheading</h2>
```

Paragraphs

Of course, no one wants to read a document that contains only headings—you need to put some text in there. The element we use to deal with blocks of text is the p element. It's not difficult to remember, as p is for paragraph. That's just as well, because you'll almost certainly find yourself using this element more than any other. And that's the beauty of XHTML: most elements that you use frequently are either very obvious, or easy to remember once you're introduced to them.

For People Who Love Lists

Let's imagine that you want a list on your web page. To include an **ordered list** (the HTML term for a numbered list) of items, we use the ol element. An **unordered list**—known as bullet points to the average person—makes use of the ul element.

In both types of list, individual points or list items are specified using the li element. So we use ol for an ordered list, ul for an unordered list, and li for a list item. Simple.

To see this markup in action, type the following into a new text document, save it as **lists.html**, and view it in the browser by double-clicking on the saved file's icon:

lists.html

```
<!DOCTYPE html PUBLIC "-//W3C//DTD XHTML 1.0 Strict//EN"
    "http://www.w3.org/TR/xhtml1/DTD/xhtml1-strict.dtd">
<html xmlns="http://www.w3.org/1999/xhtml">
  <head>
    <title>Lists - an introduction</title>
    <meta http-equiv="Content-Type"
        content="text/html; charset=utf-8"/>
  </head>
  <body>
    <h1>Lists - an introduction </h1>
    <p>Here's a paragraph. A lovely, concise little paragraph.</p>
    <p>Here comes another one, followed by a subheading.</p>
    <h2>A subheading here</h2>
    <p>And now for a list or two:</p>
    <ul>
      <li>This is a bulleted list</li>
      <li>No order applied</li>
      <li>Just a bunch of points we want to make</li>
    </ul>
    <p>And here's an ordered list:</p>
    <ol>
      <li>This is the first item</li>
      <li>Followed by this one</li>
      <li>And one more for luck</li>
    </ol>
  </body>
</html>
```

How does it look to you? Did you type it all out? Remember, if it seems like a hassle to type out the examples, you can find all the markup in the code archive, as I explained in the preface. However, bear in mind that simply copying and pasting markup, then saving and running it, doesn't really give you a feel for creating your own web site—it really will pay to learn by doing. Even if you make mistakes, it's still a better way to learn (you'll be pleased when you can spot and fix your own errors yourself). When displayed in a browser, the above markup should look like the page shown in Figure 2.9.

There are many, many different elements that you can use on your web page, and we'll learn more of them as our web site development progresses. As well as the more obvious elements that you'll come across, there are others that are not immediately clear-cut: for example, what would you use `div`, `span`, or `a` elements for? Any guesses? All will be revealed in good time.

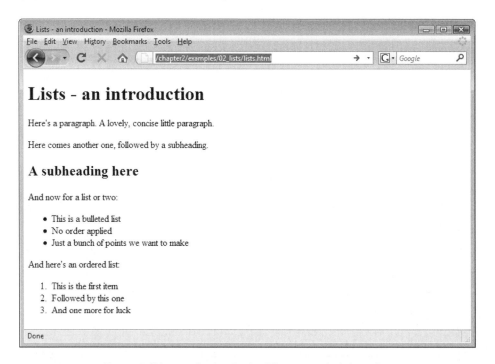

Figure 2.9. Using unordered and ordered lists to organize information

Commenting Your HTML

Back in the garage, you're doing a little work on your project car and, as you prepare to replace the existing tires with a new set, you notice that your hubcaps aren't bolted on: you'd stuck them to the car with nothing more than super glue. There must have been a good reason for doing that, but you can't remember what it was. The trouble is, if you had a reason to attach the hubcaps that way before, surely you should do it the same way again. Wouldn't it be great if you'd left yourself a note when you first did it, explaining why you used super glue instead of bolts? Then again, your car wouldn't look very nice with notes stuck all over it. What a quandary.

When you're creating a web site, you may find yourself in a similar situation. You might build a site then not touch it again for six months. Then when you revisit the work, you might find yourself going through the all-too-familiar head-scratching routine. Fortunately, there *is* a solution.

XHTML—like most programming and markup languages—allows you to use **comments.**[11] Comments are perfect for making notes about something you've done and, though they're included within your code, comments do not affect the on-screen display. Here's an example of a comment:

comments.html

```
<!DOCTYPE html PUBLIC "-//W3C//DTD XHTML 1.0 Strict//EN"
    "http://www.w3.org/TR/xhtml1/DTD/xhtml1-strict.dtd">
<html xmlns="http://www.w3.org/1999/xhtml">
  <head>
    <title>Comment example</title>
    <meta http-equiv="Content-Type"
        content="text/html; charset=utf-8"/>
  </head>
  <body>
    <p>I really, <em>really</em> like this XHTML stuff.</p>
    <!-- Added emphasis using the em element. Handy one, that. -->
  </body>
</html>
```

Figure 2.10 shows the page viewed on-screen.

Figure 2.10. The comment remains hidden in the on-screen display

Comments must start with <!--, after which you're free to type whatever you like as a "note to self." Well, you're free to type *almost* anything: you cannot type double

---

[11] http://reference.sitepoint.com/html/html-xhtml-syntax#html-xhtml-syntax__sect-comments

dashes. Why not? Because that's a signal that the comment is about to end—the - -> part.

Oh, and did you spot how we snuck another new element in there? The emphasis element, denoted with the <em> and </em> tags, is used wherever … well, do I *really* need to tell you? Actually, that last question was there to illustrate this point: did you notice that the word "really" appeared in italics? Read that part to yourself now, and listen to the way it sounds in your head. Now you know when to use the em element.

Using Comments to Hide Markup from Browsers Temporarily

There is no limit to the amount of information you can put into a comment, and this is why comments are often used to hide a section of a web page temporarily. Commenting may be preferable to deleting content, particularly if you want to put that information back into the web page at a later date (if it's in a comment, you won't have to re-type it). This is often called "**commenting out**" markup. Here's an example:

```
                                                          commentout.html
<!DOCTYPE html PUBLIC "-//W3C//DTD XHTML 1.0 Strict//EN"
    "http://www.w3.org/TR/xhtml1/DTD/xhtml1-strict.dtd">
<html xmlns="http://www.w3.org/1999/xhtml">
  <head>
    <title>Commenting out XHTML</title>
    <meta http-equiv="Content-Type"
        content="text/html; charset=utf-8"/>
  </head>
  <body>
    <h1>Current Stock</h1>
    <p>The following items are available for order:</p>
    <ul>
      <li>Dark Smoke Window Tinting</li>
      <li>Bronze Window Tinting</li>
      <!-- <li>Spray mount</li>
      <li>Craft knife (pack of 5)</li> -->
    </ul>
  </body>
</html>
```

Figure 2.11 shows how the page displays in Firefox.

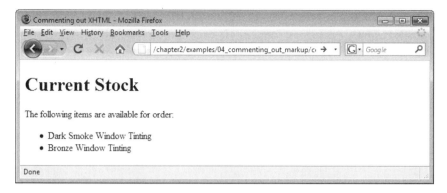

Figure 2.11. The final, commented list items are not displayed

Remember, you write a comment like this: `<!--Your comment here followed by the comment closer, two dashes and a right-angled bracket-->`.

Symbols

Occasionally, you may need to include the greater-than (>) or less-than (<) symbols in the text of your web pages. The problem is that these symbols are also used to denote tags in XHTML. So, what can we do? Thankfully, we can use special little codes called **entities** in our text instead of these symbols. The entity for the greater-than symbol is `&gt;`—we can substitute it for the greater-than symbol in our text, as shown in the following simple example. The result of this markup is shown in Figure 2.12.

```
entity.html

<!DOCTYPE html PUBLIC "-//W3C//DTD XHTML 1.0 Strict//EN"
    "http://www.w3.org/TR/xhtml1/DTD/xhtml1-strict.dtd">
<html xmlns="http://www.w3.org/1999/xhtml">
  <head>
    <title>Stock Note</title>
    <meta http-equiv="Content-Type"
        content="text/html; charset=utf-8"/>
  </head>
  <body>
    <p>Our current stock of craft knives &gt;
    OUT OF STOCK (more due in 3 days)</p>
  </body>
</html>
```

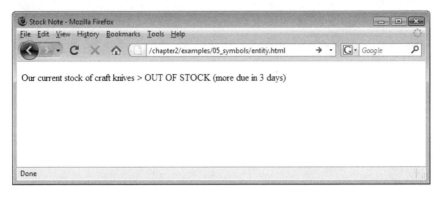

Figure 2.12. The > entity is displayed as > in the browser

Many different entities are available for a wide range of symbols, most of which don't appear on your keyboard. They all start with an ampersand (&) and end with a semicolon. Some of the most common are shown in Table 2.1.

Table 2.1. Some common entities

Entity (used in markup)	Symbol (displayed on screen)
&gt;	>
&lt;	<
&amp;	&
&pound;	£
&copy;	©
&trade;	™

Diving into Our Web Site

So far, we've looked at some very basic web pages as a way to ease you into the process of writing your own XHTML markup. Perhaps you've typed them up and tried them out, or maybe you've pulled the pages from the code archive and run them in your browser. Perhaps you've even tried experimenting for yourself—it's good to have a play around. None of the examples shown so far are worth keeping, though. You won't need to use any of these pages, but you will be using the ideas that we've introduced in them as you start to develop the fictitious project we'll complete in the course of this book: a web site for a local diving club.

The diving club comprises a group of local enthusiasts, and the web site will provide a way for club members to:

- share photos from previous dive trips
- stay informed about upcoming dive trips
- provide information about ad-hoc meet-ups
- read other members' dive reports and write-ups
- announce club news

The site also has the following goals:

- to help attract new members
- to provide links to other diving-related web sites
- to provide a convenient way to search for general diving-related information

The site's audience may not be enormous, but the regular visitors and club members are very keen to be involved. It's a fun site that people will want to come back to again and again, and it's a good project to work on. But it doesn't exist yet. You're going to start building it right now. Let's start with our first page: the site's home page.

The Homepage: the Starting Point for All Web Sites

At the very beginning of this chapter, we looked at a basic web page with nothing on it (the car chassis with no bodywork or interior). You saved the file as **basic.html**. Open that file in your text editor now, and strip out the following:

- the text contained within the opening `<title>` and closing `</title>` tags
- all the content between the opening `<body>` and closing `</body>` tags

Save the file as **index.html**.

Here's the markup you should have in front of you now:

```
                                                          index.html

<!DOCTYPE html PUBLIC "-//W3C//DTD XHTML 1.0 Strict//EN"
    "http://www.w3.org/TR/xhtml1/DTD/xhtml1-strict.dtd">
<html xmlns="http://www.w3.org/1999/xhtml">
  <head>
    <title></title>
    <meta http-equiv="Content-Type"
        content="text/html; charset=utf-8"/>
  </head>
  <body>
  </body>
</html>
```

Let's start building this web site, shall we?

Setting a Title

Remembering what we've learned so far, let's make a few changes to this document. Have a go at the following:

■ Change the title of the page to read "Bubble Under—The diving club for the south-west UK."

■ Add a heading to the page—a level one heading—that reads "BubbleUnder.com."

■ Immediately after the heading, add a paragraph that reads, "Diving club for the south-west UK—let's make a splash!" (This is your basic, marketing-type tag line, folks.)

Once you make these changes, your markup should look something like this (the changes are shown in bold):

```
                                                          index.html

<!DOCTYPE html PUBLIC "-//W3C//DTD XHTML 1.0 Strict//EN"
    "http://www.w3.org/TR/xhtml1/DTD/xhtml1-strict.dtd">
<html xmlns="http://www.w3.org/1999/xhtml">
  <head>
    <title>Bubble Under—The diving club for the south-west
        UK</title>
```

```
    <meta http-equiv="Content-Type"
       content="text/html; charset=utf-8"/>
  </head>
  <body>
    <h1>BubbleUnder.com</h1>
    <p>Diving club for the south-west UK—let's make a
       splash!</p>
  </body>
</html>
```

Save the page, then double-click on the file to open it in your chosen browser. Figure 2.13 shows what it should look like.

Figure 2.13. Displaying our work on the homepage

Welcoming New Visitors

Now, let's expand upon our tag line a little. We'll add a welcoming subheading—a second level heading—to the page, along with an introductory paragraph:

index.html *(excerpt)*

```
<body>
  <h1>BubbleUnder.com</h1>
  <p>Diving club for the south-west UK - let's make a splash!</p>
  <h2>Welcome to our super-dooper Scuba site</h2>
  <p>Glad you could drop in and share some air with us! You've
     passed your underwater navigation skills and successfully
     found your way to the start point - or in this case, our
     home page.</p>
</body>
```

Apologies for the diving terminology puns, they're truly cringe-worthy!

Hey! Where'd It All Go?

You'll notice that we didn't repeat the markup for the entire page in the above example. Why? Because paper costs money, trees are beautiful, and you didn't buy this book for weight-training purposes. In short, we won't repeat all the markup all the time; instead, we'll focus on the parts that have changed or have been added to. And remember: if you think you've missed something, don't worry. You can find all of the examples in the book's code archive.

Once you've added the subheading and the paragraph that follows it, save your page once more, then take another look at it in your browser (either hit the refresh/re-load button in your browser, or double-click on the file icon in the location at which you saved it). You should be looking at something like the display shown below in Figure 2.14.

Figure 2.14. The homepage taking shape

So, the homepage reads a lot like many other homepages at this stage: it has some basic introductory text to welcome visitors, but not much more. But what exactly is the site about? Or, to be more precise, what will it be about once it's built?

What's It All About?

Notice that, despite our inclusion of a couple of headings and a couple of paragraphs, there is little to suggest what this site is about. All visitors know so far is that the site's about diving. Let's add some more explanatory text to the page, along with some contact information:

▣ Beneath the content you already have on the page, add another heading: this time, make it a level three heading that reads, "About Us" (remember to include both the opening and closing tags for the heading element).

▣ Next, add the following text. Note that there is more than one paragraph.

> Bubble Under is a group of diving enthusiasts based in the south-west UK who meet up for diving trips in the summer months when the weather is good and the bacon rolls are flowing. We arrange weekends away as small groups to cut the costs of accommodation and travel, and to ensure that everyone gets a trustworthy dive buddy.

> Although we're based in the south-west, we don't stay on our own turf: past diving weekends have included trips up to Scapa Flow in Scotland and to Malta's numerous wreck sites.

> When we're not diving, we often meet up in a local pub to talk about our recent adventures (any excuse, eh?).

 Save Yourself Some Trouble

If you don't feel like typing out all this content, you can paraphrase, or copy it from the code archive. I've deliberately chosen to put a realistic amount of content on the page, so that you can see the effect of several paragraphs on our display.

▣ Next, add a Contact Us section, again, signified by a level three heading.

▣ Finally, add some simple contact details as follows:

> To find out more, contact Club Secretary Bob Dobalina on 01793 641207 or email bob@bubbleunder.com.

So, just to recap, we suggested using different heading levels to signify the importance of the different sections and paragraphs within the document. With that in mind, you should have something much like the following markup in the body of your document:

index.html *(excerpt)*

```
<h1>BubbleUnder.com</h1>
<p>Diving club for the south-west UK - let's make a splash!</p>
<h2>Welcome to our super-dooper Scuba site</h2>
<p>Glad you could drop in and share some air with us! You've
    passed your underwater navigation skills and successfully
    found your way to the start point - or in this case, our home
    page.</p>
<h3>About Us</h3>
<p>Bubble Under is a group of diving enthusiasts based in the
    south-west UK who meet up for diving trips in the summer
    months when the weather is good and the bacon rolls are
    flowing. We arrange weekends away as small groups to cut the
    costs of accommodation and travel and to ensure that everyone
    gets a trustworthy dive buddy.</p>
<p>Although we're based in the south-west, we don't stay on our
    own turf: past diving weekends away have included trips up to
    Scapa Flow in Scotland and to Malta's numerous wreck
    sites.</p>
<p>When we're not diving, we often meet up in a local pub
    to talk about our recent adventures (any excuse, eh?).</p>
<h3>Contact Us</h3>
<p>To find out more, contact Club Secretary Bob Dobalina on
    01793 641207 or email bob@bubbleunder.com.</p>
```

You can see how our home page is shaping up in Figure 2.15.

Figure 2.15. Viewing **index.html**

It's still not very exciting, is it? Trust me, we'll get there. The important thing to focus on at this stage is what the content of your site should comprise, and how it might be structured. We haven't gone into great detail about document structure yet, other than to discuss the use of different levels of headings, but we'll be looking at this in more detail later in this chapter. In the next chapter, we'll see how you can begin to **style** your document—that is, change the font, color, letter spacing and more—but for now, let's concentrate on the content and structure.

Clickable Email Links

It's all well and good to put an email address on the page, but it's hardly perfect. To use this address, a site visitor would need to copy and paste the address into an email message. Surely there's a simpler way? There certainly is:

```
<p>To find out more, contact Club Secretary Bob Dobalina
    on 01793 641207 or <a
    href="mailto:bob@bubbleunder.com">email
    bob@bubbleunder.com</a>.</p>
```

This clickable email link uses the a element, which is used to create links on web pages (this will be explained later in this chapter). The `mailto:` prefix tells the browser that the link needs to be treated as an email address (that is, the email program should be opened for this link). The content that follows the `mailto:` section should be a valid email address in the format *username@domain*.

Add this to the web page now, save it, then refresh the view in your browser. Try clicking on the underlined text: it should open your email program automatically, and display an email form in which the **To:** address is already completed.

The page so far seems a little boring, doesn't it? Let's sharpen it up a little. We can only keep looking at a page of black and white for so long—let's insert an image into the document. Here's how the img element is applied within the context of the page's markup:

index.html *(excerpt)*

```
<h2>Welcome to our super-dooper Scuba site</h2>
<p><img src="divers-circle.jpg" width="200" height="162"
    alt="A circle of divers practice their skills"/></p>
<p>Glad you could drop in and share some air with us! You've
    passed your underwater navigation skills and successfully
    found your way to the start point - or in this case, our home
    page.</p>
```

The img element is used to insert an image into our web page, and the attributes `src`, `alt`, `width`, and `height` describe the image that we're inserting. `src` is just the name of the image file. In this case, it's **divers-circle.jpg**, which you can grab from the code archive. `alt` is some alternative text that can be displayed in place of the image if, for some reason, it can't be displayed. This is useful for blind visitors to your site, search engines, and users of slow Internet connections. `width` and `height` should be pretty obvious: they give the width and height of the image, measured in pixels. We'll cover pixels when we look into images in more detail a bit later.

Go and grab **divers-circle.jpg** from the code archive, and put it into your web site's folder. The image is shown in Figure 2.16.

Figure 2.16. Divers pausing in a circle

Open **index.html** in your text editor and add the following markup just after the level two heading (h2):

index.html *(excerpt)*

```
<p><img src="divers-circle.jpg" width="200" height="162"
    alt="A circle of divers practice their skills"/></p>
```

Save the changes, then view the homepage in your browser. It should look like the display shown in Figure 2.17.

Figure 2.17. Displaying an image on the homepage

Adding Structure

Paragraphs? No problem. Headings? You've got them under your belt. In fact, you're now familiar with the basic structure of a web page. The small selection of tags that we've discussed so far are fairly easy to remember, as their purposes are obvious (remember: p = paragraph). But what on earth is a div?

A div is used to divide up a web page and, in doing so, to provide a definite structure that can be used to great effect when combined with CSS.

When you place content inside a div, it has no effect on the styling of the text it contains, except for the fact that it adds a break before and after the contained text. Unlike a p element, the div does not add any margins or padding. Compare the following:

```
<p>This is a paragraph.</p>
<p>This is another paragraph.</p>
<p>This is yet another paragraph.</p>
<p>And just one more paragraph.</p>

<div>This is a div.</div>
<div>The content of each div appears on a new line.</div>
<div>But unlike paragraphs, there is no additional padding.</div>
<div>A div is a generic block-level container.</div>
```

The difference can be seen in Figure 2.18.

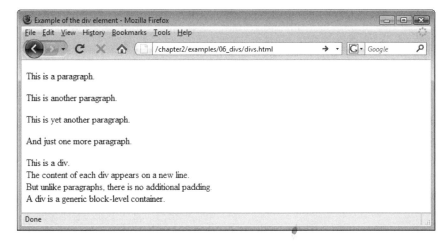

Figure 2.18. Paragraphs have additional spacing above and below, unlike div elements

The purpose of a div is to divide (hence the abbreviation 'div') up a web page into distinct sections—a basic structural framework with no styling—whereas p should be used to create a paragraph of text.

 Use Elements as Intended

Never use an XHTML element for a purpose for which it was not intended. This really is a golden rule.

Rather than leaving the paragraph tags as they are, you might decide to have something like this:

```
<div>
  <p>This is a paragraph inside a div.</p>
  <p>So is this.</p>
</div>
```

You can have as many paragraphs as you like inside that `div` element, but note that you cannot place `div` elements inside paragraphs. Think of a `div` as a container that's used to group related items together, and you can't go wrong.

If we look at our homepage in the browser, it's possible to identify areas that have certain purposes. These are listed below, and depicted in Figure 2.19. We have:

- a header area that contains:
  - the site name
  - a tag line
- an area of body content

Figure 2.19 shows how the different segments of content can be carved up into distinct areas based on the purposes of those segments.

Take the homepage we've been working on (**index.html**) and, in your text editor of choice, add `<div>` and `</div>` tags around the sections suggested in Figure 2.19. While you're adding those `div`s, add an `id` attribute to each, appropriately allocating the names `header`, `sitebranding`, `tagline`, and `bodycontent`. Remember that attribute names should be written in lowercase, and their values should be contained within quotation marks.

 No Sharing `ids`

`id` attributes are used in XHTML to uniquely identify elements, so no two elements should share the same `id` value. You can use these `ids` later, when you're dealing with elements via CSS or JavaScript.

Figure 2.19. Noting distinct sections in the basic web page

h1, header, and head

An `id` attribute set to `header` should not be confused with headings on the page (`h1`, `h2`, and so on); nor is it the same as the `head` of your HTML page. The `id=` attribute could just as easily have been named `topstuff` or `pageheader`. It doesn't matter, so long as the attribute name describes the *purpose* of that page section to a fellow human being (or to yourself 12 months after you devised it, and have forgotten what you were thinking at the time!).

To get you started, I've done a little work on the first part of the page. In the snippet below, that section has been changed to a `div` with an `id` attribute:

index.html *(excerpt)*

```html
<div id="header">
  <h1>BubbleUnder.com</h1>
  <p>Diving club for the south-west UK - let's make a splash!</p>
</div> <!-- end of header div -->
```

Now, try doing the same: apply `div`s to the parts of the content that we've identified as "site branding" and "tag line."

Nesting Explained

We already know that divs can contain paragraphs, but a div can also contain a number of other divs. This is called **nesting**. It's not tricky, it's just a matter of putting one div inside the other, and making sure you get your closing tags right. Nesting elements can help to logically group sections of a web page together, just as you might do in the real world by placing a selection of small boxes containing similar items inside a larger box.

```
<div id="outer">
  <div id="nested1">
    <p>A paragraph inside the first nested div.</p>
  </div>
  <div id="nested2">
    <p>A paragraph inside the second nested div.</p>
  </div>
</div>
```

As Figure 2.19 shows, some nesting is taking place: the "site branding" and "tag line" divs are nested inside the "header" div.

The Sectioned Page: All Divided Up

All things being well, your XHTML should now look like this:

```
                                                              index.html
<!DOCTYPE html PUBLIC "-//W3C//DTD XHTML 1.0 Strict//EN"
    "http://www.w3.org/TR/xhtml1/DTD/xhtml1-strict.dtd">
<html xmlns="http://www.w3.org/1999/xhtml">
  <head>
    <title>Bubble Under - The diving club for the south-west
        UK</title>
    <meta http-equiv="Content-Type"
        content="text/html; charset=utf-8"/>
  </head>
  <body>
    <div id="header">
      <div id="sitebranding">
        <h1>BubbleUnder.com</h1>
      </div>
      <div id="tagline">
        <p>Diving club for the south-west UK - let's make
```

```
                a splash!</p>
          </div>
        </div> <!-- end of header div -->
        <div id="bodycontent">
          <h2>Welcome to our super-dooper Scuba site</h2>
          <p><img src="divers-circle.jpg" width="200" height="162"
              alt="A circle of divers practice their skills"/></p>
          <p>Glad you could drop in and share some air with us! You've
              passed your underwater navigation skills and
              successfully found your way to the start point - or in
              this case, our home page.</p>
          <h3>About Us</h3>
          <p>Bubble Under is a group of diving enthusiasts based in
              the south-west UK who meet up for diving trips in the
              summer months when the weather is good and the bacon
              rolls are flowing. We arrange weekends away as small
              groups to cut the costs of accommodation and travel and
              to ensure that everyone gets a trustworthy dive
              buddy.</p>
          <p>Although we're based in the south-west, we don't stay on
              our own turf: past diving weekends away have included
              trips up to Scapa Flow in Scotland and to Malta's
              numerous wreck sites.</p>
          <p>When we're not diving, we often meet up in a local pub
              to talk about our recent adventures (any excuse,
              eh?).</p>
          <h3>Contact Us</h3>
          <p>To find out more, contact Club Secretary Bob Dobalina on
              01793 641207 or
              <a href="mailto:bob@bubbleunder.com">email
              bob@bubbleunder.com</a>.</p>
        </div> <!-- end of bodycontent div -->
      </body>
</html>
```

Indenting Your Markup

It's a good idea to indent your markup when nesting elements on a web page, as is demonstrated with the items inside the `div` section above. Indenting your code can help resolve problems later, as you can more clearly see which items sit inside other items. Note that indenting is only really useful for the person—perhaps just you—who's looking at the source markup. It does not affect how the browser interprets or displays the web page.[12]

Notice that, in the markup above, comments appear after some of the closing `div` tags. These comments are optional, but again, commenting is a good habit to get into as it helps you fix problems later. Often, it's not possible to view your opening and closing `<div>` tags in the same window at the same time, as they're wrapped around large blocks of XHTML. If you have several nested `<div>` tags, you might see something like this at the end of your markup:

```
    </div>
  </div>
</div>
```

In such cases, you might find it difficult to work out which `div` is being closed off at each point. It may not yet be apparent why this is important or useful, but once we start using CSS to style our pages, errors in the XHTML can have an impact. Adding some comments here and there can really help you debug later.

```
    </div> <!-- end of inner div -->
  </div> <!-- end of nested div -->
</div> <!-- end of outer div -->
```

How does the web page look? Well, we're not going to include a screen shot this time, because adding those `div` elements should make no visual difference at all. The changes we just made are structural ones that we'll build on later.

---

[12] The one exception to this is the `pre` element. Pre is short for pre-formatted, and any text marked up with this element appears on the screen exactly as it appears in the source; in other words, carriage returns, spaces, and any tabs that you've included will be evident. The `pre` element is usually used to show code examples.

Show a Little Restraint

Don't go overboard adding `div`s. Some people can get carried away as they section off the page, with `<div>` tags appearing all over the place. Overly enthusiastic use of the `div` can result in a condition that has become known as "div-itis." Be careful not to litter your markup with superfluous `<div>` tags just because you can.

Splitting Up the Page

We've been making good progress on our fictitious site … but is a web site really a web site when it contains only one page? Just as the question, "Can you have a sentence with just one word?" can be answered with a one-word sentence ("Yes"), so too can the question about our one-page web site. But you didn't buy this book to learn how to create a one-page web site, did you?

Let's take a look at how we can split the page we've been working on into separate entities, and how these pages relate to each other.

First, let's just ensure that your page is in good shape before we go forward. The page should reflect the markup shown in the last large block presented in the previous section (after we added the `<div>` tags). If not, go to the code archive and grab the version that contains the `div`s (**/chapter2/website_files/06_adding_struc-ture_with_divs/index.html**). Save it as **index.html** in your web site's folder (if you see a prompt that asks whether you want to overwrite the existing file, click **Yes**).

Got that file ready? Let's break it into three pages. First, make two copies of the file:

- Click on the **index.html** icon in Windows Explorer or Finder.
- To copy the file, select **Edit > Copy**.
- To paste a copy in the same location, select **Edit > Paste**.
- Repeat the process once more.

You should now have three HTML files in the folder that holds your web site files. The **index.html** file should stay as it is for the time being, but take a moment to rename the other two in lowercase only. Select each file in turn, choosing **File > Rename**, if you're using Windows; Mac users, simply select the file by clicking on it, then hit **Return** to edit the filename.

■ Rename one file as **contact.html**.

■ Rename the other one as **about.html**.

 Where's My File Extension?

If your filename appears as just **index** in Windows Explorer, your system is currently set up to hide extensions for files that Windows recognizes. To make the extensions visible, follow these simple steps:

1. Launch Windows Explorer.

2. Vista users, select **Organize > Folder and Search Options...**; Windows XP users, select **Tools > Folder Options...**

3. Select the **View** tab.

4. In the **Advanced Settings** group, make sure that **Hide extensions for known file types** does not have a tick next to it.

We have three identical copies of our XHTML page. Now, we need to edit the content of these pages so that each page includes only the content that's relevant to that page.

To open an existing file in Notepad, select **File > Open...**, and in the window that appears, change **Files of type** to **All Files**. Now, when you go to your **Web** folder, you'll see that all the files in that folder are available for opening.

Opening a file in TextEdit is a similar process. Select **File > Open...** to open a file, but make sure that **Ignore rich text commands** is checked.

In your text editor, open each page in turn and edit them as follows (remembering to save your changes to each before you open the next file):

index.html   Delete the "About Us" and "Contact Us" sections (both the headings and the paragraphs that follow them), ensuring that the rest of the markup remains untouched. Be careful not to delete the `<div>` and `</div>` tags that enclose the body content.

about.html	Delete the introductory spiel (the level two heading and associated paragraphs, including the image) and remove the "Contact Us" section (including the heading and paragraphs).
contact.html	You should be getting the hang of this now. This time, we're removing the introductory spiel and the "About Us" section. (If you're not sure you've got it right, keep reading: we'll show the altered markup in a moment.)

Now, each of the three files contains the content that suits its respective filename, but a further change is required for the two newly created files. Open **about.html** in your text editor and make the following amendments:

- Change the contents of the `title` element to read "About BubbleUnder.com: who we are; what this site is for."

- Change the level three heading `<h3>About Us</h3>` to a level two heading. In the process of editing our original homepage, we've lost one of our heading levels. Previously, the "About Us" and "Contact Us" headings were marked up as level three headings that sat under the level two "Welcome" heading. It's not good practice to skip heading levels—an `h2` following `h1` is preferable to an `h3` following an `h1`.

Next, open **contact.html** in your text editor and make the following changes:

- Amend the contents of the `title` element to read, "Contact Us at Bubble Under."
- Change the level three heading to a level two heading, as you did for **about.html**.

If everything has gone to plan, you should have three files named **index.html**, **about.html**, and **contact.html**.

The markup for each should be as follows:

index.html

```
<!DOCTYPE html PUBLIC "-//W3C//DTD XHTML 1.0 Strict//EN"
    "http://www.w3.org/TR/xhtml1/DTD/xhtml1-strict.dtd">
<html xmlns="http://www.w3.org/1999/xhtml">
  <head>
    <title>Bubble Under - The diving club for the south-west
        UK</title>
    <meta http-equiv="Content-Type"
        content="text/html; charset=utf-8"/>
  </head>
  <body>
    <div id="header">
      <div id="sitebranding">
        <h1>BubbleUnder.com</h1>
      </div>
      <div id="tagline">
        <p>Diving club for the south-west UK - let's make a
            splash!</p>
      </div>
    </div> <!-- end of header div -->
    <div id="bodycontent">
      <h2>Welcome to our super-dooper Scuba site</h2>
      <p><img src="divers-circle.jpg"
          alt="A circle of divers practice their skills"
          width="200" height="162"/></p>
      <p>Glad you could drop in and share some air with us! You've
          passed your underwater navigation skills and
          successfully found your way to the start point - or in
          this case, our home page.</p>
    </div> <!-- end of bodycontent div -->
  </body>
</html>
```

about.html

```
<!DOCTYPE html PUBLIC "-//W3C//DTD XHTML 1.0 Strict//EN"
    "http://www.w3.org/TR/xhtml1/DTD/xhtml1-strict.dtd">
<html xmlns="http://www.w3.org/1999/xhtml">
  <head>
    <title>About Bubble Under: who we are, what this site is
        for</title>
    <meta http-equiv="Content-Type"
```

```
          content="text/html; charset=utf-8"/>
    </head>
    <body>
      <div id="header">
        <div id="sitebranding">
          <h1>BubbleUnder.com</h1>
        </div>
        <div id="tagline">
          <p>Diving club for the south-west UK - let's make a
             splash!</p>
        </div>
      </div> <!-- end of header div -->
      <div id="bodycontent">
        <h2>About Us</h2>
        <p>Bubble Under is a group of diving enthusiasts based in
           the south-west UK who meet up for diving trips in the
           summer months when the weather is good and the bacon
           rolls are flowing. We arrange weekends away as small
           groups to cut the costs of accommodation and travel and
           to ensure that everyone gets a trustworthy dive
           buddy.</p>
        <p>Although we're based in the south-west, we don't stay on
           our own turf: past diving weekends away have included
           trips up to Scapa Flow in Scotland and to Malta's
           numerous wreck sites.</p>
        <p>When we're not diving, we often meet up in a local pub
           to talk about our recent adventures (any excuse,
           eh?).</p>
      </div> <!-- end of bodycontent div -->
    </body>
</html>
```

contact.html

```
<!DOCTYPE html PUBLIC "-//W3C//DTD XHTML 1.0 Strict//EN"
    "http://www.w3.org/TR/xhtml1/DTD/xhtml1-strict.dtd">
<html xmlns="http://www.w3.org/1999/xhtml">
  <head>
    <title>Contact Us at Bubble Under</title>
    <meta http-equiv="Content-Type"
        content="text/html; charset=utf-8"/>
  </head>
  <body>
    <div id="header">
      <div id="sitebranding">
```

```
            <h1>BubbleUnder.com</h1>
          </div>
          <div id="tagline">
            <p>Diving club for the south-west UK - let's make a
                splash!</p>
          </div>
        </div> <!-- end of header div -->
        <div id="bodycontent">
          <h2>Contact Us</h2>
          <p>To find out more, contact Club Secretary Bob Dobalina on
              01793 641207 or <a
              href="mailto:bob@bubbleunder.com">email
              bob@bubbleunder.com</a>.</p>
        </div> <!-- end of bodycontent div -->
      </body>
</html>
```

Linking Between Our New Pages

We've successfully created a three-page web site, but there's a small problem: there are no links between the pages. Try for yourself: open **index.html** in a web browser and take a look at the display. How will you get from one page to another?

To enable site visitors to move around, we need to add navigation. Navigation relies on **anchors**, which are more commonly referred to as links. The XHTML for an anchor, or link, is as follows:

```
<a href="filename.html">Link text here</a>
```

The a element might not be intuitive (it stands for "anchor"), but you'll get to know this one very quickly: it's what the Web is built on.

■ The a element contains the **link text** that will be clicked (which, by default, appears on the screen as blue, underlined text).

■ The href attribute refers to the URL to which you're linking (be that a file stored locally on your computer, or a page on a live web site). Unfortunately, again, href is not immediately memorable (it stands for "hypertext reference"), but you'll use it so often that you'll soon remember it.

Don't Click Here!

The link text—the words inside the anchor element, which appear underlined on the screen—should be a neat summary of that link's purpose (for example, email bob@bubbleunder.com). All too often, you'll see people asking you to "Click here to submit an image," or "Click here to notify us of your change of address" when "Submit an image," or "Notify us of your change of address" more than suffices. Never use "Click here" links—it really is bad linking practice and is discouraged for usability and accessibility reasons.[13]

Let's create a simple navigation menu that you can drop into your pages. Our navigation is just a list of three links. Here's the markup:

```
<ul>
  <li><a href="index.html">Home</a></li>
  <li><a href="about.html">About Us</a></li>
  <li><a href="contact.html">Contact Us</a></li>
</ul>
```

We'll place all of this inside a `div`, so we can quickly and easily see what this block of XHTML represents.

```
<div id="navigation">
  <ul>
    <li><a href="index.html">Home</a></li>
    <li><a href="about.html">About Us</a></li>
    <li><a href="contact.html">Contact Us</a></li>
  </ul>
</div> <!-- end of navigation div -->
```

Now, we just need to paste this markup into an appropriate place on each of our pages. A good position would be just after the header has finished, before the main body content starts.

---

[13] *Why 'Click here' is bad linking practice* [http://www.cs.tut.fi/~jkorpela/www/click.html], Jukka Korpela.

In the code below, the navigation block appears in position on the homepage:

index.html

```
<!DOCTYPE html PUBLIC "-//W3C//DTD XHTML 1.0 Strict//EN"
    "http://www.w3.org/TR/xhtml1/DTD/xhtml1-strict.dtd">
<html xmlns="http://www.w3.org/1999/xhtml">
  <head>
    <title>Bubble Under - The diving club for the south-west
        UK</title>
    <meta http-equiv="Content-Type" content="text/html;
        charset=utf-8"/>
  </head>
  <body>
    <div id="header">
      <div id="sitebranding">
        <h1>BubbleUnder.com</h1>
      </div>
      <div id="tagline">
        <p>Diving club for the south-west UK - let's make a
            splash!</p>
      </div>
    </div> <!-- end of header div -->
    <div id="navigation">
      <ul>
        <li><a href="index.html">Home</a></li>
        <li><a href="about.html">About Us</a></li>
        <li><a href="contact.html">Contact Us</a></li>
      </ul>
    </div> <!-- end of navigation div -->
    <div id="bodycontent">
      <h2>Welcome to our super-dooper Scuba site</h2>
      <p><img src="divers-circle.jpg" width="200" height="162"
          alt="A circle of divers practice their skills"/></p>
      <p>Glad you could drop in and share some air with us!
          You've passed your underwater navigation skills and
          successfully found your way to the start point - or in
          this case, our home page.</p>
    </div> <!-- end of bodycontent div -->
  </body>
</html>
```

You should now be looking at a page like the one shown in Figure 2.20.

Figure 2.20. Displaying simple navigation on the page

Add the block of links to **contact.html** and **about.html**, then try clicking on the links that you've just added. It should be possible to flick between all three pages, as shown in Figure 2.21.

This is a landmark: you're now the creator of a working, navigable web site. Let's now discuss a few more XHTML elements that you can add to your pages.

Figure 2.21. Navigating the web site

The `blockquote` (Who Said That?)

We're going to add a sound bite—well, a written quote, to be precise—to the About Us page. Here are the lines:

> "Happiness is a dip in the ocean followed by a pint or two of Old Speckled Hen. You can quote me on that!"

We'll add the quote after the final paragraph in **about.html** using a `blockquote`[14] element; here's the markup you'll need:

about.html *(excerpt)*

```
<blockquote>
  <p>"Happiness is a dip in the ocean followed by a pint or two of
     Old Speckled Hen. You can quote me on that!"</p>
</blockquote>
```

---

[14] http://reference.sitepoint.com/html/blockquote/

Or is it? Who's doing the talking? Well, it's our dear (fictional) Club Secretary, Bob Dobalina:

about.html (excerpt)

```
<p>Or as our man Bob Dobalina would put it:</p>
<blockquote>
  <p>"Happiness is a dip in the ocean followed by a pint or two of
     Old Speckled Hen. You can quote me on that!"</p>
</blockquote>
```

The quotation can contain as many paragraphs as you like, as long as each one starts and ends correctly, and the opening `<blockquote>` tag is closed off properly.

Figure 2.22 shows how the `blockquote` above will appear on the page.

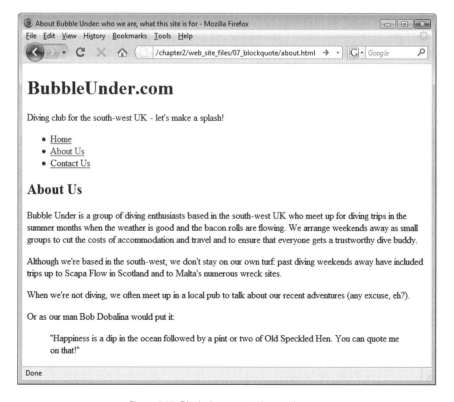

Figure 2.22. Displaying a quotation on the page

Displaying `blockquotes`

In most browsers, your use of `blockquote` will see the quoted text indented in the page display. This effect can be overridden if it's not to your taste, but that's something we'll cover in a later chapter. On the flip side, you should *never* use the `blockquote` element for the purposes of indenting text. This is very poor form. Only use `blockquote` for its intended purpose: to present a quotation. There are other, better ways to create visual indentations, namely CSS.

The `cite` Element

If the quote to which you've referred is written elsewhere—in a magazine, for instance, or a book, or even your own web site—you can add some information to communicate the quote's source. One way is to use the `cite` element. A citation, by default, will style the text in italics. Here's how the markup would look for a citation:

```
<p>I remember reading <cite>Salem's Lot</cite> by Stephen King as
    a child, and being very scared of the dark for days after.</p>
```

So what do we do if something is both a quotation *and* a citation? The `blockquote` element has a `cite` attribute for this very purpose:

```
<blockquote cite="http://www.petermoore.net/sftb/chapter1.htm">
   <p>It didn't take long for a daily routine to form: when they
       left for work in the morning I'd still be in bed. And when
       they came home they'd find me sitting on the sofa, drinking
       beer and watching TV soaps.</p>
</blockquote>
```

We're not using the `cite` element (or the `cite` attribute) in the diving web site, but you may find them useful in your own web site projects.

strong and em

We mentioned the `em` element earlier in this chapter. It's a fairly straightforward element to remember. If you can imagine yourself adding some kind of inflection as you say a word, then emphasis is probably what you need. If you're looking to strike a slightly more forceful tone, then you should consider "going in `strong`".

By default, adding `em` will style text in italics, while using `strong` makes the text bold. You can combine the two if you want, but usually, one or the other will suffice. The examples below should help you understand what these elements are used for. Figure 2.23 shows how they appear in the browser.

```
<p>Although Jimmy was told to <strong>never</strong> put his hands
    on the exhaust pipe, he <em>still</em> couldn't help
    himself.</p>
```

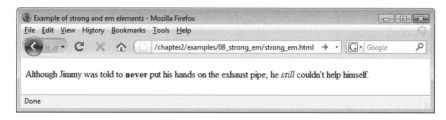

Figure 2.23. Displaying different emphasis styles in the browser

Taking a Break

The chapter's almost at an end, so why take a break? Well, this is just an excuse for a headline pun. We have one more element to look at: the break element.

The break element (`br`)[15] basically replicates what happens when you hit the carriage return on an old typewriter. To create a paragraph on an old typewriter, you'd hit **Enter** twice to give the necessary spacing. In XHTML, the fact that you're marking up a paragraph with `<p>` and `</p>` tags means the spacing is worked out for you automatically. However, if you just want to signify the start of a new line, rather than a new paragraph, the element you need is `br`, as demonstrated in this limerick:[16]

```
<p>The limerick packs laughs anatomical,<br/>
Into space that is quite economical.<br/>
But the good ones I've seen,<br/>
So seldom are clean,<br/>
And the clean ones so seldom are comical.</p>
```

---

[15] http://reference.sitepoint.com/html/br/
[16] http://en.wikipedia.org/wiki/Limerick_(poetry)

Avoid Multiple Breaks

It's all too easy to resort to using multiple breaks in a web page to achieve a visual effect. If you find yourself doing this, something's wrong: you almost certainly need to look for a more suitable technique (we'll look at how this visual effect should be achieved later). Be careful in your use of br.

Note that br is an empty element, just like meta and img, so in XHTML it's written as <br/>.

Summary

Wow—what a great start we've made. In this chapter, you've built a single web page gradually into three linked pages. You've become familiar with the most commonly used XHTML tags, as well as some of the less common ones that you can apply to your web pages. But, somehow, despite all your efforts, the web pages are still looking a little on the bland side. We're going to fix that very soon: in the next chapter, we'll start to add some splashes of color, and make the site look a little more like a fun diving site and less like a boring old Word document.

Chapter 3

Adding Some Style

In Chapter 1 and Chapter 2, we stepped through the process of setting up your computer so that we could develop web sites, and pulled together the beginnings of a web site with which you could impress your friends and family. The trouble is, when you came to show off your fledgling site to your nearest and dearest, they weren't *that* impressed. What have you done wrong?

The answer is: nothing. It's true that the web site may look a little bland at present, but the underlying structure on which it's built is rock-solid. To return to our automotive analogy, you now have a perfect chassis and some decent bodywork, and, while your car's not making people turn their heads just yet, it's only a matter of time. Just let them see what you can do with this rolling shell!

In this chapter, we'll begin the process of adding that lick of paint to your site. The tool for the job is **Cascading Style Sheets—CSS** to those in the know (or with limited typing abilities). Let's take a look at what CSS can do for you.

What is CSS?

As this chapter revolves almost exclusively around CSS, it's probably a good idea to begin with a basic discussion of what CSS is, and why you should use it. As we've already mentioned, CSS stands for Cascading Style Sheets, but that's too much of a mouthful for most people—we'll stick with the abbreviation.

CSS is a language that allows you to change the appearance of elements on the page: the size, style, and color of text, background colors, border styles and colors—even the position of elements on the page. Let's take a look at some CSS in action; we'll start by learning about **inline styles**.

Inline Styles

If you're familiar with Microsoft Word (or a similar word processing package), you may well have created your fair share of flyers, advertisements, or personal news-letters (as well as the more mundane letters to the local authorities and so on). In doing so, you've probably used text formatting options to color certain parts of your text. It's as simple as highlighting the words you want to change, then clicking on a color in a drop-down palette. The same effect can be achieved in XHTML using a little bit of inline CSS. This is what it looks like:

```
<p style="color: red;">The quick brown fox jumps over
    the lazy dog.</p>
```

In the example above, we use a `style` attribute inside the opening `<p>` tag. Applying a style to a specific XHTML element in this way is known as using an "inline style."

 But Wait a Minute: Inline Styles?

> If you have dabbled with CSS before you may be thinking at this stage, "But this isn't the right way to do it," to which I say "Just wait a short while—all will be explained soon." We just need to run through these basics first before approaching the best way of doing this.

The `style` attribute can contain one or more **declarations** between its quotation marks. A declaration is made up of two parts: a **property**, and a **value** for that property. In the example above, the declaration is `color: red` (`color` being the property and `red` being its value).

If you wanted to, you could add another declaration to the example above. For instance, as well as having the text display in red, you might want it to appear in a bold typeface. The property that controls this effect is `font-weight`; it can have a range of different values, but mostly you'll use `normal` or `bold`. As you might expect, you'd use the following markup to make the paragraph red and bold:

```
<p style="color: red; font-weight: bold;">The quick brown fox
    jumps over the lazy dog.</p>
```

Notice that a semicolon separates the two declarations. You could carry on adding styles in this way, but beware, this approach can be messy. There are cleverer ways to apply styling, as we'll see very soon.

Adding Inline Styles

Open **about.html** in your text editor, and add an inline style. We want to make the text in the first paragraph after the "About Us" heading bold and blue. Refer to the previous example as you create the style.

Does the markup for your paragraph look like this?

```
<p style="color: blue; font-weight: bold;">Bubble Under is a group
    of diving enthusiasts based in the south-west UK who meet up
    for diving trips in the summer months when the weather is good
    and the bacon rolls are flowing. We arrange weekends away as
    small groups to cut the costs of accommodation and travel and
    to ensure that everyone gets a trustworthy dive buddy.</p>
```

If your markup looks like that shown here, save **about.html** and take a look at it in your browser. It should appear like the page shown in Figure 3.1.

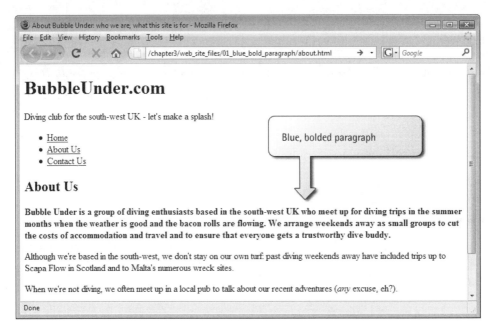

Figure 3.1. Content displayed using blue and bold styles

The span Element

You can easily color a whole paragraph like this, but more often than not, you'll want to pick out just specific words to highlight within a paragraph. You can do this using a span element, which can be wrapped around any content you like. Unlike p, which means paragraph, or blockquote, which signifies a quotation, span has no meaning. A span is little more than a tool for highlighting the start and end of a section to which you want to apply a style.[1] Instead of making that whole paragraph blue, we might want just the first two words, "Bubble Under," to be blue and bold. Here's how we can use the span element to achieve this:

```
<p><span style="color: blue; font-weight: bold;">Bubble
    Under</span> is a group of diving enthusiasts based in the
    south-west UK who meet up for diving trips in the summer
    months when the weather is good and the bacon rolls are
    flowing. We arrange weekends away as small groups to cut the
    costs of accommodation and travel and to ensure that everyone
    gets a trustworthy dive buddy.</p>
```

---

[1] Applying a span also gives you the ability to do some other clever things to your web page using JavaScript, but for our purposes, its scope is limited to what it allows you to do using CSS.

When we view that markup in a browser, we see the display shown in Figure 3.2.

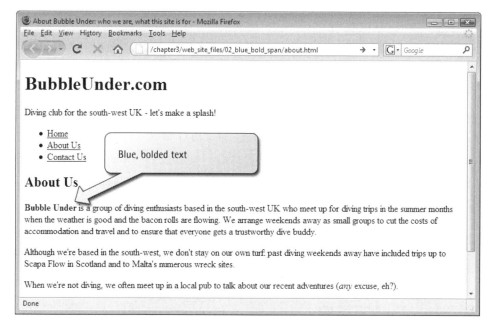

Figure 3.2. Using the span element to pick out specific words for styling

Let's take a quick look at other ways that we can apply inline styles (don't worry, this isn't part of our project site; feel free to experiment).

```
<p style="font-style: italic">The quick brown fox jumps over the
    lazy dog.</p>
```

Not surprisingly, that CSS declaration will italicize all the text in the paragraph. Here's another example, in which span is used to highlight specific words:

```
<p>The quick brown fox <span style="font-style: italic;
    font-weight: bold">jumps</span> over the lazy dog.</p>
```

Embedded Styles

Inline styles are a simple, quick way to apply some CSS effects to specific sections of a document, but this is not the best method of styling a page. Wouldn't it be better if you could set styles in just one place, rather than having to type them out every time you wanted to use them?

Embedded style sheets are a logical step up. An **embedded style sheet** is a section you add to the start of a web page that sets out all the styles that will be used on that page. To do this, you need to use the `style`[2] element inside the `head`:

```html
<head>
  <title>Bubble Under - The diving club for the south-west
      UK</title>
  <meta http-equiv="Content-Type"
      content="text/html; charset=utf-8"/>
  <style type="text/css">
    p {
      font-weight: bold;
    }
  </style>
</head>
```

In the markup shown above, we've moved the inline style into an embedded style sheet. The embedded style sheet starts with a `<style type="text/css">` tag and, predictably, ends with a `</style>` tag. The actual style declarations are enclosed in a set of **curly braces**: { and }. The p that appears before the first curly brace tells the browser what elements the style rules are for; in this case, we're making the text inside every p element bold. The p is called the **selector**, and it's a great tool for quickly and easily changing the appearance of lots of elements on your page. The selector instructs the browser to apply all the declarations between the curly braces to certain elements. The selector, curly braces, and declarations combine to form what's called a **rule**.

In this case, our style sheet contains one rule: "Please style all the paragraphs on this page so that the text appears in a bold font."

---

[2] http://reference.sitepoint.com/html/style/

If we wanted to, we could add more declarations to our rule. For instance, if we wanted to make the text bold and blue, we'd add the declaration `color: blue` to our rule:

```
<style type="text/css">
  p {
    font-weight: bold;
    color: blue;
  }
</style>
```

Jargon Break

Okay, okay. There's been an awful lot of jargon so far. Let's recap: Figure 3.3 brings the theory into focus.

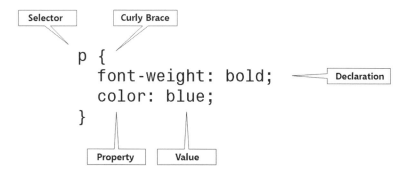

Figure 3.3. The anatomy of a rule

Why Embedded Styles Are Better than Inline Styles

In the example provided in Figure 3.3, text in all paragraphs will display in bold, blue type. This is useful because it saves you having to type <p style="font-weight: bold; color: blue"> every time you start a new paragraph—a clear benefit over inline styles.

If you wanted to change the color of all paragraphs text to red, you need only to change it in the style sheet at the top of the page:

```
<style type="text/css">
  p {
    font-weight: bold;
    color: red;
  }
</style>
```

That's efficiency for you. For this reason, an embedded style sheet is a marked improvement over inline styles. But what if you have a web site that comprises many pages? If you want to make your changes across the whole site, using embedded style sheets in the way I demonstrated above is still not quite the perfect solution. Why not? Because, to make a site-wide change, you'd have to edit the embedded style sheet on every single page of that site. The best solution is to use an external style sheet.

External Style Sheets

Why External Style Sheets Are Better than Embedded Styles

An **external style sheet** provides a location in which you can place styles that can be applied on all of your web pages. This is where the true power of CSS lies, and it's for this reason that we haven't spent too much time applying inline styles or embedded styles to our diving club project site.

The Bad Old Days

In the past, or The Bad Old Days as we'll call them, people would create web sites on a page-by-page basis, and style them on a page-by-page basis using all manner of nasty elements of which I dare not even speak! Sometimes, these sites grew beyond the webmaster's wildest imagination. "Fantastic," thought Mr or Mrs Webmaster. "My web site now has over 200 pages! Soon I'll be bigger than Microsoft." A few months later, the webmaster decided to redesign the web site and realized, with considerable horror, that he or she would have to alter each and every single web page in order to redesign the site in a consistent manner. Every page needed 20 or more different tweaks, and each tweak had to be applied consistently to every page of the site. Inevitably, some pages were missed and eventually the redesign plan was unceremoniously dropped. In short, the ugly web site remained ugly for a whole lot longer before dying a nasty death through sheer negligence (indeed, there are many such legacy documents littered around the Web today). This need not be the case though.

CSS gives you the power to set styling rules in one place. When you want to make changes to your web site, you make changes in that one place, and your whole web site changes automatically to reflect those new styles.

Happy Days! CSS Support Is Here

The good news is that the large majority of web browsers in use today offer excellent support for CSS (though this has not always been the case, which is why some people were slow to adopt CSS-based design in the past). Some browsers can choke on a few of the more advanced CSS techniques, but, by and large, you can style your web pages using CSS and be confident that what you see on your screen is the same view that 99.5% of your intended audience will see.

Creating an External CSS File

If you are to make use of all the benefits that an external style sheet can provide, you'll first need to create a CSS file that can be shared among all the pages of your web site. Open your text editor and enter the following:

```
                                                                    style1.css
/*
CSS for Bubble Under site
*/

p {
  font-weight: bold;
  color: blue;
}
```

Save the file in the same folder as your HTML files, naming it **style1.css**; you can save a CSS file in the same way you saved your HTML files.

Note that the first few lines we typed into our CSS file will not actually do anything. Like HTML, CSS allows you to add comments. It's a shame that the tags for HTML comments are different from those for CSS comments, but they perform exactly the same function: they allow you to make notes about your work without affecting the on-screen display. In CSS, a comment starts with a /* and ends with a */; the browser ignores anything in between. Above, we used the comment simply to make a note about the purpose of the file, namely that it is the CSS for the Bubble Under site. We've also added a rule to turn the type in all our paragraphs bold and blue.

Linking CSS to a Web Page

Before your CSS can have any effect, you need to link it to the web page, or pages, to which you want the styles to apply. To do this, you need to add a link[3] element to the head of each and every web page that will be styled using CSS. Our site contains just three pages at the moment, so this will be nice and easy. The link element simply links a file to the page on which the element appears; in this case, the linked file is a style sheet.

Below, the new line appears in the context of the homepage:

```
                                                     index.html (excerpt)

<head>
  <title>Bubble Under - The diving club for the south-west
      UK</title>
  <meta http-equiv="Content-Type"
      content="text/html; charset=utf-8"/>
  <link href="style1.css" rel="stylesheet" type="text/css"/>
</head>
```

Let's take a look at what the markup means.

The href attribute tells the web browser where the style sheet file (**style1.css**) can be found, in the same way that the href attribute is used in an anchor to point to the destination file (e.g. <a href="home.htm">Home</a>).

The rel="stylesheet" and type="text/css" parts of the link tag tell the browser what kind of file is being linked to, and how the browser should handle the content. You should always include these important attributes when linking to a **.css** file.

---

[3] http://reference.sitepoint.com/html/link/

Empty Element Alert!

The `link` element is another of those special empty elements we discussed in Chapter 2: it does not have separate start and end tags. `link` is a complete element in its own right, and ends using the space and forward slash required by XHTML.

Now that we know how to link our pages to our CSS file, let's try it out on our project site:

▥ Open each of your web pages—**index.html**, **about.html**, and **contact.html**—in your text editor. Add the following line just before the closing `</head>` tag in each of those files:

```
<link href="style1.css" rel="stylesheet" type="text/css"/>
```

▥ Be sure to save each page. Then, try opening each one in your web browser.

All of your paragraphs should now display in bold, blue text. If so, congratulations—you've now linked one style sheet to three separate pages. If you change the color specified in your **.css** file from blue to red, you should see that change reflected across your pages the next time you open them. Go ahead, give it a try.

Now, using blue, bold text might be a good way to make sure your style sheets are correctly linked, but it's not necessarily the design effect we want to use. Remove the **p** rule from your style sheet, but leave the comment, and let's start building our style sheet for real.

Starting to Build Our Style Sheet

The style sheet is ready to be used: it's saved in the right location, and all of your web pages (all three—count 'em) are linked to it correctly. All we need to do is set some styles.

One of the first changes that people often make to a web site's default styling is to alter the font (or typeface) that's used. On Windows, most browsers use Times New Roman as the default—it's the font that has been used in all the screen shots we've seen so far. For many people, though, it's a little bit dull, probably because this font is used more than any other. It's very easy to change fonts using CSS's `font-family` property.

The best place to use this is within the `body` element, as shown below:

```
                                                            style1.css

/*
CSS for Bubble Under site
*/

body {
    font-family: Verdana;
}
```

Here, I've chosen to use the Verdana font. It's applied to the `body` element because `body` contains every element that you will see on the web page. The nature of the way in which CSS is applied means that every element contained in the `body` element will take on the same font (unless another font is specified for a given element or elements within `body`—but more on that a little later).

Great: Verdana it is! But … what if some people who view your site don't have Verdana installed on their computers? Hmm, that's a tricky one. The short answer is that the browser will make its best guess about which font it should use instead, but we don't have to make the browser do *all* the guesswork. The `font-family` property allows us to enter multiple fonts in the order in which we'd prefer them to be used. So, we could type the following:

```
body {
    font-family: Verdana, Helvetica, Arial, sans-serif;
}
```

This translates as: "Please style everything in the body of my web page so that the text appears as Verdana. Failing that, please try using Helvetica and, failing that, Arial. If none of the above are installed, just use whatever sans-serif font is available."

We'll use this selection of fonts in our diving site, so let's open the style sheet file and play around with some CSS.

- Type the above CSS into **style1.css**.
- Save the file, then open the homepage (**index.html**) in your browser.

If everything went to plan, your web page (all three of them, actually) should display slightly differently than they did before. Figure 3.4 shows the appearance of our newly-styled homepage.

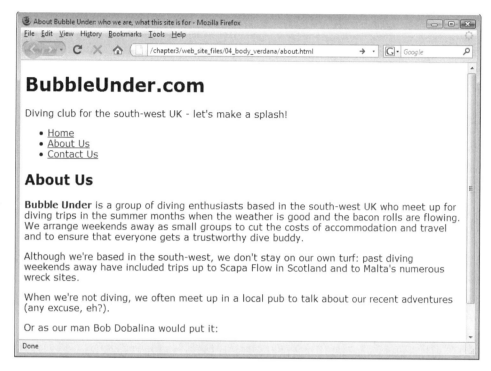

Figure 3.4. A font change in the style sheet affects the body of our web pages

Sans-serif Fonts: Better for On-screen Viewing

A serif font is one that has all those little flourishes at the ends of each letter. These flourishes, which are shown in Figure 3.5, are known as **serifs**. They're great for reading printed material, as they give a little shape to the words, making them easier to read.

However, on the screen, serif fonts can become a little messy, especially when they're used for smaller type—there simply aren't enough pixels on the screen to do these little flourishes justice. For this reason, you'll notice that many web sites use **sans-serif** fonts (from French, translating as "without serif") when the font size is set quite small.

Note that when you refer to a sans-serif font in CSS, you must hyphenate the two words, i.e. `sans-serif`.

Figure 3.5. Highlighting the serifs of a serif font (Georgia)

Stylish Headings

The first element that we'll style is our level 1 headings, denoted by the h1 element. Let's add some rules to our CSS file to see what's possible when it comes to those headings. In your text editor, add the following to **style1.css**:

```
h1 {
    font-family: "Trebuchet MS", Arial, Helvetica, sans-serif;
}
```

Save the CSS file and refresh your view of the homepage in your browser. Can you see what's changed? All the first-level headings now display in the Trebuchet MS font, while everything else displays in Verdana.

The font we've chosen is another sans-serif font, but it's different enough to provide plenty of contrast with the paragraphs, as Figure 3.6 illustrates.

Some Font Names Deserve Quotes

In the code example above, "Trebuchet MS" appeared in quotation marks. You don't need to bother wrapping quote marks around font names, unless the font comprises several words, such as "Courier New" or "Times New Roman." A single-word font name, such as Arial or Verdana, does not need to be wrapped inside quotes.

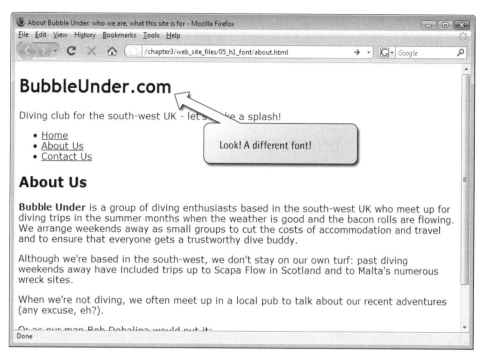

Figure 3.6. h1 headings displayed in one sans-serif font (Trebuchet MS) while paragraph text displayed in another (Verdana)

Have a quick look around all three pages of the web site and you'll see that your new styles have been applied to all your web pages. Let's go a step (or two) further.

What's Going on? Nothing's Changed!

If you try refreshing your browser's view of a page and nothing appears to change, first check that you saved the changes you made to the CSS file. If you have saved the altered file, check that you typed the CSS exactly as described. If you did, you may be experiencing a caching problem with your browser.

Web browsers "cache" some content. **Caching** is when your browser accesses files previously saved to the hard drive when you visit a given web page, rather than downloading new files each time. For example, you enter the URL, and the browser pulls the page stored in its cache. This speeds up the process of displaying a web page that has been loaded before. Unfortunately, your cache can soon become out-of-date, and when that happens, the page you visit might not display the most recent data.

This happens most frequently with images, but it can also occur using CSS files. The good news is that you have control over your browser's cache settings. Therefore, the amount of space the cache takes up on your hard disk before cached content is replaced with newer data can be adjusted. You can poke around your browser's settings for terms like "Cache" or "Temporary Internet Files" to change these settings; however, most users opt to leave their caches to the default settings.

If you're positive that you've made the necessary changes to your CSS file (and saved them) correctly, you may need to force-reload the CSS file in your browser.

To stop the caching problem and force the browser to retrieve the most up-to-date version of your CSS file, simply hold down the **Shift** key and click on the **Refresh** (or **Reload**) icon on your browser's toolbar.

A Mixture of New Styles

Let's change the look of the site a little more—we'll add more styles to the body, and change the look of the navigation. Copy the CSS below into your **style1.css** file (or copy it from the book's code archive):

style1.css

```
/*
CSS for Bubble Under site
*/

body {
  font-family: Verdana, Helvetica, Arial, sans-serif;
  background-color: #e2edff;
  line-height: 125%;
  padding: 15px;
}

h1 {
  font-family: "Trebuchet MS", Helvetica, Arial, sans-serif;
  font-size: x-large;
}

li {
  font-size: small;
}
```

```
h2 {
  color: blue;
  font-size: medium;
  font-weight: normal;
}

p {
  font-size: small;
  color: navy;
}
```

Save the CSS file, then click **Reload** (or **Refresh**) in your browser. Hopefully, you'll be looking at a page like the one shown in Figure 3.7.

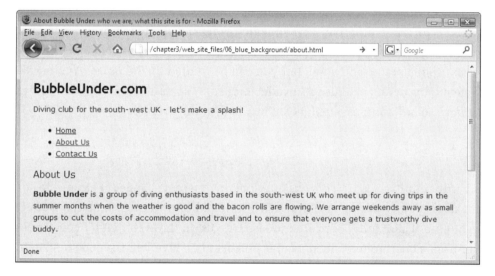

Figure 3.7. Applying subtle changes to the CSS that affects the display of the font

A New Look in a Flash!

We've introduced quite a few new style declarations here. Let's examine a few of them in the order in which they appear in the CSS file:

```
                                                     style1.css (excerpt)

body {
    font-family: Verdana, Helvetica, Arial, sans-serif;
    background-color: #e2edff;
    line-height: 125%;
    padding: 15px;
}
```

The `background-color` property can be applied to most elements on a web page, and there are many different ways in which you can specify the color itself. One is to use recognized color names[4] such as navy, `blue`, `red`, `yellow`, and so on. These are easy to remember and spell, but you can be limited by the range. Another way of referencing colors is to use a **hexadecimal** color specification. Yes, you're right: that *does* sound a little scary. I mean, just look at the code for it:

```
background-color: #e2edff;
```

It's hardly intuitive, is it? This obscure-looking reference (`#e2edff`) translates to a light shade of blue. You could not, as a beginner, begin to guess that this would be a light blue. Thankfully there are numerous tools on the Web that let you choose a color from a chart (often called a **color picker**), then give you the code to match. Take a look at some of these tools,[5] and you'll soon be able to find the hexadecimal numbers you need to create your ideal color schemes.

What the Heck's Hex?

Colors in HTML are often written as a hexadecimal color specification. You might remember the hexadecimal counting system from your high school math class. Or maybe you were asleep up the back of the room. Never mind. Hexadecimal is that weird counting system that goes up to 16 instead of 10; the one you thought you'd never have any practical use for. Well, you do now!

---

[4] http://reference.sitepoint.com/html/color-names
[5] A good selection of links to color scheme tools is available at http://www.clagnut.com/blog/260/.

That's right: when you count in hexadecimal, there are not ten, but **16 digits**. The hexadecimal sequence looks like this:

```
0, 1, 2, 3, 4, 5, 6, 7, 8, 9, A, B, C, D, E, F, 10, 11, 12…
```

Eh? What's happening here? Well, as you can see, after we reach 9, instead of going straight to 10 (as we do when counting in decimal) we go through A, B, C, D, E, and F before we finally hit 10. That gives us six extra digits to use when we count. Sound confusing? Well, as it so happens, computers can count in hexadecimal far better than humans can!

The key here is that all of those numbers that we know and love in the decimal system, like 2,748, 15,000,000, and 42, can be represented in hexadecimal. And Table 3.1 proves it!

Table 3.1. Decimal to Hexadecimal Conversion

Decimal	Hexadecimal
7	7
15	F
2,748	ABC
15,000,000	E4E1C0
42	2A

When a color is expressed as a hexadecimal number, such as `ff0000`, that number actually comprises three values that are joined together. The values represent the proportions of red (the `ff` part), green (the first two zeros), and blue (the second two zeros) that are mixed to create the specified color. Those three primary colors can be combined to display any color on the screen, similar to the way a television set uses different amounts of red, green, and blue to create a single dot on its screen.[6] In this example, `ff` is the value for red, while the green and blue values are zero. It may not surprise you, then, to learn that `#ff0000` will give you the color red.

The `line-height` property is an interesting one. By increasing that value (we used 125% in our example), you can increase the space between lines of text—which

---

[6] If you thought the primary colors were red, blue, and yellow you're not wrong! Head over to http://en.wikipedia.org/wiki/Primary_color to learn all about the additive and subtractive methods of color mixing.

can greatly increase legibility. Try tweaking this value, save your CSS file, and see how the new value affects the text on your web page.

The `padding` property is used to provide space between the outside edge of the element in question and the content that sits inside it. Because we're referring to the `body` element, you can think of the outside edge as being the top, bottom, and sides of the browser's **viewport** (that being the part of the browser where the web page is viewable, not including any of the browser's tool bars, menus, or scroll bars). We'll take a look at `padding` in more detail in Chapter 4.

The value we've given to this property specifies how much space must exist between the edge of the viewport and the content. In this case, we've specified 15px, or 15 pixels. We mentioned pixels before, when we specified the size of an image, but what is a **pixel**? Basically, one pixel is one of the tiny dots that make up what you see on the computer screen. The screen itself is made up of hundreds of thousands of these pixels, so a 15-pixel border won't take up too much space on your screen!

Now, to the paragraph styles:

style1.css *(excerpt)*

```
p {
   font-size: small;
   color: navy;
}
```

We've already shown that it's possible to change the color of text in a paragraph; now, we're going to settle on the appropriate color of navy.

Let's see what's changed with the list item style:

style1.css *(excerpt)*

```
li {
   font-size: small;
}
```

The size of the list items has changed ever so slightly through our application of the `font-size` property. Here, we've decided to set the font size using the `small` keyword, but we could just as easily have used the percentage or pixel methods. As we've already seen—there are many ways to skin a cat using CSS! Font-size keywords range from `xx-small` to `xx-large` and offer a quick way to style text. Unfortunately, different browsers implement font-size keywords slightly differently, and unfortunately you can't be guaranteed that an `xx-large` font will render at the same size in all browsers. However, unless you're extremely worried about precise sizing, these keywords make a good starting point.[7]

We've also introduced a new rule for the `h1` element (the main heading on our web pages, which displays the site name) and, once again, used a `font-size` property to specify the size of the text (extra large!).

style1.css (excerpt)

```
h1 {
  font-family: "Trebuchet MS", Helvetica, Arial, sans-serif;
  font-size: x-large;
}
```

The `h2` element also receives a minor makeover:

style1.css (excerpt)

```
h2 {
  color: blue;
  font-size: medium;
  font-weight: normal;
}
```

Browsers usually display headings in bold type, but we can have them display in standard type by giving the `font-weight` property a value of `normal`.

A Beginner's Palette of Styling Options

We've looked at some examples of styles that can be applied to your web pages through CSS, but the examples we've seen have been a mixed bag (and deliberately so). There are so many more from which you can pick and choose—too many possibilities, in fact, for us to be able to list them all here. However, this section lists

---

[7] For more reasons than we have space to discuss, text sizing in CSS is a topic that causes heated debate in some circles. As you become familiar with CSS, you may want to learn more about the other text-sizing techniques that it offers. A good place to start would be SitePoint's CSS discussion forum at http://www.sitepoint.com/launch/cssforum/.

some of the basic properties and values with which you might like to experiment. Feel free to try any of these in your CSS file. Note that we'll be adding to this list in subsequent chapters; it's by no means exhaustive!

`color` `background-color`	As we've seen, both of these properties can take color keywords (e.g. `red`, `blue`, or `green`) or hexadecimal color specifications such as `#ff0000`.
`font-family`	This property takes a list of font names, containing any fonts you choose in order of preference. Be sure to provide options that users are likely to have on their computers (e.g. Arial, Verdana, etc.). This list should end using one of the "generic" CSS fonts such as `serif` or `sans-serif`, which any browser that supports CSS will recognize.
`font-size`	This property can be any one of the following:

font size keywords

- `xx-small`
- `x-small`
- `small`
- `medium`
- `large`
- `x-large`
- `xx-large`

relative font sizes

- a percentage (e.g. `140%`)
- em units (e.g. `1.2em`; `1em` is equal to the height of the M font character)

fixed font sizes

- pixels (e.g. `20px`)
- points (e.g. `12pt`, as you may be used to using in Microsoft Word)

Fixed font sizes are not always a great idea, as they cannot easily be scaled up or down to suit the reader's needs. Relative font sizes are definitely the preferred option.

font-weight   bold or normal

font-style   normal or italic

text-decoration   none, underline, overline, or line-through

 Backing It Up!

Before you experiment using the CSS properties above, it might be an idea to make a backup of your CSS file, just in case you run into difficulties. Remember that you can download all the examples used in this chapter from the code archive if you accidentally mangle your CSS file. If this happens, don't worry! It's all part of the learning process, and you can be sure that no animals will be harmed in the process.

Recap: the Style Story so Far

Let's allow ourselves a moment to reflect. Our site now boasts a CSS file using a selection of attractive styles. We're in the enviable position of being able to change the site at a whim by altering just that one CSS file. Let's try styling some more of the elements on our web pages.

Changing the Emphasis

◼ Open **about.html** in your text editor.

◼ Find the paragraph about meeting up in a local pub and add an emphasis element as shown here:

about.html *(excerpt)*

```
<p>And when we're not diving, we often meet up in a local pub
    to talk about our recent adventures (<em>any</em> excuse,
    eh?).</p>
```

■ Save the page, then view it in your web browser; it should appear as shown in Figure 3.8. As you can see, emphasis elements appear in italics by default. We're going to use CSS to change that default style.

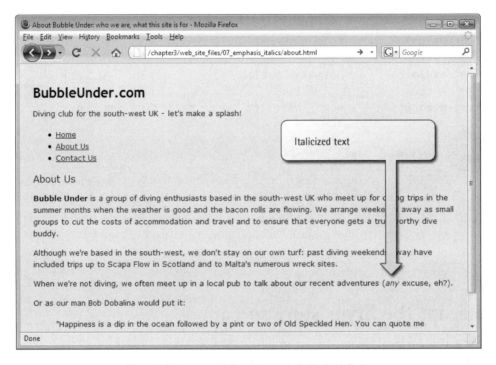

Figure 3.8. Using emphasis to set type to italics by default

■ Open **style1.css** (if you haven't already opened it for editing) and add the following rule below the others:

style1.css *(excerpt)*

```
em {
  font-style: normal;
  text-transform: uppercase;
}
```

■ Save the CSS file, then refresh your browser's view of the About Us page. Does your page look like Figure 3.9?

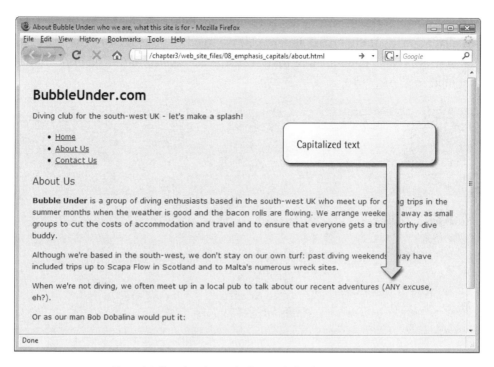

Figure 3.9. Changing the emphasis to capitalized text from italics

Now, whenever you add an em element to any web page of your site (assuming that page is linked to **style1.css**), the emphasized text will appear in capital letters, not italics. But this raises an interesting point: when should you override a browser's default style for one of your own choosing? Presumably, the default styles that browsers use were selected carefully; how can you be sure that redefining the styles is a good idea? Aren't italics a suitable style for emphasis? They probably are. As they say in the Spider-Man film, "With great power comes great responsibility," so be sure to exercise caution. Just because you *can* change a default style doesn't always mean you should.

Perhaps a compromise is in order. Let's change the emphasis so that it's still italic, but also appears in uppercase letters. All we need to do is remove the `font-style` declaration; the em element will then revert to its default italicized appearance, as depicted in Figure 3.10:

style1.css *(excerpt)*

```
em {
    text-transform: uppercase;
}
```

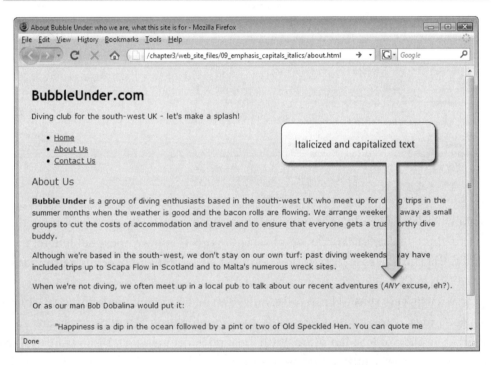

Figure 3.10. Emphasis displayed as uppercase italics

Emphasis or Italics?

You might well be asking yourself, "If I want an italic font, can't I use an italic element?" In fact, HTML provides an i element for just this purpose, but its use isn't recommended. Why not? Well, marking text as i says nothing about its meaning; i only communicates how it should be presented on the screen. Such elements are referred to as **presentational** HTML elements, and they should be avoided. Likewise, the b element (for bold), another old HTML element, should not be used. The preferred option is to use strong or, if you just want to display headings in bold, use CSS.

Why is this important? It might not seem a big deal as you look at the italicized text in your web browser. But imagine if you were blind, and you used software that read web pages aloud to you, instead of displaying them on the screen. This program (called a **screen reader**) might read text marked up with an em element using slight emphasis, and text marked up with strong in a more powerful voice (though this, of course, depends on the screen reader being used). But what would it do with text marked up with i or b? Well, these elements say nothing about the meaning of the text, so it would not treat them in any special way—thus potentially losing the meaning that you were trying to convey. A search engine (e.g. Google, Yahoo) *may* also place more importance on a user's search terms that appear within a strong element than a b element (although the search engine companies never give anything solid away about how their search algorithms work!).

One other presentational tag that you might see others use, but should *never* copy, is the u element. Wrap this around some text and needless underlining occurs that only serves to confuse users. This is because in web pages, underlined text normally signifies a link—which the u element most definitely isn't!

Looking at Elements in Context

Here's a riddle for you: which of these items is bigger? A pen or a sheep? Well, the answer is either, depending on the context. If you were a farmer, you'd swear that the pen is bigger. After all, you spend many hours a week rounding up herds of sheep into a big, solid pen. If, however, you're an office worker, you'd opt for the sheep being the larger of the two—after all, you'd find it a lot easier to pick up a pen and flip it around your fingers.

Context can change a situation quite drastically, and we can use context to our advantage in CSS. We can style an element in a number of different ways, depending on its position. Let's head back to our example site for another lesson. Don't be sheepish, now!

Currently, we have styled paragraphs so that they appear in a navy blue, sans-serif font (Verdana, specifically), as does almost everything else on the page:

style1.css (excerpt)

```css
body {
  font-family: Verdana, Helvetica, Arial, sans-serif;
}

p {
  font-size: small;
  color: navy;
}
```

This is all well and good, but there's one paragraph on our site that's a little different than the others in terms of its purpose. Can you spot which one it is? It's our first paragraph, the one in the tag line. Here's the XHTML for that section:

index.html (excerpt)

```html
<div id="tagline">
  <p>Diving club for the south-west UK - let's make a splash!</p>
</div>
```

It's different because it's not really part of the document content and, as such, it might benefit from some different styling. The fact that this particular paragraph is contained within a specific div element—which has an id attribute of tagline—can be useful. Because it's contained within its own div, we can set a rule for this paragraph and this paragraph only.

■ Open the CSS file for editing, and add the following after the first paragraph rule:

style1.css (excerpt)

```css
#tagline p {
  font-style: italic;
  font-family: Georgia, Times, serif;
}
```

Save the file, then refresh the About Us page (or any of the three, for that matter) in your browser. Your page should now look similar to the one shown in Figure 3.11.

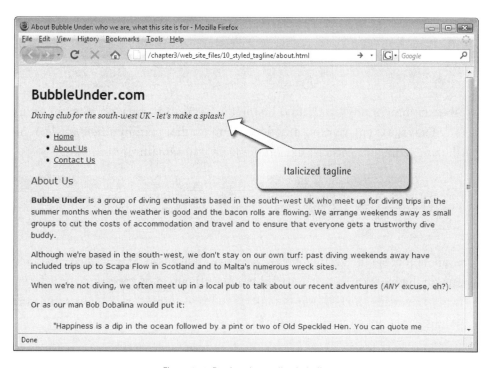

Figure 3.11. Putting the tag line in italics

What's happening here? Perhaps a CSS-to-English translation is required. This CSS rule means, "For any paragraph element that occurs inside an element that has an id of `tagline`, set the text to italics and the font to Georgia, Times, or some other serif font if you don't have either of those."

Getting a Positive ID

The # notation in the CSS refers to an element with a specific `id` attribute—in this case, `tagline`. We'll learn more about selecting `id`s and manipulating them in subsequent chapters.

Contextual Selectors

`#tagline p` is known as a **contextual selector**. Here are some other examples (with their English translations):

```
#navigation a {
   text-decoration: none;
}
```

Translation: for any link found inside the navigation area (an element with an id of `navigation`), remove any decoration on that text; in other words, remove the underline (any other links on the page will remain underlined).

```
#footer p {
   line-height: 150%;
}
```

Translation: set the vertical height between lines of text contained in paragraphs inside the footer area (e.g. a `div` element with an id of `footer`) to 150%. This would override the browser default of 100%, or other line-height values that might be set, for example, for the body text.

```
h1 strong {
   color: red;
}
```

Translation: for any text inside a level one heading that's marked up as `strong`, set the color to red (any other instance of `strong` on the page will not be set to red).

```
h2 a {
   text-decoration: none;
}
```

Translation: don't underline the text of any link inside a level two heading (the default setting underlines all links, so any other links on the page will remain underlined).

Grouping Styles

If you want to apply the same style to different elements on a web page, you don't have to repeat yourself. For example, let's say that you want to set heading levels one through three in yellow text with a black background. Perhaps you'd do this:

```
h1 {
  color: yellow;
  background-color: black;
}

h2 {
  color: yellow;
  background-color: black;
}

h3 {
  color: yellow;
  background-color: black;
}
```

That's very messy and repetitive. Plus, once you have a lot of styles on the page, it is even more difficult to maintain. Wouldn't it be great if you could reduce some of that work? You can! Here's how:

```
h1, h2, h3 {
  color: yellow;
  background-color: black;
}
```

Translation: if the element is a level one heading, a level two heading, or a level three heading, set the text to yellow and the background to black.

 Comma = "Or"

You can think of the commas in CSS selectors (like the one above) as the word "or."

Let's try grouping some styles in our project site. We don't have any h3 headings yet, but we will soon.

■ Edit your CSS file (**style1.css**) by adding the following to the bottom of it:

```
                                                          style1.css (excerpt)

h1, h2, h3 {
    font-family: "Trebuchet MS", Helvetica, Arial, sans-serif;
    background-color: navy;
    color: white;
}
```

■ Save the file, then refresh the About Us page in your browser. You should be
looking at a page like the one shown in Figure 3.12.

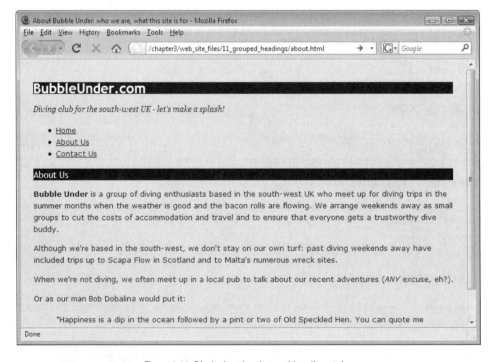

Figure 3.12. Displaying the changed heading styles

That CSS really does kill several birds with one stone (figuratively speaking, of
course; I did say no animals would be harmed!). Not only do you have the convenience of being able to style many pages from one central location (your CSS file), but
you have the added convenience of being able to style many elements in one go.
Your CSS file becomes easier to manage and—a nice little side-benefit—smaller,
and therefore quicker to download.

Filenames for Your Style Sheets

Although we've been working with **style1.css** for some time, you may be wondering why we named the file this way. The name is deliberate. You might want to add another style to your web site at a later date, and numbering is a basic way to keep track of the styles you can apply to a site.

You might be thinking, "Why not name it something like **marine.css** because it uses marine colors, references to sea animals, and so on?" That's a fair question, but it's important to remember with CSS is that you can always change the styles later, and your naming convention might, at a later date, bear no relevance to the styles a file contains. For example, you can edit **marine.css** such that all the colors in your web site are changed to ochres, browns, and sandy yellows. This ability to change the web site's design in one action is the whole point of CSS! With the new design, your web site might have an earthy/desert feel to it, yet you could still have 200 or more pages referring to a style sheet by the filename of **marine.css**. It's not quite right, is it? This is why I've chosen an abstract name for the CSS file, and I recommend that you do the same for the web sites you develop.

But something interesting is happening in our CSS file: it appears that we may have a conflict in our rules. Or have we?

Which Rule Wins?

When we added the grouped declaration for the headings, we changed some styles that we'd set previously. A look at the source shows that the level two heading, h2, has been set to be blue *and* white in different places in our style sheet:

style1.css (excerpt)

```
h2 {
  color: blue;
  font-size: medium;
  font-weight: normal;
}
⋮
h1, h2, h3 {
  font-family: "Trebuchet MS", Helvetica, Arial, sans-serif;
  background-color: navy;
  color: white;
}
```

Because the declaration specifying that the h2 should be white comes later, it has overridden the earlier one. It doesn't matter if you've defined an h2 to be blue 100 times through your style sheet; if the last definition says it should be white, then white it will be!

Recapping Our Progress

Time for another breather. What have we learned? Well, we've learned some more styles that you can apply in CSS, we've seen how you can style certain elements depending on their context, and more recently, we've discussed how you can group elements that need to be styled in the same way. There's one thing that we've touched on only briefly, yet it demands more attention because it's so fundamental to the way the Web functions. That topic is links.

Styling Links

Links are everywhere on the Web: they truly are the basis of everything you see online. Nowadays, we're used to seeing highly decorative web pages adorned by a wealth of different images and features. Take a step back in time, though, and you'll find that the World Wide Web was little more than a collection of linked documents. Go back to the earliest browsers and you'll see that those links were underlined, which remains the case today. By default, a browser uses the following color scheme for links:

blue   an unvisited link

purple a link to a web page that you've previously visited

red   an active link (one you're clicking on; you may have noticed links flash red momentarily when you initially click on them)

This color scheme isn't to everyone's taste, but it's what we're stuck with for now. At least, it's what we *would* be stuck with if we couldn't use CSS to redefine those colors.

At its most basic, a CSS style for links might look like this:

```
a {
  font-weight: bold;
  color: black;
}
```

Now, instead of being blue and having a normal font weight, your links appear in bold, black type. Try adding that to your **style1.css** file, then save it and see how it affects your web pages—Figure 3.13 illustrates this.

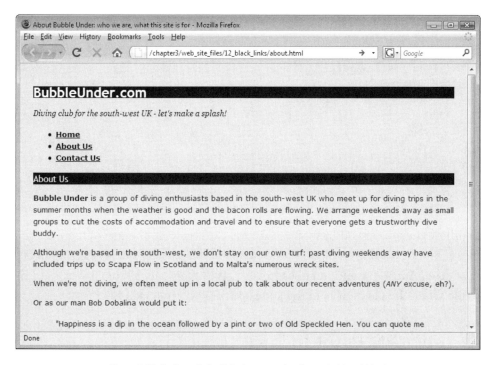

Figure 3.13. Styling all the links in our navigation to bold and black

Link States

As I mentioned previously, there are different types of links (unvisited, visited, active) that you'll come across on a web page. There's one other state that I haven't mentioned, but it's one with which you're probably familiar: the **hover** state (which occurs when you pass your cursor over the link). In CSS, you can change the styling of all these link states using **pseudo-classes**, which sounds complicated but really is fairly straightforward. You can think of a pseudo-class as being like an internal class the browser automatically applies to the link while it's in a certain state. Here is some CSS that shows the color/style scheme for the different link states:

```
a {
  font-weight: bold;
}

a:link {
  color: black;
}

a:visited {
  color: gray;
}

a:hover {
  text-decoration: none;
  color: white;
  background-color: navy;
}

a:active {
  color: aqua;
  background-color: navy;
}
```

The different states are addressed within the CSS through the use of the a element selector, and by adding a colon (:) and the pseudo-classes link, visited, hover, and active. Adding pseudo-classes to your style sheet means the browser applies the rule when the element is in the state specified by the pseudo-class.

 Getting Your Link States in Order

Browsers usually aren't fussy about the order in which you specify rules in your CSS file, but links should always be specified in the order shown above: link, visited, hover, and active. Try to remember the letters LVHA. The more cynical users might find it easier to remember this mnemonic with the phrase, "Love? Ha!" We can thank Jeffrey Zeldman for that little gem.[8]

---

[8] *Designing With Web Standards*, Jeffrey Zeldman, New Riders.

Let's change the styles for different link states in our project site:

- Open the project site's CSS file (**style1.css**), and add the above CSS at the bottom of the file.

- Save the CSS file.

- Open any of the three web pages in your browser (or hit **Reload**) to see how the styled links display.

Figure 3.14 shows the three different link states: the home link is unvisited, the link to the About Us page shows that it has been visited previously (shown in gray), and the link to the Contact Us page is being hovered over by the user's cursor.

Feel free to experiment in the CSS file with the different foreground and background colors, and other text formatting styles that were detailed in the table earlier in this chapter.

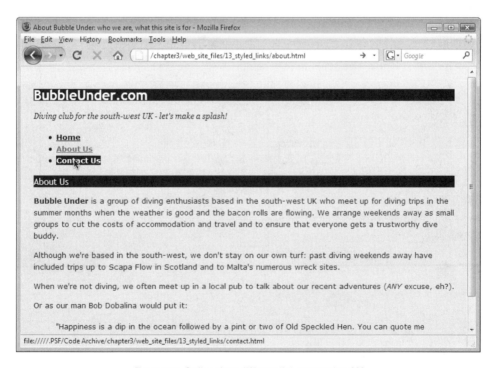

Figure 3.14. Styling three different link states using CSS

Clearing Your History

Your browser automatically stores a certain amount of your browsing history, and uses this information to decide whether a link has been visited or not (and, hence, how the link should be displayed). If you're building a site and testing links, you might want to check how an unvisited link looks but, because of your browsing history, they may all show as having been visited. This is almost certainly the case with our three-page project site—the links in your navigation list are probably all gray. To reset this, you can clear your browser's history. In IE, select **Tools** > **Internet Options**. You'll see a button under **Browsing History** that reads **Delete**. Click on this and it will bring up a **Delete Browsing History** dialog with more options, as shown in Figure 3.15; make sure that the **History** checkbox has been ticked, then click the **Delete** button on that dialog. Afterwards, reload the web page. Any links you may have visited will now appear as unvisited. (The process for clearing history in older versions is a little easier—just look for the button on the **Internet Options** dialogue that says **Clear History**).

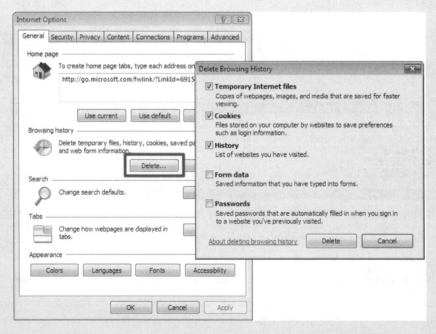

Figure 3.15. Clearing the history in IE displays unvisited link styles again

Other browsers have similar options, which may be found in locations such as **Tools** > **Options** or **Preferences** > **Privacy**. I won't list all the different methods for deleting your history from various browsers here, but if you rummage around, you should be able to find them without too much difficulty.

Class Selectors

To date, we've discussed the ways in which we can style various elements, such as paragraphs and headings; we've also seen how we can style elements in specific areas of the page using the id attribute. However, implementing broad-brush styles, such as coloring the text in all p elements navy, is very much a blanket approach to design. What if you want some of those paragraphs (or any elements, for that matter) to look a little different than the rest? **Class selectors** are the answer.

A class selector lets you define a style that can be used over and over again to style many different elements. So, for example, let's say you wanted to make some parts of your text stand out—to make them look slightly more appealing or fun than other parts of the document.

You could do so in your CSS like this:

```
.fun {
    color: #339999;
    font-family: Georgia, Times, serif;
    letter-spacing: 0.05em;
}
```

Here, we've created a style rule for a class called "fun." The fact that it's a class selector is denoted by the period at the beginning of the class name. We've slipped another property into this rule: letter-spacing defines the space between each of the letters. We've set a spacing of 0.05em here. 1em is the height of the M character in any font, so 0.05em is 5% of that height. It doesn't sound like much of a difference, but when it comes to typography, subtle changes are usually more effective than extreme modifications.

In order to make use of the style once it has been added to your style sheet, all you need to do is add the class="fun" attribute to an element:

```
<p class="fun">A man walks into a bar; you would've thought he'd
    see it coming!</p>
```

Let's apply some classes to our project site. First, we'll need to add the style rule shown above to the style sheet we're working on:

- Open **style1.css** and add the CSS from the above block to the bottom of that file.
- Save **style1.css**, then open **about.html**.
- Find the paragraph that's contained inside the `blockquote` element.
- Add the `class="fun"` attribute to the paragraph's opening tag.

This is how your markup should look right now:

about.html *(excerpt)*

```
<blockquote>
  <p class="fun">"Happiness is a dip in the ocean followed by a
      pint or two of Old Speckled Hen. You can quote me on
      that!"</p>
</blockquote>
```

Note that the `class` attribute was applied at the paragraph level. If there were a few paragraphs in our man Bob's quotation, it could look like this:

```
<blockquote>
  <p class="fun">"Happiness is a dip in the ocean followed by a
      pint or two of Old Speckled Hen. You can quote me
      on that!"</p>
  <p class="fun">"Join us for a weekend away at some of our
      favorite dive spots and you'll soon be making new
      friends.</p>
  <p class="fun">"Anyway, about time I got on with some
      <em>proper</em> work!"</p>
</blockquote>
```

There's a lot of repetition in there. Surely there's a tidier way to apply this style? There sure is:

```
<blockquote class="fun">
  <p>"Happiness is a dip in the ocean followed by a pint or two of
      Old Speckled Hen. You can quote me on that!</p>
  <p>"Join us for a weekend away at some of our favorite dive
      spots and you'll soon be making new friends.</p>
  <p>"Anyway, about time I got on with some <em>proper</em>
      work!"</p>
</blockquote>
```

In this example, we apply that `class` of `fun` to the `blockquote` element, so everything contained in that element inherits the style of the parent container. This saves us from having to apply these different classes all over our pages (an affliction that has become known as class-itis—a not-too-distant relation of div-itis, which we discussed in Chapter 2).

 ## class vs id

So far, we've looked at both `class` selectors (which involve periods: ".") and `id` selectors (which involve pound or hash signs: "#"). Are you confused by them? It's true that these selectors are similar, but there is one important difference: *a specific id can only be applied to one XHTML element*. So, for example, on any web page, there can only be one element with an `id` of `mainnavigation`, and only one with an `id` of `header`. A class, on the other hand, can appear as many times as required.

 ## Limiting Classes to Specific Elements

Imagine you want to italicise any `blockquote` element that has a `class` attribute with the value `fun`, but not other elements with that class value. Think it sounds tricky? Not with CSS! Take a look:

```css
.fun {
  font-family: Georgia, Times, serif;
  color: #339999;
  letter-spacing: 0.05em;
}

blockquote.fun {
  font-style: italic;
}
```

Now, any text inside a pair of `<blockquote class="fun">` and `</blockquote>` tags will appear in italics.

By prefixing our normal class selector with an element name, we're telling the browser to apply the following declarations to that element-and-class combination only. It's as simple as *element.class*, but make sure you don't leave any spaces!

Specifically Speaking

Those with an eagle eye will have noticed that not all of the `fun` styles in the previous example are actually applied to the quotation. The `font-family` and `letter-spacing` declarations take effect, but the color change does not! The reason for this can be explained with the concept of **specificity**.

Specificity simply means the rule that is the most specific is the one that is applied. Determining which rule is the most specific is a little bit complex, but understandable. In our style sheet, the specificity is easy to determine: the `.fun` rule is applied to the `blockquote` element and properties are inherited by the `p` elements, but property values are only inherited in the absence of any other declaration. We have another color declaration in our project site—the one that we created at the start of the chapter that states that all paragraphs should be navy-colored:

```
p {
   color: navy;
}
```

The rule with the element selector `p` has a greater specificity for the `p` elements because the selector specifically targets `p` elements, whereas the `.fun` rule does not. Imagine if, however, we added another rule like this:

```
.fun p {
   color: green;
}
```

The effect would be this: all paragraph text would be navy, except for the paragraphs inside elements with the `class fun`, which would be green. This is because the `.fun p` selector is more specific for those paragraphs. Note that, unlike the conflicting rules we encountered in the section called "Which Rule Wins?", this battle between style rules has no relation to the order in which they appear in the style sheet.

Specificity can be confusing, so don't lose too much sleep over it—for now, it's enough just to be aware of the concept, as this may be the reason why one of your styles doesn't take effect when you're convinced it should. Specificity is covered in great depth in the SitePoint CSS Reference[9] if you'd like to explore it further.

---

[9] http://reference.sitepoint.com/css/specificity/

Styling Partial Text Using `span`

So, a class can be applied in many different places—perhaps to a specific paragraph, or to a block of several paragraphs contained in a `blockquote`, or to a `div` that holds many different types of content. But what would you do if you wanted to apply the style to a very small section of text—maybe just a couple of words, or even just a couple of letters, within a paragraph? For this, once again, you can use the `span` element.

Earlier in this chapter I showed how you could use the `span` element in conjunction with inline styles to pick out and style specific words within a paragraph. The exact same technique can be used with classes: we simply place an opening `<span>` tag at the point at which we want the styling to begin, and the closing `</span>` tag at the point at which the styling should end. The advantage of this technique over the inline style demonstrated earlier is, of course, that with this technique, the style is defined in a single location, so you could potentially add the "fun" class to many different elements on many different pages with a minimum of hassle. When you decide that you want to have a different kind of fun (so to speak), you need only change your style sheet (**style1.css**) for that new style to be reflected across your site:

```
<p><span class="fun">Bubble Under</span> is a group of diving
    enthusiasts based in the south-west UK who meet up for diving
    trips in the summer months when the weather is good and the
    bacon rolls are flowing. We arrange weekends away as small
    groups to cut the costs of accommodation and travel and to
    ensure that everyone gets a trustworthy dive buddy.</p>
```

Try applying the span element to your "About Us" page as suggested in the above XHTML code. If you save the changes and check them in your browser (remember to hit **Reload**), your page should look like the one shown in Figure 3.16.

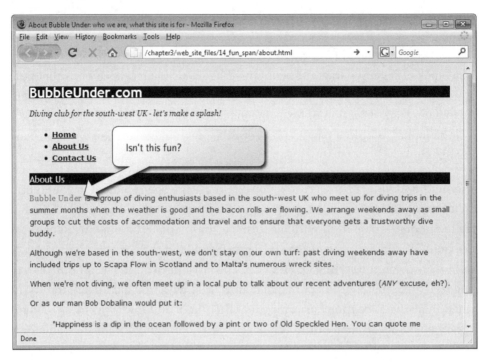

Figure 3.16. Applying the `fun` class to two specific words

Don't Throw (Needless) **spans** into the Works

The span element is nearly always used with a class attribute. There's not normally a good reason to apply a span element to your XHTML on its own, although you may see some web sites that do.

Before you apply a span to any given element on your web page, take a moment to think about whether there's another element that's better suited to the task. For example, it's advisable not to do this:

```
<p>Do it <span class="shouty">now</span>!</p>
```

A more appropriate choice would be to use the **strong** element:

```
<p>Do it <strong>now</strong>!</p>
```

Think of the meaning of what you're writing, and aim for an XHTML element that suits the purpose. Other examples might be em, cite, and blockquote.

Summary

It's been another busy chapter, but my, how our site's blossoming! A chapter or two ago, we hadn't even built a web page, but now we're at the stage where we know how to apply a (virtual) lick of paint to any type of XHTML element on a page, to a specific section of a web page depending on its `id`, or to arbitrary portions of a page—sometimes in several different places—using class selectors.

The web site is starting to look a little more colorful, but the layout is still fairly basic. In the next chapter, we'll look at how it's possible to change the layout of elements on a page—their position, shape, size, and more—using CSS. Styling text? Been there, done that. Let's move to the next level!

Shaping Up Using CSS

For many years, web developers regarded CSS as a tool that could be used to style text on web pages, and add a splash of color here and there, but little more. And for a long time, that was all you could *realistically* use it for, because browser support for CSS was so poor. Thankfully, progress has been made!

You've now reached a point at which many budding web designers stop experimenting with CSS. Not you! In this chapter, we're going to delve a little further into the capabilities of CSS as we use it to:

- change the shape and size of specific areas of content
- change backgrounds and border styles
- position items anywhere on the web page

Let's begin, then, by seeing how we can use CSS to change the shape and size of items on a web page. However, before we can understand this technique, we need to grasp the difference between **block-level elements** and **inline elements**.

Block-level Elements vs Inline Elements

Any given web page comprises two basic types of elements: block-level elements and inline elements. It's important to appreciate the differences between these element types, particularly where CSS is concerned.

The Basic Rules of Block-level and Inline Elements

I'm going to revert to analogies for a moment here—bear with me.

I've moved house recently. When was the last time you moved? It's amazing how much stuff we seem to amass, especially those little trinkets that collect dust on the mantelpiece. You have to find some small boxes to put these bits and pieces in so they don't get damaged, and of course you then need some larger packing boxes into which you can put those smaller boxes.

So on the day before the move—possibly earlier if you're more organized than I am—you start to place your trinkets into small boxes (here's a tip: shoe boxes work well). You then place those shoe boxes into bigger boxes, along with some books and those video tapes of the X-Files that you know you'll never watch but can't bring yourself to throw away. This process continues through the night, and eventually (usually about three minutes before the moving truck is due to arrive) all of your stuff is finally packed and ready to go (whew!).

If you think of the different types of boxes as block-level elements, and your other stuff—the books, videos and trinkets—as inline elements, you'll start to understand the difference between the element types. Armed with that knowledge, we can state the rules for these elements as follows:

- A block-level element can contain other block-level elements, as well as inline elements.

- An inline element can only contain other inline elements.

Block-level Elements

As I explained above, a block-level element is any element that can contain other elements (block-level and inline). To identify a block-level element, look for any element that:

- is normally displayed *on its own line* (or across multiple lines)

Other elements probably appear above or below it, but not on either side (not by default, anyway).

■ is being used as a *container* for one or more other elements

Here are a few examples of common block-level elements:

■ h1, h2, h3, and so on, through to h6
■ p
■ div
■ blockquote
■ ul and ol
■ form[1]

When you create a paragraph of text, you do not need to tell the browser to add a carriage return, start a new line, then add another carriage return at the end of the paragraph—the opening <p> and closing </p> tags do that for you. Consider the text that appears on our site's "About Us" page:

about.html (excerpt)

```
<h2>About Us</h2>
<p><span class="fun">Bubble Under</span> is a group of diving
    enthusiasts based in the south-west UK who meet up for diving
    trips in the summer months when the weather is good and the
    bacon rolls are flowing. We arrange weekends away as small
    groups to cut the costs of accommodation and travel and to
    ensure that everyone gets a trustworthy dive buddy.</p>
<p>Although we're based in the south-west, we don't stay on our
    own turf: past diving weekends away have included trips up to
    Scapa Flow in Scotland and to Malta's numerous wreck
    sites.</p>
<p>When we're not diving, we often meet up in a local pub to
    talk about our recent adventures (<em>any</em> excuse,
    eh?).</p>
<p>Or as our man Bob Dobalina would put it:</p>
<blockquote class="fun">
    <p>"Happiness is a dip in the ocean followed by a pint or two
        of Old Speckled Hen. You can quote me on that!"</p>
</blockquote>
```

---

[1] Forms will be discussed in detail in Chapter 7.

The heading (h2) and the three paragraphs are all block-level elements. They represent blocks of content, where clearly defined breaks above and below each block appear. This is clear in Figure 4.1, where some of the block-level elements are outlined.

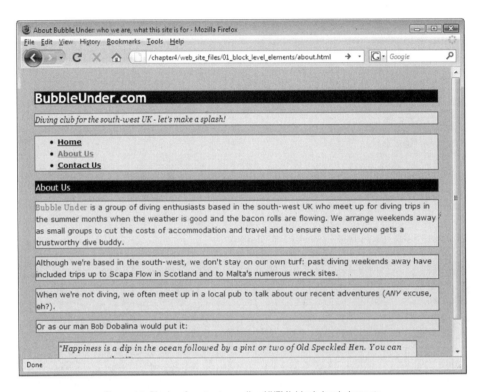

Figure 4.1. Blocks of content revealing XHTML block-level elements

Inline Elements

An easy way to identify an *in*line element is to remember that it sits *in*side another element. As we established in my packing analogy, we can have a box of old photos, or a box containing just one photo, but we can't have a photo full of boxes—it's physically impossible! Similarly, it's against the specifications to use an inline element to contain a block-level element. A good example of an inline element is span (used in Chapter 3), to group words together in order to apply a style:

about.html *(excerpt)*

```
<p><span class="fun">Bubble Under</span> is a group of diving
   enthusiasts based in the south-west UK who meet up for diving
   trips in the summer months when the weather is good and the
   bacon rolls are flowing. We arrange weekends away as small
   groups to cut the costs of accommodation and travel and to
   ensure that everyone gets a trustworthy dive buddy.</p>
```

Other examples of inline elements include:

- em
- strong
- cite
- a

Looking at the example markup above, any one of those inline elements could be applied to the words "Bubble Under":

```
<p><em>Bubble Under</em> is a group of diving enthusiasts…</p>
<p><strong>Bubble Under</strong> is a group of diving
   enthusiasts…</p>
<p><cite>Bubble Under</cite> is a group of diving enthusiasts…</p>
<p><a href="http://www.bubbleunder.com/">Bubble Under</a> is a
   group of diving enthusiasts…</p>
```

In fact, even the image element, img, is inline, although we don't use it in the same way as the elements mentioned above. Instead, img doesn't provide any information to the browser about how text should be treated; an image is simply an image.

Inline Begets Inline

It's perfectly okay to nest one inline element inside another. Here's an example of an inline element that contains another inline element:

```
<p><span class="fun"><a href="http://www.bubbleunder.com/">Bubble
   Under</a></span> is a group of diving enthusiasts based in
   the south-west UK who meet up for diving trips in the summer
   months when the weather is good and the bacon rolls are
   flowing. We arrange weekends away as small groups to cut the
   costs of accommodation and travel and to ensure that everyone
   gets a trustworthy dive buddy.</p>
```

Actually, to refer to the separate examples we saw previously, even the markup shown below would constitute acceptable and valid XHTML (although it may seem like overkill):

```
<p><strong><em><cite><a href="http://www.bubbleunder.com/">Bubble
    Under</a></cite></em></strong> is a group of diving
    enthusiasts...</p>
```

 Watch Your Symmetry

One of the rules of XHTML is that opening and closing tags should be symmetrical: if you open one tag, then another, those tags should be closed in reverse order. In the example above, the tags are correctly opened and closed as follows (indenting is for effect only):

```
<strong>
  <em>
    <cite>
      <a href="http://www.bubbleunder.com/">
        Bubble Under
      </a>
    </cite>
  </em>
</strong>
```

This rule of symmetry applies to *any* kind of element—block-level or inline—and can be checked using online validators (we'll cover this in Chapter 8).

Inline Elements Can Never Contain Block-level Elements

The previous example showed the perfectly acceptable usage of an inline element that contained other inline elements. Now, I'm going to turn that on its head and show you what you should *never* do:

```
<span class="fun"><p>Bubble Under is a group of diving enthusiasts
    based in the south-west UK who meet up for diving trips in the
    summer months when the weather is good and the bacon rolls are
    flowing. We arrange weekends away as small groups to cut the
    costs of accommodation and travel and to ensure that everyone
    gets a trustworthy dive buddy.</p></span>
```

Why is this wrong? Well, what we have here is an inline element, span, wrapped around a block-level element, p, and so this markup is invalid. Bad, naughty markup! We don't discuss validity until the section called "Validating Your Web Pages" in Chapter 8. For now, just remember: block-level elements can only be contained within other block-level elements.

Recap: Block-level and Inline Elements

If you think I've belabored the point of differences between these two types of elements, please accept my humble apologies. Often, people don't appreciate the differences between block-level and inline elements. It's a very important point, though, because these two element types have very different capabilities where CSS is concerned. Let's look at this in detail now.

Styling Inline and Block-level Elements

Inline elements allow for a limited range of styling options, as outlined below (this is a simplified recap of the discussion from Chapter 3):

- change colors (text and background)

- change font properties (size, font family, and other decorative transformations such as underlining, etc.)

This is all fairly superficial, cosmetic stuff, to be honest. However, with block-level elements, you have a much wider range of CSS tools at your disposal, such as:

- Give a block of text a fixed width or height.

- Create padding effects to prevent text from pushing right up against the edge of the block in which it's contained.

- Move a block to any location on the web page, regardless of the position in which it appears in the markup.

In this chapter, we'll see examples of all these techniques—for which the markup is available for download from the code archive. Then, we'll apply the techniques to our project site. Let's begin by looking at how you can shape up and size blocks of content.

Sizing Up the Blocks

By default, a block-level element will take up 100% of the available width (whatever the size of its parent container, be that another `div` element, or even the document's `body`) and whatever height it needs. So far, the paragraphs we've created have fit this description, but, if you wish, you can change these defaults.

Setting a Width

Let's imagine that you have a document that comprises many paragraphs, and you would like to draw attention to one of them in some way other than simply changing the font. For starters, you could try changing the paragraph width. Here's the CSS that does just that (as well as making the font bold):

```css
.attentiongrab {
  width: 50%;
  font-weight: bold;
}
```

I've used a class selector here; do you remember it from the last chapter? It will let us apply this particular style as many times as we like. Here's some XHTML to go with the above CSS:

```html
<p>We've stayed in quite a few caravan parks and camp sites over
    the last couple of months, and I've started to notice a few
    things that seem to suggest that there are some unwritten
    rules of staying at these places. Unwritten until now, that
    is.</p>
<p>Everyone else on site will be better prepared and better
    equipped than you. It's a fact. No matter what extras you
    might carry, someone a couple of plots down will still have
    more. Utensil envy is rife.</p>
<p class="attentiongrab">When you first park, the distance
    between the power supply and your van's power socket will be
    precisely 2 inches longer than the inadequate power lead that
    you own.</p>
```

```
<p>On the hottest evenings, you will be parked next to someone
    with a very flashy van that's equipped with an air-con unit.
    It will be facing you, blowing out hot air and taunting you
    with its efficient hum.</p>
```

Figure 4.2 shows how the text appears on the screen.

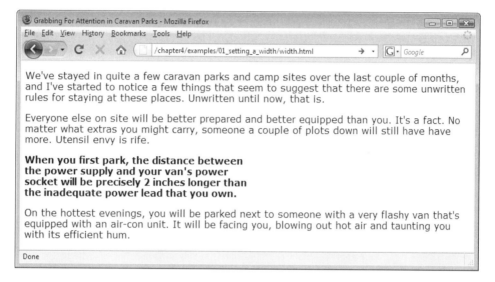

Figure 4.2. Reducing a paragraph's width to 50% of neighboring paragraphs

Setting a Height

The process for setting the height of a block of content is just as simple as setting the width—although you probably won't have as much use for styling the `height` of paragraph text as you will for styling the `width`. A case where you may want to set a specific `height` is in a navigation area (assuming that the number of navigation items in the list doesn't vary dramatically between different pages).

Consider this XHTML:

```
<div id="mainnavigation">
  <h3>Site Navigation</h3>
  <ul>
    <li><a href="home.html">Home</a></li>
    <li><a href="recent.html">Recent Work</a></li>
    <li><a href="portfolio.html">Portfolio</a></li>
    <li><a href="testimonials.html">Testimonials</a></li>
    <li><a href="contact.html">Contact</a></li>
  </ul>
</div>
```

As with our project site, the navigation area is contained in a div that has an id attribute (mainnavigation). As we saw at the beginning of this chapter, a div is a block-level element and, as such, we can play around with it. Let's specify a height and width for it in CSS:

```
#mainnavigation {
  background-color: #ffcc33;
  color: navy;
  font-weight: bold;
  width: 200px;
  height: 400px;
}
```

Note that I've also added a splash of background color (#ffcc33) to make the resized block easier to see.

In the CSS, I've used the width *and* height properties, applying pixel values to achieve a rectangular shape. Figure 4.3 shows how the page looks in the browser.

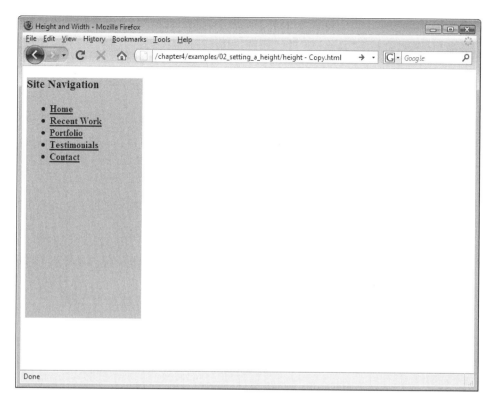

Figure 4.3. Displaying the `div` set to 200 pixels wide, 400 pixels high

What If the Navigation Area Gets Too Big?

I mentioned that we could set a height for a navigation block in this way, "assuming that the number of navigation items in the list doesn't vary dramatically between different pages." Well, you know what they say about assumptions! What would happen if the navigation *did* grow too big for the space we'd allowed for it? The answer to this question depends on the browser, actually.

■ In Firefox 3, and IE7 and 8, the height attribute is honored and the list items overflow out of the bottom of that `div`, beyond the yellow background.

■ In older versions of IE (version 6 and below), the yellow background area expands vertically as the navigation grows.

These differences are depicted in Figure 4.4.

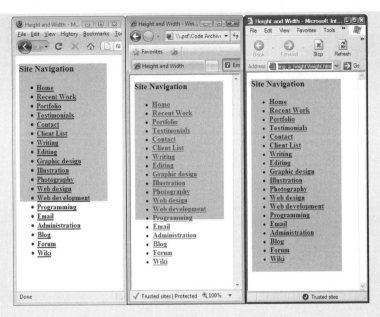

Figure 4.4. Firefox 3 and IE8 behave differently to IE6, as content outgrows its allotted area

Arguably, IE6's behavior of ignoring the height and stretching the background to fit is the preferable reaction to this quandary, but it's a poor implementation of CSS standards. So, if you can, beware of setting a height in situations like the above when it's likely the content will outgrow its container. That said, if you *do* set a height and run out of room later, the beauty of CSS is that you can simply make a change in that one place to give your navigation a little more breathing space site-wide.[2]

Adding Borders to Block-level Elements

You can use block-level elements to apply a range of border effects, including:

- different border thicknesses
- various border styles (solid lines, dotted lines, and more)
- a range of border colors

---

[2] There is a CSS property that you can use to control the behavior of content that overflows a fixed area. This is best used on sections of a web page in which the amount of content is likely to vary quite a lot. For more information, see "The overflow property" on SitePoint's CSS Reference: http://reference.sitepoint.com/css/overflow/.

The CSS properties we can use to achieve these effects are: `border-width`, `border-style`, and `border-color`.

Example Borders

Let's see some examples in action.

Simple Black Border

Figure 4.5 depicts a basic, entry-level border: a solid black line, five pixels wide.

> When you first park, the distance between the power supply and your van's power socket will be precisely 2 inches longer than the inadequate power lead that you own.

Figure 4.5. A simple black border

The CSS for this effect is as follows:

```
.highlight {
  border-width: 5px;
  border-style: solid;
  border-color: black;
}
```

Naming Your Classes

You'll notice here that I've used the class name `highlight`. I've used that name because I'm imagining a hypothetical situation where I wanted to highlight a particular paragraph within a page of content. This is good practice. The basic rule is to use names that describe the purpose or meaning of the content to which the class names are applied.

It may be tempting, however, to name your classes according to how they appear visually. For instance, I could've used the class name `blackborder` for the above example. But there's a very simple reason why I didn't go down that path: what if, one day, I decided to use a red border as my way to emphasize a section? By using the class name `highlight`, I can change the way paragraphs are highlighted easily in the future, without being confused by the labeling or having to adopt a new class name every time it appeared in the XHTML.

Inset Border

If a solid line doesn't do it for you, you could try an `inset` border, which gives the effect shown in Figure 4.6.

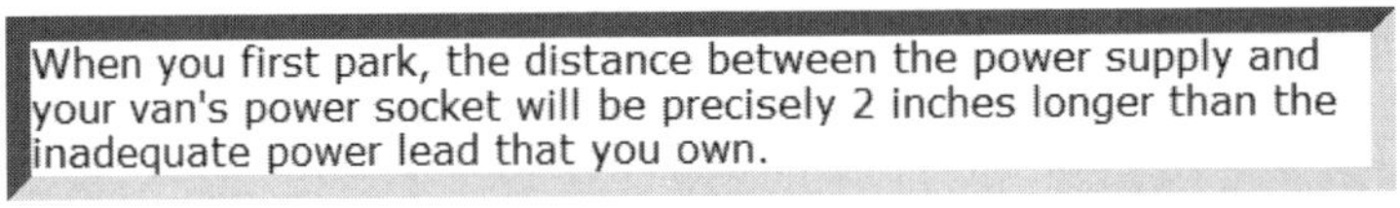

When you first park, the distance between the power supply and your van's power socket will be precisely 2 inches longer than the inadequate power lead that you own.

Figure 4.6. An inset border

The color applied in this example is a shade of gray (shown here as a hexadecimal code):

```
.highlight {
  border-width: 10px;
  border-style: inset;
  border-color: #999999;
}
```

Colored Ridge Border

You can apply some color in combination with a border style to create a two-tone effect. In Figure 4.7, a ridged effect works nicely with the red border color (again, you don't have to take my word for it with regards to the color: check out the file in the code archive for yourself).

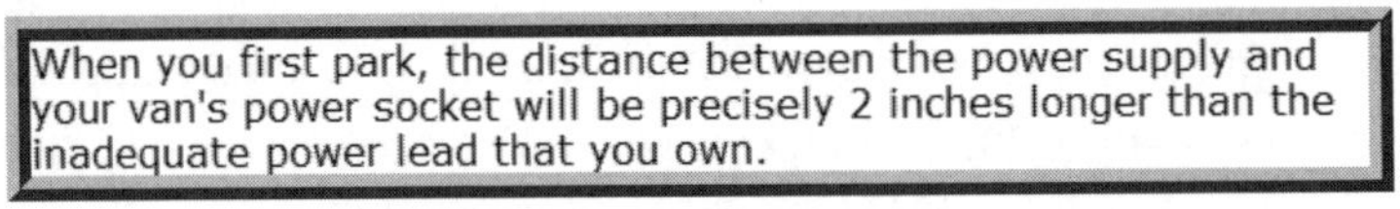

When you first park, the distance between the power supply and your van's power socket will be precisely 2 inches longer than the inadequate power lead that you own.

Figure 4.7. A colored ridge border

The code that creates this effect is shown below:

```
.highlight {
  border-width: 10px;
  border-style: ridge;
  border-color: red;
}
```

Bold Border Effects

You're not limited to using solid lines for the border, though. The examples depicted in Figure 4.8 and Figure 4.9 show `dotted` and `dashed` effects respectively; both borders are set to purple with a ten-pixel thickness.

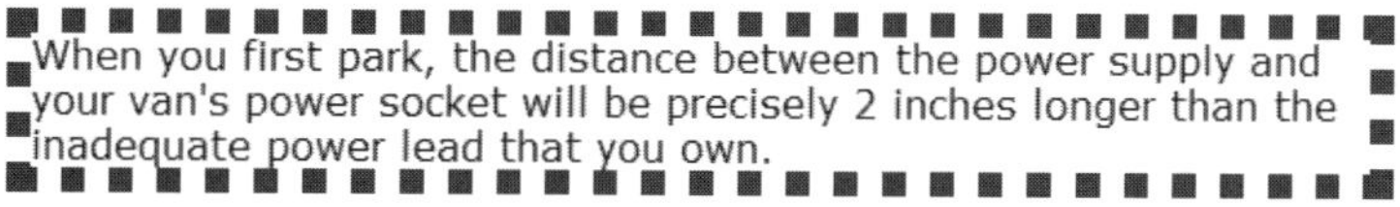

Figure 4.8. A bold, dotted border

```
.highlight {
  border-width: 10px;
  border-style: dotted;
  border-color: purple;
}
```

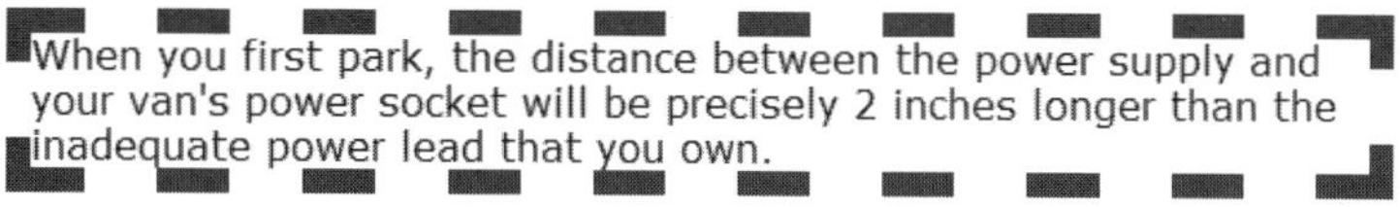

Figure 4.9. A bold, dashed border

```
.highlight {
  border-width: 10px;
  border-style: dashed;
  border-color: purple;
}
```

All the border styles above are a bit intense. Let's have a look at some more refined examples.

Simple Gray Border

The example depicted in Figure 4.10 uses a simple, single-pixel, gray border.

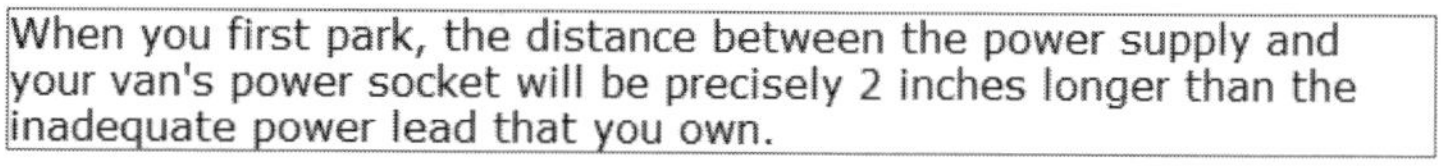

Figure 4.10. A simple gray border

Here's the CSS that achieves this effect:

```
.highlight {
  border-width: 1px;
  border-style: solid;
  border-color: gray;
}
```

Simple Gray Border (Version 2!)

In Figure 4.11, the border has been thickened a little more (to two pixels), but doesn't appear too bold because we've altered the color to a lighter shade (silver).

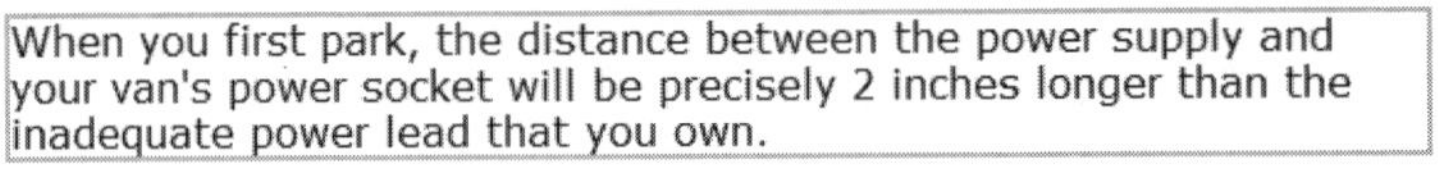

> When you first park, the distance between the power supply and your van's power socket will be precisely 2 inches longer than the inadequate power lead that you own.

Figure 4.11. Another simple gray border

```
.highlight {
  border-width: 2px;
  border-style: solid;
  border-color: silver;
}
```

Dotted Red Border

The red border in Figure 4.12 doesn't seem too severe because it's only one pixel wide; its dotted appearance lightens the effect even more.

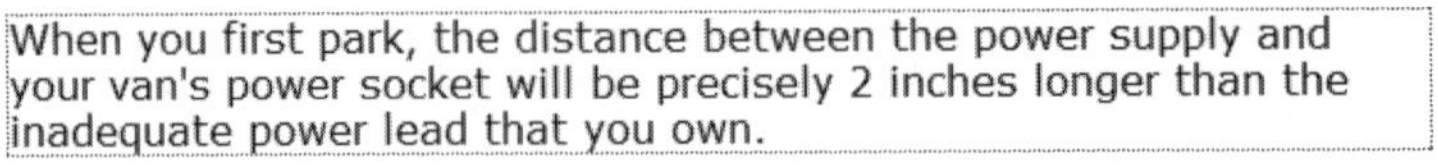

> When you first park, the distance between the power supply and your van's power socket will be precisely 2 inches longer than the inadequate power lead that you own.

Figure 4.12. A dotted red border

Here's the CSS for this border:

```
.highlight {
  border-width: 1px;
  border-style: dotted;
  border-color: red;
}
```

Dashed Gray Border

The dashed version shown in Figure 4.13 is not quite as subtle as the single pixel dotted border, but you will certainly find uses for this style.

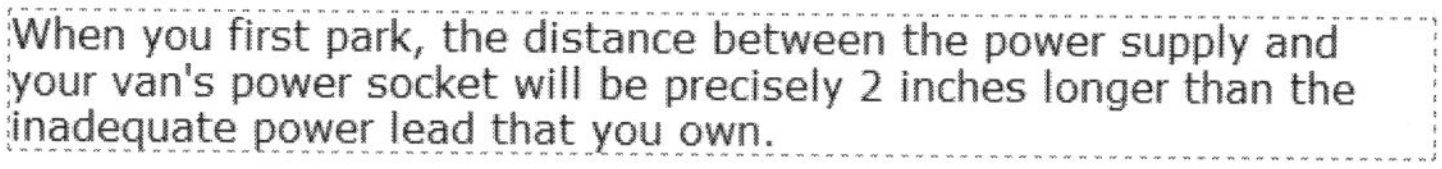

When you first park, the distance between the power supply and your van's power socket will be precisely 2 inches longer than the inadequate power lead that you own.

Figure 4.13. A dashed gray border

```
.highlight {
  border-width: 1px;
  border-style: dashed;
  border-color: gray;
}
```

Double Borders

You can set a double border on block-level elements, as Figure 4.14 shows.

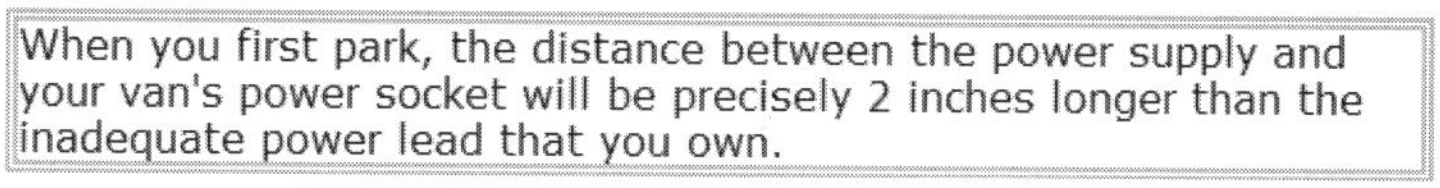

When you first park, the distance between the power supply and your van's power socket will be precisely 2 inches longer than the inadequate power lead that you own.

Figure 4.14. Double border

The markup that creates this effect appears below:

```
.highlight {
  border-width: 5px;
  border-style: double;
  border-color: silver;
}
```

Styling Individual Sides of an Element

As well as applying borders to all the sides of a block-level element, you can style individual edges of the element using `border-top`, `border-bottom`, `border-left`, and `border-right`. Here's an example of a block that has different styles applied to each of its sides:

```
.highlight {
  border-top-width: 1px;
  border-top-style: solid;
  border-top-color: red;
  border-bottom-width: 3px;
  border-bottom-style: dotted;
  border-bottom-color: blue;
  border-left-width: 5px;
  border-left-style: dashed;
  border-left-color: yellow;
  border-right-width: 7px;
  border-right-style: double;
  border-right-color: fuchsia;
}
```

Let's be honest: as Figure 4.15 shows all too clearly, this looks pretty ugly! However, you can use any of those CSS properties on its own. For example, `border-bottom` is often used by itself effectively to create dividing lines between sections of page content.

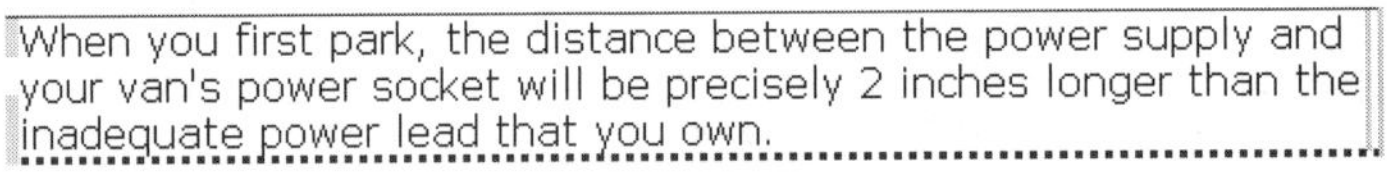

> When you first park, the distance between the power supply and your van's power socket will be precisely 2 inches longer than the inadequate power lead that you own.

Figure 4.15. Displaying a different border for each side of the element

Shorthand Border Styles

As we saw in the previous example, there is a large number of CSS declarations. Wouldn't it be nice if you could set up a border using just one declaration, instead of three? Good news: you can!

```
.highlight {
  border: 5px solid black;
}
```

This is a shorthand method for styling borders, and browser support for this style of CSS notation is excellent. Given that it saves you a little typing, and also saves on file download sizes (albeit by a pinch), this is the method I recommend for styling borders. You can even use `border-top`, `border-bottom`, `border-left`, and `border-right` to style individual sides using this shorthand notation.

Border Styles You Can Use

The examples above demonstrated most of the styles that you can use. Below is a list of all the different options that are available to you; feel free to experiment with whatever combinations you like.

border thickness

> This can be specified using pixels (px), points (pt), or ems.
>
> Alternatively, you could just use one of the border thickness keywords: thin, medium, or thick.

border style

> A border can take any of the following styles:
> - solid (the default value)
> - double
> - dotted
> - dashed
> - groove
> - ridge
> - inset
> - outset

border color

> Border color is specified in the same way as the colors of other elements—either as a hexadecimal code, or as one of the color keywords.

Recap: What Have We Learned?

In this chapter, we've seen how block-level elements can be shaped and sized, and how the border styles can be changed. Until now, I've been using generic examples to explain the possibilities that are available. Now, we're going to apply some of these styles to our project site, using only a smattering here and there; be aware that the overuse of borders can make a web site look very blocky and, possibly, quite ugly.

Shaping and Sizing Our Diving Site

Let's make some minor changes to the project site, beginning with the body element. Open up **style1.css** and find the rule for the body element (it should be the first item that occurs after the comment). Add a declaration to style the whole page with a border, like so:

```
                                                  style1.css (excerpt)

body {
   font-family: Verdana, Helvetica, Arial, sans-serif;
   background-color: #e2edff;
   padding: 15px;
   line-height: 125%;
   border: 4px solid navy;
}
```

Take a look at any of the pages in your browser, and they should be similar to the display depicted in Figure 4.16.

Next, let's make some changes to the navigation area. Earlier, in Chapter 2, I suggested adding id attributes to key sections of the web pages. We'll make use of those attributes in this procedure.

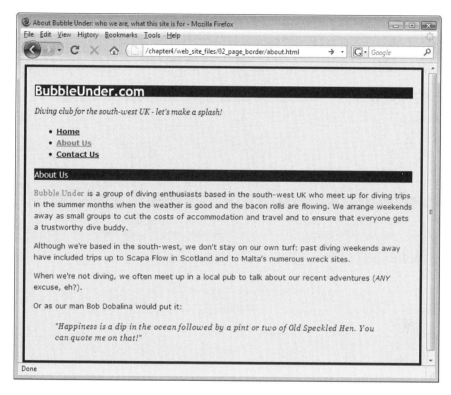

Figure 4.16. Surrounding the entire web page with a border

In **style1.css**, add a new rule for the `navigation` id. Set the area's width to 180 pixels, and add a dotted navy border that's one pixel wide. Your CSS should look like this:

style1.css (excerpt)

```
#navigation {
  width: 180px;
  border: 1px dotted navy;
}
```

Save **style1.css**, then take a look at your web site in a browser. Figure 4.17 shows what you should see.

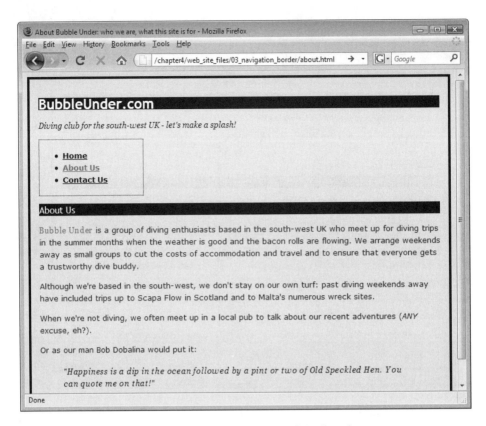

Figure 4.17. The navigation displaying definite dimensions

Another tweak we'll make to the navigation is changing the background color:

```
                                                        style1.css (excerpt)

#navigation {
  width: 180px;
  border: 1px dotted navy;
  background-color: #7da5a8;
}
```

I've chosen another shade of blue (remember from Chapter 3 that a range of color picker tools are available to help you find the hexadecimal codes for different colors). The result of this work is shown in Figure 4.18.

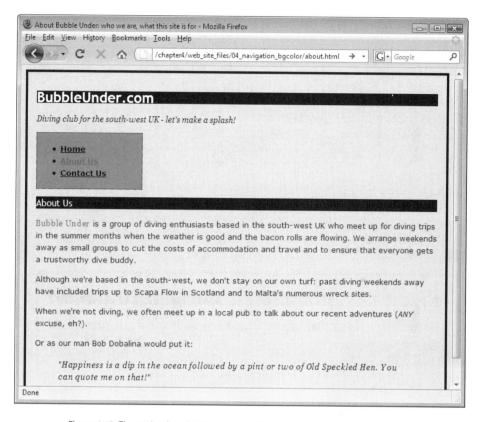

Figure 4.18. The navigation displaying as a distinct, functional area of the web page

That looks better, but the background color we've chosen makes the `visited` link text a bit difficult to read. Let's fix that by choosing a darker color for the visited link. Find the rule for visited links and change it to the following:

```
a:visited {
  color: navy;
}
```

That's much better! Next, let's style the tag line a little more by applying a background color and border effect to set it off nicely. In your style sheet, find the markup that styles the tag line, and add the declaration shown in bold below:

```
#tagline p {
  font-style: italic;
  font-family: Georgia, Times, serif;
  background-color: #bed8f3;
  border-top: 3px solid #7da5d8;
  border-bottom: 3px solid #7da5d8;
}
```

Figure 4.19 shows how this markup displays in the browser.

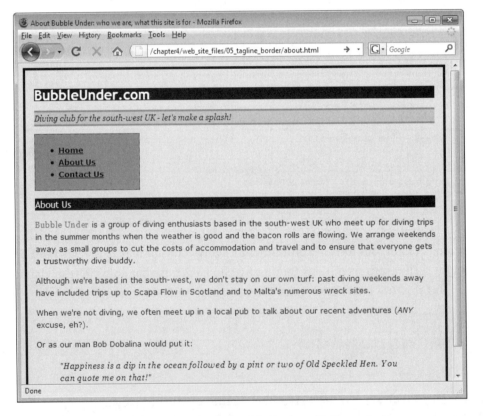

Figure 4.19. Highlighting the tag line with a border and background color

Finally, let's change the styling of the h2 headings so that they look a bit different from the h1s (it *is* possible to go overboard with that dark background effect). Now is also a good time to rearrange some of our rules which, if you've just been adding to the bottom of the file, may be jumbled all over the place, rather than appearing in a logical order. Cut and paste all of the heading rules so they appear together, to make them easier to locate later on:

```css
h1, h2, h3 {
   font-family: "Trebuchet MS", Helvetica, Arial, sans-serif;
}

h1 {
  font-size: x-large;
  background-color: navy;
  color: white;
}

h2 {
  color: navy;
  font-size: 130%;
  font-weight: normal;
}
```

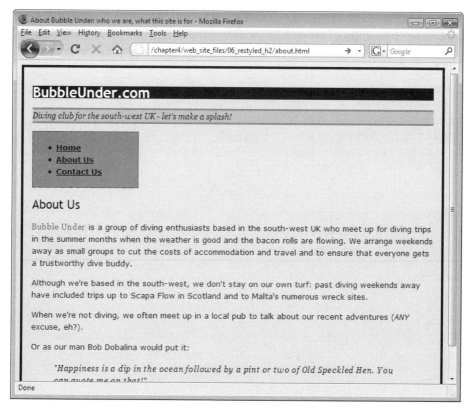

Figure 4.20. Varying the heading styles

We've chosen a new height of 130% for our h2 headings, which (in most browsers) is a bit bigger than large, but slightly smaller than x-large. The page now displays like the one shown in Figure 4.20.

Adding Padding

If you take a look at the headings on the project site, and at the borders that I demonstrated earlier in this chapter, you'll notice that the text sits right next to the border; it looks a little uncomfortable, don't you think? To remedy this, let's add some padding—extra buffer space between the border and the text. Not surprisingly, the CSS property for this extra space is padding.

Here are three different ways we can apply padding to a block-level element: using pixels, ems, and percentage values:

```css
.pixelpadding {
  padding: 30px;
  border: 1px dashed gray;
}
.empadding {
  padding: 2em;
  border: 1px dashed gray;
}
.percentagepadding {
  padding: 5%;
  border: 1px dashed gray;
}
```

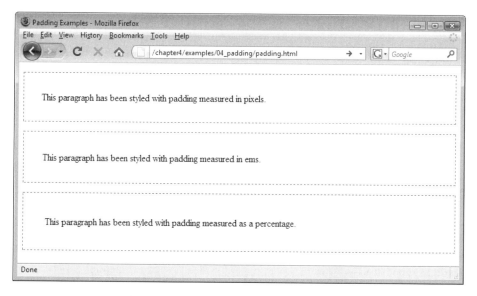

Figure 4.21. Three methods of padding, all achieving the same result on screen

Figure 4.21 shows how these CSS styles render on the screen.

Which Unit of Measurement is Best?

Which method of measurement should you use for your padding: pixels, ems, or percentages? If each of the examples above creates the same effect on the web page, what difference does your choice make? The answer is: it depends on how you want your design to behave.

If you intend your design to change with the browser window, then percentages is the way to go. Any value that's set using percentages will change as the size of the browser window changes: the bigger the browser window, the bigger your padding will become.

If you want your design to scale well with different font sizes, then you should use ems, because the measurements will be based on how your users set the font size in their browsers. If users increase their browsers' font sizes, then sizes set in ems will also increase accordingly.

If you're after a precise design with graphical elements that line up exactly, regardless of browser window size or font setting, then setting sizes in pixels is the most predictable method of all. A pixel will *nearly* always represent a single dot on the user's screen. Why nearly? Because most browsers now offer a page zoom facility which will magnify everything in proportion, over which you have little control.

Introducing Padding to the Project Site

Adding a bit of breathing space to your layout sure can improve it. Let's take a moment to address an issue on the project site—namely, the first-level headings.

Find the section in **style1.css** in which you set the color and size of your h1, and add padding as shown below:

style1.css (excerpt)

```
h1 {
  font-size: x-large;
  background-color: navy;
  color: white;
  padding-top: 2em;
  padding-bottom: .2em;
  padding-left: .4em;
}
```

Next, let's give our headings a bit of head room:

style1.css (excerpt)

```
h2 {
  color: navy;
  font-size: 130%;
  font-weight: normal;
  padding-top: 15px;
}
```

Finally, find the tag line, and give that some padding, too. Use the values below:

style1.css (excerpt)

```
#tagline p {
  font-style: italic;
  font-family: Georgia, Times, serif;
  background-color: #bed8f3;
  border-top: 3px solid #7da5d8;
  border-bottom: 3px solid #7da5d8;
  padding-top: .2em;
  padding-bottom: .2em;
  padding-left: .8em;
}
```

Refresh the view in your browser and you'll see the clear improvement shown in Figure 4.22.

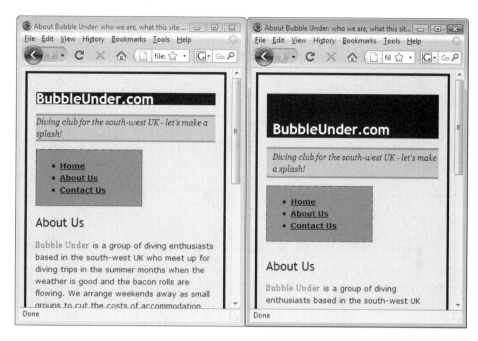

Figure 4.22. Before and after: the benefits of extra padding

Margins

So, you've learned that you can size a block-level element, give it a border of your choosing, and apply padding to that its content doesn't bump right up against its edges. Let's take a look at another very useful CSS property: the margin property.

margin allows us to specify how much space should exist *outside* an element's border. The only difference between the CSS for the two paragraphs shown in Figure 4.23 is that the declaration margin: 30px has been added to the second one.

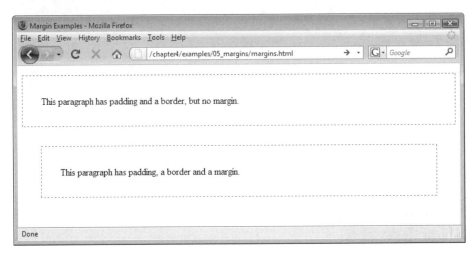

Figure 4.23. The difference between `padding` and `margin` is clearer when a border is present

We're going to change the margin of two elements for now: the `ul` and `h2` elements. Different browsers apply different default top margin values to these elements. Rather than relying on the defaults, let's set a value of 15 pixels, so there's no confusion about the size of this margin:

style1.css *(excerpt)*

```css
h2, ul {
  margin-top: 15px;
}
```

The Box Model

What we've been looking at in this chapter is the **box model**. A block-level element can be manipulated using a combination of `margin`, `border`, `padding`, `height`, and `width` values. These properties can be seen together in Figure 4.24.

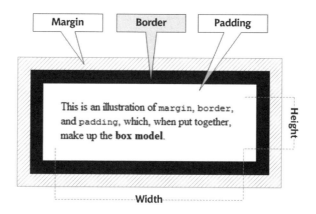

Figure 4.24. The Box Model explained

The Broken Box Model

If you're using IE version 6 or later (to check, go to **Help** > **About Internet Explorer** and look for **Version**), you shouldn't have too many problems sizing and manipulating block-level elements as I've described here, as long as you've included a doctype at the beginning of your web page. If you do not specify a doctype, IE reverts to **quirks mode**.

In quirks mode, IE calculates widths and heights using a different—incorrect—method. This problem arises because IE versions 4 and 5, which were among the first browsers to support CSS, got some of the details wrong (such as the box model). Microsoft fixed those problems in IE6, but in the interim many sites on the Web had been written to use Microsoft's incorrect interpretation of the CSS rules. Microsoft was in a prickly situation: professional web developers demanded that Microsoft fix the bugs, but if it complied, users would be left to battle with most web pages not displaying as intended, sometimes with horrible results.

Microsoft's answer was to use a technique called **doctype switching**. If developers included a doctype, their pages would be displayed according to the correct rules. Pages without a doctype (most of the pages on the Internet at that time didn't bother with doctypes) would be displayed in quirks mode: the same way they appeared in IE5.

If you stick to advice given in this book and use the markup provided, you should not experience any problems relating to quirks mode. However, if you do see noticeable differences between web pages viewed in IE and in other browsers, you may be experiencing the "broken box model" problem. If you think this is the case, your best course of action would be to head over to SitePoint's CSS Forum[3] and ask your questions.

Positioning Elements Anywhere You Like!

Without any intervention, a web browser will simply display the items on the page in the same order as they appear in the source. So, if your markup contains a heading followed by navigation, a second heading, three paragraphs of text, then a quotation, that's precisely what you'll see on the screen, in that exact order. And until now, this has been the way we've approached our project site, adding content in the order in which we've wanted it to appear on the page. But in this next section, I'm going to show you some of the really powerful effects that CSS can achieve: you're going to learn how to position certain sections of the site in very specific areas on the screen.

CSS Layouts: a Million and One Ways to Skin a Cat

With regards to CSS layouts, there are many, many different ways that you can approach this task. One person may naturally opt for one method, while another will take a completely different approach. I cannot possibly teach you every different available method. If, having read this book, you want to investigate the topic further, I'd recommend that you pick up a copy of another SitePoint book: *HTML Utopia: Designing Without Tables Using CSS*.[4]

Showing the Structure

When you're about to lay out your web page using CSS, remember this useful tip: temporarily add a border to each section you're planning to move. Borders make it much easier to see the effects of your markup; afterwards, you'll simply need to remove that temporary style. Let's remind ourselves of the specific sections in our web site:

---

[3] http://www.sitepoint.com/launch/cssforum/
[4] http://www.sitepoint.com/books/css2/

```
                                                         contact.html
<!DOCTYPE html PUBLIC "-//W3C//DTD XHTML 1.0 Strict//EN"
    "http://www.w3.org/TR/xhtml1/DTD/xhtml1-strict.dtd">
<html xmlns="http://www.w3.org/1999/xhtml">
  <head>
    <title>Contact Us at Bubble Under</title>
    <meta http-equiv="Content-Type"
        content="text/html; charset=utf-8"/>
    <link href="style1.css" rel="stylesheet" type="text/css"/>
  </head>
  <body>
    <div id="header">
      <div id="sitebranding">
        <h1>BubbleUnder.com</h1>
      </div>
      <div id="tagline">
        <p>Diving club for the south-west UK - let's make a
            splash!</p>
      </div>
    </div> <!-- end of header div -->
    <div id="navigation">
      <ul>
        <li><a href="index.html">Home</a></li>
        <li><a href="about.html">About Us</a></li>
        <li><a href="contact.html">Contact Us </a></li>
      </ul>
    </div>
    <div id="bodycontent">
      <h2>Contact Us</h2>
      <p>To find out more, contact Club Secretary Bob Dobalina on
          01793 641207 or email
          <a href="bob@bubbleunder.com">bob@bubbleunder.com</a>.
          </p>
    </div> <!-- end of bodycontent div -->
  </body>
</html>
```

Let's add a new (but temporary) rule to our style sheet (**style1.css**) to apply a border to each of the elements. Insert this rule at the end of the style sheet, so that it overrides any border styles you might have set earlier:

```
                                                        style1.css (excerpt)

#header, #sitebranding, #tagline, #navigation, #bodycontent {
  border: 1px solid red;
  padding: 2px;
  margin-bottom: 2px;
}
```

Here, I've applied some padding, as well as a bottom margin, to make it easier for us to see the items that are nested (the `sitebranding` and `tagline` sections are inside the `header` section). Let's see what that CSS has done to our web pages; Figure 4.25 shows the document displayed in the browser.

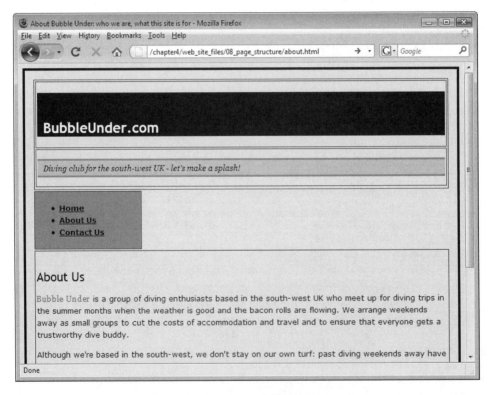

Figure 4.25. Revealing the page structure with red borders

It looks a bit ugly, doesn't it? It's going to get even uglier—for a short while—as we move the text about. You know how it is when you move furniture around in your house: while you're halfway through the job, it can seem a little chaotic, but you know that it will all work out in the end. That's exactly what's going to happen with our project site.

Now, let's start moving these boxes around!

Absolute Positioning

Perhaps the easiest method for positioning items using CSS is **absolute positioning**. Using absolute positioning, we specify top and left positions (or coordinates) for the item in question. Imagine directing a store owner to retrieve a piece of jewelry for you from the shop window with the words, "Can I have the watch that's five along and three down?"

Using absolute positioning is as simple as adding a `position: absolute` declaration to your CSS rule, then specifying where you'd like that element positioned. In the following example, we use `top` and `left` to position a `div` 200 pixels from the top of the browser viewport, and 200 pixels from its left edge:

```
<!DOCTYPE html PUBLIC "-//W3C//DTD XHTML 1.0 Strict//EN"
    "http://www.w3.org/TR/xhtml1/DTD/xhtml1-strict.dtd">
<html xmlns="http://www.w3.org/1999/xhtml">
  <head>
    <title>Absolute Positioning</title>
    <meta http-equiv="Content-Type"
        content="text/html; charset=utf-8"/>
    <style type="text/css">
      #redblock {
        position: absolute;
        top: 200px;
        left: 200px;
        color: white;
        background-color: red;
        width: 90px;
        height: 90px;
        padding: 5px;
      }
    </style>
  </head>
  <body>
    <h1>Absolute Positioning</h1>
    <div id="redblock">This is the red block.</div>
    <p>The red block is positioned 200 pixels from the top and 200
        pixels from the left.</p>
  </body>
</html>
```

Figure 4.26 shows the resulting display.

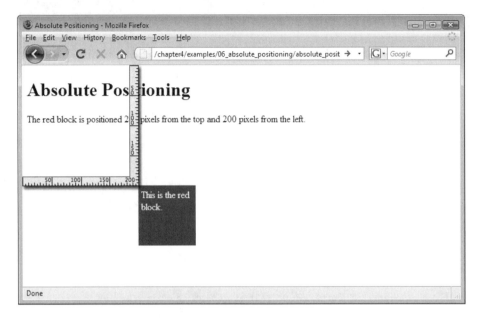

Figure 4.26. Absolute positioning in action

Getting Ready to Move into Position

We're now going to position every element on our page using fixed coordinates relative to the browser window's top and left sides. Because of this, it's worth taking the time to undo some stylistic changes that can complicate matters. We'll now undo the `padding` and `border` properties that we set on the `body` element earlier.

- Open **style1.css** and remove the `padding` and `border` declarations on the `body` element.

- In their place, add two new declarations to set both `padding` and `margin` to zero.

The `body` element rule in your style sheet should now look like this:

style1.css *(excerpt)*

```css
body {
  background-color: #e2edff;
  font-family: Verdana, Helvetica, Arial, sans-serif;
  line-height: 125%;
```

```
    padding: 0;
    margin: 0;
}
```

Nothing is Always Nothing

What's the difference between zero feet, zero meters, and zero furlongs? Well, there's no difference—they're all measuring a zero distance, so the unit is unimportant.

This principle applies in the above CSS—hence, we haven't added a qualifying unit of measurement for the `padding` and `margin` properties. If we want a value of nothing, we don't need to specify a unit of measurement, because whatever the unit might be, it amounts to nothing!

Refresh the view in your browser and you should see a page like the one shown in Figure 4.27.

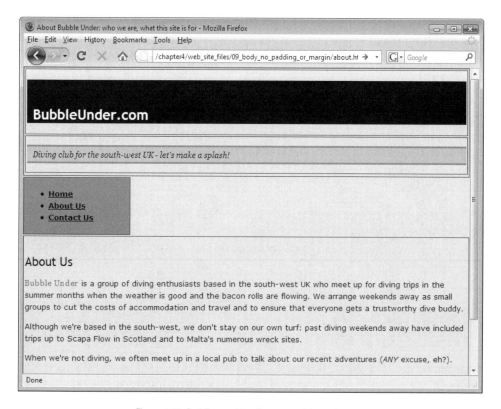

Figure 4.27. Padding and border removed from the body

The headings in the page—BubbleUnder.com (h1) and About Us (h2)—are surrounded by margins, which the browser inserts by default if we don't specify margins of our own. It's a good idea to remove them—what we're aiming to do is "trim off the fat" and try to get each heading as close as possible to the top-left of its containing div. This will make the headings easier to position, and ensure that the page looks the same in different browsers.

▓ In **style1.css**, scroll down the page to find the h1 rule.

▓ Add a declaration to set the margin to zero:

```
                                                        style1.css (excerpt)

h1 {
   font-size: x-large;
   background-color: navy;
   color: white;
   padding-top: 2em;
   padding-bottom: .2em;
   padding-left: .4em;
   margin: 0;
}
```

▓ Locate the #tagline p rule and remove its margins, too:

```
                                                        style1.css (excerpt)

#tagline p {
   font-style: italic;
   font-family: Georgia, Times, serif;
   background-color: #bed8f3;
   border-top: 3px solid #7da5d8;
   border-bottom: 3px solid #7da5d8;
   padding-top: .2em;
   padding-bottom: .2em;
   padding-left: .8em;
   margin: 0;
}
```

▓ Refresh the page in your browser. The gaps that previously appeared above and below the headings should have disappeared, as shown in Figure 4.28.

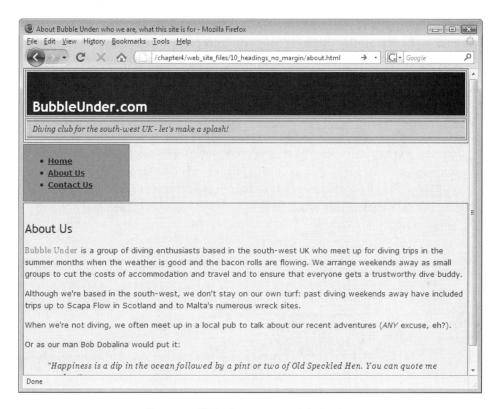

Figure 4.28. Eliminating space around the headings

Now, hold your breath: this is where it *can* get really ugly! However, trust me, I'll get you through this quickly and painlessly (and you'll appreciate why I've suggested adding the red borders to the page elements while their positions are shifting).

▧ Add the following to the end of your CSS file:

```
                                                    style1.css (excerpt)

#navigation, #bodycontent, #header {
    position: absolute;
}
```

▧ Save the style sheet.

▧ Refresh the view in your browser.

▧ Enter a state of shock when you see how bad the page looks!

Your page should look like someone has picked it up, thrown it in the air, and let it fall back to Earth: all the different parts of your page should look like they've landed in a pile, as in Figure 4.29. Don't worry: this is normal!

Avoiding the Messy Part

In case you're wondering why the layout is deliberately being messed up, and whether you're going to have to do this every time you create a web site in future, don't despair. Many web designers skip this intermediate step, and go straight to positioning items where they want them to appear. This ability comes with practice. I think it's important to understand the process properly first, before we dispense with these basics.

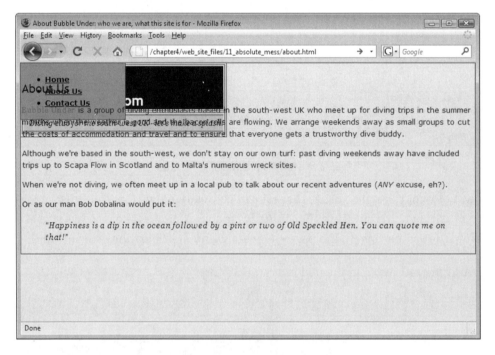

Figure 4.29. Absolute positioning makes the page a mess

What's happened here? Well, the three sections of the page now sit on top of each other, all absolutely positioned at the top left corner of the page. Why? Because that's what we've told the browser to do with them. All it knows is to position them *absolutely*; it doesn't know *where* to position them, so they just sit there in a pile: the header area first, the navigation on top of that, and finally, the bodycontent, king of the heap!

Let's begin to fix the site by moving the navigation and main content area to appear below the header area. In **style1.css**, add the following rule:

style1.css *(excerpt)*

```
#navigation, #bodycontent {
  top: 120px;
}
```

This should move the blocks down so that the header is no longer obscured. Figure 4.30 shows how the markup displays.

What we've done here is tell the browser to move both the `navigation` and `bodycontent` areas to an absolute position that's 120 pixels from the top of the web page—no questions asked! The browser has honored that request. Now we're going to throw it another request: move the `bodycontent` area to the right so that it no longer obscures the `navigation`. As the navigation was previously set to a `width` of 180 pixels, let's try moving the `bodycontent` section to the right by 200 pixels; that should easily move it clear (and leave some space between it and the navigation).

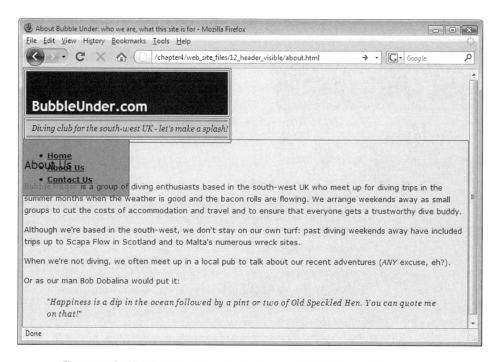

Figure 4.30. Pushing the navigation and content down 120 pixels to reveal the header area

Here's what you need to add to **style1.css**. I've included all of the CSS relating to positioning that we added in the previous few steps, so you can check that everything's okay with your style sheet:

style1.css *(excerpt)*

```css
#navigation, #bodycontent, #header {
  position: absolute;
}

#navigation, #bodycontent {
  top: 120px;
}

#bodycontent {
  left: 200px;
}
```

Let's see how that markup looks in the browser; your page should display as shown in Figure 4.31.

Figure 4.31. Distinguishing navigation from content with the help of positioning

We still need to address a few maintenance issues before this looks like a finished page:

▪ The header area and tag line aren't stretching to fill the width of the web page.

▪ There is some unnecessary space around the h1 element and the tag line.

▪ The red borders and padding between block elements need to be removed (they've served their purpose admirably).

▪ A comment or two should be added to the CSS, to explain what we've done here.

We're going to complete all these tasks in one go. By now, you should be feeling confident enough to have a go at it yourself. As always, don't worry if you do get a bit stuck: the solution awaits you on the other side of this discussion. Let's get this web site looking completely shipshape!

▪ Position the navigation and body content 107 pixels from the top, instead of 120 pixels—this will allow for a snugger fit when we remove the red borders.

▪ Next, tell the browser that the header div and the tag line should fill the available width (i.e., they need to take up 100% of the width).

▪ The red borders that were applied to the various divs earlier (for the purposes of seeing the layout more clearly) need to be removed. Delete the entire rule.

▪ Finally, it would be a good idea to add a comment above all the positioning code to note what you've been doing. This will allow you to easily identify this section's job and note that it controls positioning, rather than cosmetic effects.

How did you get on? Here's the style sheet again (at least, the part of it that we've been concentrating on for positioning purposes). The most recent changes are shown in bold:

style1.css *(excerpt)*

```
/*
This section deals with the position of items on the screen.
It uses absolute positioning - fixed x and y coordinates measured
from the top-left corner of the browser's content display.
*/
```

```
#navigation, #bodycontent, #header {
  position: absolute;
}

#navigation, #bodycontent {
  top: 107px;
}

#bodycontent {
  left: 200px;
}

#header {
  width: 100%;
}
```

So, the big question is, what's this markup done to our web site? Let's take a look. Does your display resemble Figure 4.32?

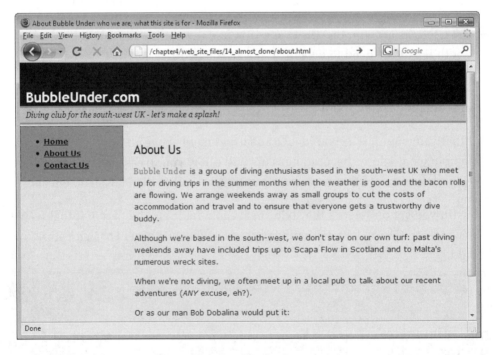

Figure 4.32. A conventional web page layout

I'm almost happy with it. How about you? The header and tag line might complement each other better if they had matching borders. Give the header a top border of three pixels, using the same shade of blue that we used for the tag line. And let's remove the dotted border around the navigation box—it doesn't quite fit our new design:

style1.css *(excerpt)*

```
#navigation {
  width: 180px;
  background-color: #7da5d8;
}

#header {
  border-top: 3px solid #7da5d8;
}
```

Save the changes in **style1.css**, refresh the view in your browser, and see how it looks—hopefully like Figure 4.33!

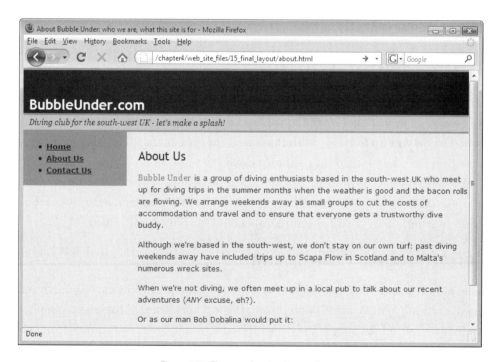

Figure 4.33. The completed web page layout

What We've Achieved: Full CSS Layout

Finally, the page is set out as intended, with the navigation on the left (where you'd expect it to be), the content on the right, and a header (and tag line) that stretches all the way along the top. We've achieved a full CSS layout—which will truly help us out in the future should we want to redesign the look of the site—and it applies to all pages on the site. You may not have noticed, but throughout this whole chapter we haven't touched the page content once, nor the actual XHTML : everything has been changed through the CSS. We've seen how the content can be manipulated using a combination of borders, padding, widths, sizes, and positioning in CSS. Now, visualize what this project web site will look like a couple of years from now, with many, many pages of content. Just think how easy it will be to redesign!

Want the navigation to sit on the right-hand side? No problem. Just change the co-ordinates for the navigation in the CSS, move the content to the left as if you're moving a piece in a slide puzzle, and before you know it, the whole site will have changed. This is the true power of using CSS to build sites (but then you've never known any other way, you lucky soul!).

Other Layout Options

As I mentioned earlier, there are many different ways that you could approach a CSS layout. In this book, I've opted to choose the simplest, most trouble-free method to get you up to speed with the idea; however, it would be remiss of me not to mention the other positioning techniques you can use. Don't worry—I'm not going to ask you to re-do the web site all over again! Instead, I'll provide some general examples (as I did with the border styles earlier in this chapter). First, let's take a look at one more aspect you should know about absolute positioning.

More Absolute Positioning

So far, all our positioning has been relative to the viewport. Whenever you've positioned anything, you've positioned it from the top left corner of the page. When you start to play around with absolutely positioned elements, and you start putting them inside each other, a different approach is required.

To illustrate, let's take our red box example from before, and add a yellow box:

```
<!DOCTYPE html PUBLIC "-//W3C//DTD XHTML 1.0 Strict//EN"
    "http://www.w3.org/TR/xhtml1/DTD/xhtml1-strict.dtd">
<html xmlns="http://www.w3.org/1999/xhtml">
  <head>
    <title>Absolute Positioning</title>
    <meta http-equiv="Content-Type"
        content="text/html; charset=utf-8"/>
    <style type="text/css">
      #redblock {
        position: absolute;
        top: 200px;
        left: 200px;
        background-color: red;
        width: 100px;
        height: 100px;
      }
      #yellowblock {
        position: absolute;
        top: 20px;
        left: 20px;
        background-color: yellow;
        color: red;
        width: 50px;
        height: 50px;
        padding: 5px;
      }
    </style>
  </head>
  <body>
    <h1>Absolute Positioning</h1>
    <div id="redblock">
      <div id="yellowblock">Yellow!</div>
    </div>
    <p>The red block is positioned absolutely using coordinates of
        200 pixels from the top, and 200 pixels from the left.</p>
    <p>The yellow block inside is positioned 20 pixels from the
        top of its parent element, and 20 pixels to the left.</p>
  </body>
</html>
```

Here, we've put a div with the id yellowblock inside our redblock div, and positioned it absolutely, 20 pixels from the top, and 20 pixels from the left. Where do you think the yellow block is going to appear? The display is illustrated in Figure 4.34.

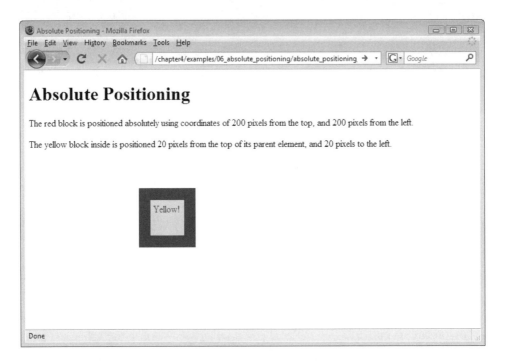

Figure 4.34. The yellow block appears inside the red block

How did it end up there? Well, whenever you absolutely position an element (e.g. the red box above), everything inside that element (the yellow box, in this example) is positioned in relation to that containing element. Don't worry if this is a bit confusing—it may seem like a pretty advanced concept at this stage, but we won't be using it in our project site. However, I wanted to mention it so that you're not confused when you come to play around with positioning on your own sites.

Relative Positioning

With absolute positioning, items are positioned from a very specific start point: the top left corner of the viewport, or the top left corner of a containing element. With **relative positioning**, any value that you apply will be implemented *relative to the item's original location before this positioning rule was applied.* Here is some example CSS. Notice the rule that is applied to elements with the nudged class:

```
p {
  background-color: #ccc;
}
```

```
.nudged {
  position: relative;
  top: 10px;
  left: 10px;
}
```

Here's some XHTML in which the class name nudged is applied to the middle paragraph:

```
<p>Next came a massage that I was not expecting. It started with a
   bit of manipulation of the temples, followed by the barber's
   attempt to drag the top half of my face down towards my chin
   (and vice-versa) with his big burly hands. I'm sure it's good
   for you. I wasn't sure it was good for me, though. He then
   made his way down to my shoulders and managed to pull me
   around in such a way that I squealed like a girl. This was not
   relaxing -- this was painful! Evidently I was knotted up. I
   must have needed it, I reasoned.</p>
<p class="nudged">There was an audible crack as he grabbed my head
   and twisted it to the right, all of it quite unexpected. To
   the left, no cracking sound. And we weren't quite done
   yet...</p>
<p>To finish off, the barber got a pair of tongs. He took a ball
   of cotton wool and wrapped it tightly around the tip of the
   tongs, so that it looked like a large cotton bud. He then
   doused the cotton wool in what must have been pure alcohol,
   set it on fire, and began to fling it at my face. Using one
   hand to cover the top of my ear and my hair, he flashed it
   against my ear, singeing the small hairs in and around the
   ear.</p>
```

The class could have been applied to any paragraph (or any other block-level element, for that matter). Figure 4.35 shows the text with the original position of the paragraph, and the effect after the class name has been added to the p element.

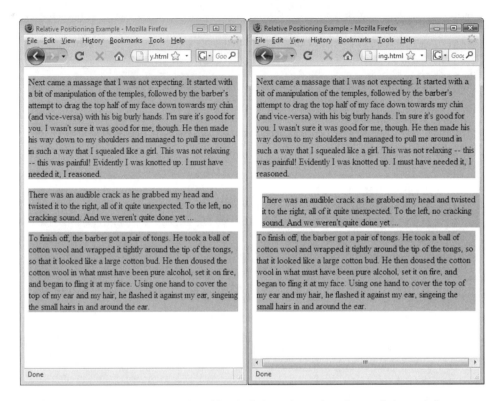

Figure 4.35. The middle paragraph positioned relative to the previous element—before and after

Notice how the markup has moved our paragraph across and down by ten pixels, so that neither the left-hand nor right-hand sides of that paragraph line up with the others. It really has been *nudged*, rather than simply indented from the left-hand side.

In case you're wondering, the text in the example above is describing the "joys" of a traditional Turkish shave. It's fun … if you like that kind of thing!

Benefits of Relative Positioning

Relative positioning is an improvement over the absolute positioning technique that I proposed in the discussion of our project site. If text sizes are increased in the browser, the document can **reflow**—that is, adjust the layout to suit the new text size—more freely if relative positioning is used. (In IE, you would use **View** > **Text Size** > **Larger** or **Largest**.) With the fixed header area (a space of 107 pixels), a large increase in text sizes could potentially cause text to exceed the allotted space and intrude onto the content or navigation area, as shown in Figure 4.36.

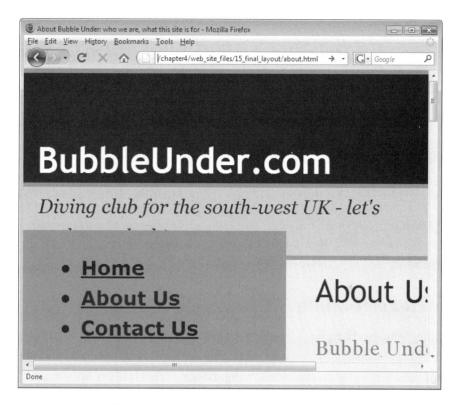

Figure 4.36. Sometimes, very large font sizes and fixed position layouts don't mix

So, why didn't we use the relative positioning method instead of absolute positioning on our project site? Well, using relative positioning for a CSS layout is not easy to accomplish; you might even be put off at an early stage in your CSS career if you get it wrong. In practice, a well-seasoned web developer will use a mixture of absolute, relative, and **floated positioning** schemes.

 Stretching Your Wings with Elastic Design

There is an approach to building web pages called **elastic** web design, where all measurements are specified using ems—borders, margins, padding, everything. Yet, it certainly falls into the realm of advanced web design, so we're not going to tackle it in this book. However, as an indication of what is possible, try making this small change to our project's style sheet.

Locate the line that positions our navigation and body content areas 107 pixels from the top of the viewport, and replace it with the following:

```
style1.css (excerpt)

#navigation, #bodycontent {
   top: 6.54em;
}
```

Save the file and refresh your browser. You shouldn't notice any difference—until you change the font size. Because the `div` elements are positioned using `ems`, the design holds together much better, even for large font sizes. The number 6.54 might seem unusual; I determined it by trial and error to be the distance from the top of the viewport to the bottom of the tag line, regardless of the font size in use.

Earlier in this chapter, we discussed the choices available for units of measurement, and this is one case when a definite advantage is gained by using `ems`. Read more in Patrick Griffith's article on elastic design.[5]

Floated Positioning

A technique favored by many web developers is to use **CSS floats**—making use of the CSS `float` property to lay out a page. Put simply, when you float an area of content, you move it to one side, allowing other content to flow around it. With careful planning, you can float several items on a page, creating effects similar to the multi-column layouts we see in newspapers. Let's take a look at a very simple example of a float:

```
#nav {
   float: right;
   width: 300px;
   background-color: yellow;
}
```

This will move a block with an `id` of `nav` to the right of the web page, setting it to just 300 pixels wide. The text that follows it moves up the page to fill the space that's been vacated by the floated element. Here's the XHTML that achieves this effect:

---

[5] http://www.alistapart.com/articles/elastic/

```
<div id="nav">
  <ul>
    <li><a href="index.html">This is an area of navigation
        items</a></li>
    <li><a href="index.html">which is floated on the
        right.</a></li>
    <li><a href="turkish.html">Turkish Shaving Stories.</a></li>
    <li><a href="http://www.bubbleunder.com/">Diving
        Stories.</a></li>
  </ul>
</div> <!-- end of nav div -->
<h1>Turkish Shaving Stories</h1>
<p>Next came a massage that I was not expecting. It started with a
    bit of manipulation of the temples, followed by the barber's
    attempt to drag the top half of my face down towards my chin
    (and vice-versa) with his big burly hands. I'm sure it's good
    for you. I wasn't sure it was good for me, though. He then
    made his way down to my shoulders and managed to pull me
    around in such a way that I squealed like a girl. This was not
    relaxing -- this was painful! Evidently I was knotted up. I
    must have needed it, I reasoned.</p>
<p>There was an audible crack as he grabbed my head and twisted it
    to the right, all of it quite unexpected. To the left, no
    cracking sound. And we weren't quite done yet ...</p>
<p>To finish off, the barber got a pair of tongs. He took a ball
    of cotton wool and wrapped it tightly around the tip of the
    tongs, so that it looked like a large cotton bud. He then
    doused the cotton wool in what must have been pure alcohol,
    set it on fire, and began to fling it at my face. Using one
    hand to cover the top of my ear and my hair, he flashed it
    against my ear, singeing the small hairs in and around the
    ear.</p>
```

Figure 4.37 shows the effect as it displays in the browser.

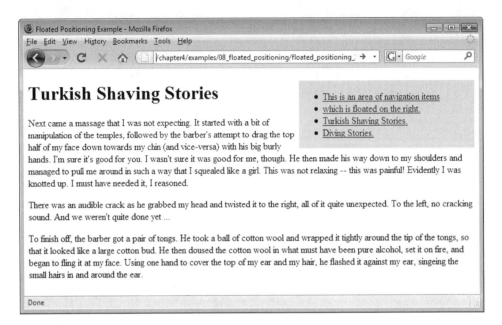

Figure 4.37. A simple CSS float at work

If you want to avoid having the text wrap around the item to form an L shape, apply the CSS `padding` property to the content area. In the example above, the navigation is set to display 300 pixels wide, so if we add a padding value of 310 pixels on the right of the content area, this should do the trick. Here's an updated version of the file:

```
#nav {
    float: right;
    width: 300px;
    background-color: yellow;
}

.contentconstrained {
    padding-right: 310px;
}
```

The class attribute value `contentconstrained` should be applied to a `div` that can surround all the paragraphs that it needs to affect, like so:

```
<div id="nav">
  <ul>
    <li><a href="index.html">This is an area of navigation
        items</a></li>
    <li><a href="index.html">which is floated on the
        right.</a></li>
    <li><a href="turkish.html">Turkish Shaving Stories.</a></li>
    <li><a href="http://www.bubbleunder.com/">Diving
        Stories.</a></li>
  </ul>
</div> <!-- end of nav div -->
<div class="contentconstrained">
<h1>Turkish Shaving Stories</h1>
<p>Next came a massage that I was not expecting. It started with a
    bit of manipulation of the temples, followed by the barber's
    attempt to drag the top half of my face down towards my chin
    (and vice-versa) with his big burly hands. I'm sure it's good
    for you. I wasn't sure it was good for me, though. He then
    made his way down to my shoulders and managed to pull me
    around in such a way that I squealed like a girl. This was not
    relaxing -- this was painful! Evidently I was knotted up. I
    must have needed it, I reasoned.</p>
<p>There was an audible crack as he grabbed my head and twisted it
    to the right, all of it quite unexpected. To the left, no
    cracking sound. And we weren't quite done yet ...</p>
<p>To finish off, the barber got a pair of tongs. He took a ball
    of cotton wool and wrapped it tightly around the tip of the
    tongs, so that it looked like a large cotton bud. He then
    doused the cotton wool in what must have been pure alcohol,
    set it on fire, and began to fling it at my face. Using one
    hand to cover the top of my ear and my hair, he flashed it
    against my ear, singeing the small hairs in and around the
    ear.</p>
</div> <!-- end of contentconstrained div -->
```

Figure 4.38 shows the outcome.

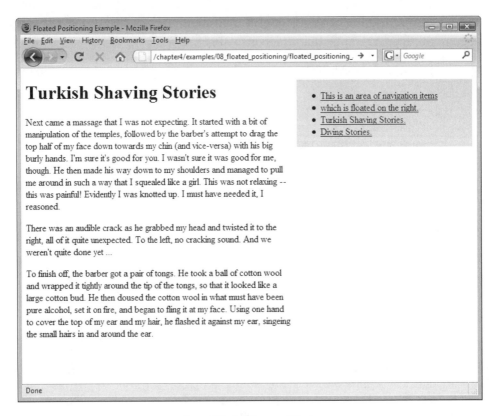

Figure 4.38. A tidier use of floats

We won't use floats much on our project site, but we will float the image of the circle of divers (remember them from Chapter 2?) on the front page. However, because we don't want to float every image on the site, we can't just apply our CSS to every img element. Instead, we'll refer to this image as our feature image, and name the img element accordingly, using a class selector. We'll also give it some margins, so that it sits nicely next to our welcome message.

Edit your homepage (**index.html**) and make the following change to your markup:

```
                                                index.html (excerpt)

<div id="bodycontent">
  <h2>Welcome to our super-dooper Scuba site</h2>
  <p><img src="divers-circle.jpg" class="feature" width="200"
      height="162" alt="A circle of divers practice their
      skills"/></p>
  <p>Glad you could drop in and share some air with us! You've
```

```
         passed your underwater navigation skills and successfully
         found your way to the start point - or in this case, our
         home page.</p>
   </div> <!-- end of bodycontent div -->
```

Now add the following to our style sheet to float our image to the right of the body content:

style1.css *(excerpt)*

```
.feature {
  float: right;
  margin: 10px;
}
```

Save your changes and refresh your browser to see the result (depicted in Figure 4.39).

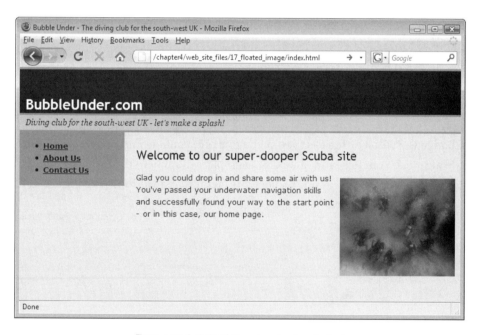

Figure 4.39. A circle of divers learning how to float

This is as far as I'm going to take you with floats. They have a habit of becoming complex and difficult to get right once you have a few floats on the page. If you want to learn more about using floats to create flexible and exciting layouts, I can recommend two other SitePoint books that go into more detail, namely *The CSS Anthology: 101 Essential Tips, Tricks & Hacks*[6] and, in particular, *HTML Utopia: Designing Without Tables Using CSS.*[7]

Styling Lists

Our standard navigation list can benefit from a little more styling. By default, the bullet points are small black blobs, but you can change these easily to some different, pre-defined shapes. Let's head back to our project's style sheet, to see how this works.

▓ In **style1.css**, find the `li` element selector.

▓ Add the following declaration (new addition shown in bold):

style1.css *(excerpt)*

```
li {
    font-size: small;
    list-style-type: circle;
}
```

▓ Save the CSS file and refresh the view in your browser.

▓ Change the value of `list-style-type` to `disc`, `square`, and `none`, saving the CSS file after each change, and checking each page display in the browser. We'll stick with the `none` option on our project site, which should look like Figure 4.40.

---

[6] http://www.sitepoint.com/books/cssant2/
[7] http://www.sitepoint.com/books/css2/

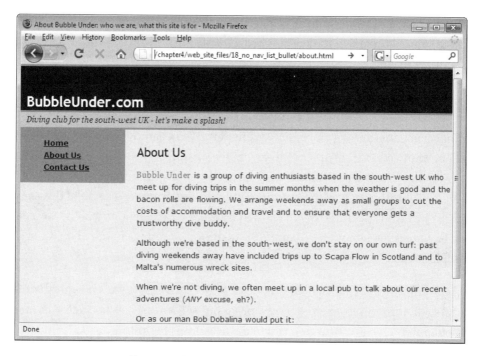

Figure 4.40. Applying different list bullet styles in CSS

It is possible to use CSS to style lists to a much greater extent, including:

- making the links appear as buttons by using the CSS `border` and `padding` properties
- creating a larger clickable area for the link (rather than just the text itself)
- setting list items out in a horizontal line

These more advanced techniques are discussed and explained thoroughly in *The CSS Anthology: 101 Essential Tips, Tricks & Hacks*[8] by Rachel Andrew. The book devotes almost a whole chapter to styling navigation, in fact, and presents many different styles that you can try out. I strongly advise you to grab a copy if you want to learn some really cool CSS tricks (once you've got the basics under your belt, of course!).

---

[8] http://www.sitepoint.com/books/cssant2/

In the meantime, if you want to play around with some styled lists to see what's possible, please do take a look at the List-O-Matic[9] tool, which I built to make this task a little easier.

Summary

This has been another very productive chapter. We began by learning about the difference between inline and block-level elements. Next, we looked at the various ways in which we can style block-level elements, such as adding a `border`, `padding`, and sizing. This theory was then put into practice as we applied some of these styles to the project web site. Finally, we learned how the entire structure of the web pages could be re-jigged—site-wide—using CSS positioning, and we touched on the styling of list elements.

I hope you now have first-hand experience with the ways in which centralizing all your presentation rules—colors, fonts, or layout schemes—can be such a bonus. In a later chapter, I'll show how you can make use of this technique quickly and easily.

In the next chapter, I'm going to guide you through the use of images on your web site, including background images that are set using CSS, and inline images that you can drop into your web pages as content (like the image of the divers in a circle that we first saw in Chapter 2).

---

[9] http://www.accessify.com/tools-and-wizards/developer-tools/list-o-matic/

Chapter 5

Picture This! Using Images on Your Web Site

Back in Chapter 2, we made a simple concession to avoid having the web site look bland: we added the image of divers (using the img[1] element). This really needed to be done: first and foremost, the Web is a visual medium, and while great writing may keep a particular audience captivated, the saying "a picture tells a thousand words" is as true as it ever was. The problem is that we glossed over a discussion of all the different actions you can perform using images in our haste to form that first visual element on the page.

In this chapter, we're going to pick up where we left our discussion on images. We'll see how you can use them to enhance a site's content, and apply them as decorative backgrounds. I'll also explain some simple techniques for managing and adjusting images, using some of the software that I suggested you download in the section called "Not Just Text, Text, Text" in Chapter 1.

Let's begin by taking a look at **inline images**.

---

[1] http://reference.sitepoint.com/html/img/

Inline Images

Let's take just a brief moment to remind ourselves what the XHTML for an inline image looks like:

```
<img src="divers-circle.jpg" width="200" height="162"
    alt="A circle of divers practice their skills"/>
```

You've probably seen this line several times since Chapter 2—yet not really paid it any attention. A refresher of its constituent parts is in order:

Anatomy of the Image Element

- The element name is img. Note that this is an empty element, not using a separate closing tag[2]—the final forward slash indicates that everything it needs to display that element's content is contained within the attributes' values.

- The src attribute defines the source of the image: the location and file name which the browser needs to display the image. In our example, the file name is divers-circle.jpg.

- The alt attribute is an important attribute, which I'll explain in detail below.

- The height and width attributes tell the browser the dimensions at which the image should be displayed. This is particularly useful if the user's web connection speed is a little slow; the browser can then reserve the appropriate space for the image before it has downloaded.

Both the height and width attributes are extremely handy, yet, unlike the src and alt attributes, they are not essential to the image element. However, because of their usefulness, most people choose to leave them in.

The alt Attribute: Making Images Useful to Everyone

In our diving site example, the img element has an alt attribute using the value A circle of divers practice their skills. What's this for? Well, the alt attribute

---

[2] If you look at the source of other web sites, you may spot img tags that do not have a trailing forward slash. In earlier versions of HTML (such as version 4.01), it was not necessary to close the tag in this way.

provides an *alt*ernative text version of the image that most people see on the screen. I say most, because not everyone can see this image. Here are a few scenarios to consider:

- The person browsing your site is blind (see the note Screen Readers: Hearing the Web below).
- The user is accessing your web site on a slow connection and has temporarily disabled images to speed the process up.
- The user is on a *very* slow connection—so slow, in fact, that images simply take too long to load.

In all of these examples, the `alt` attribute provides an alternative for these users to receive the information they need. Figure 5.1 shows what the users in the second and third scenarios will see.

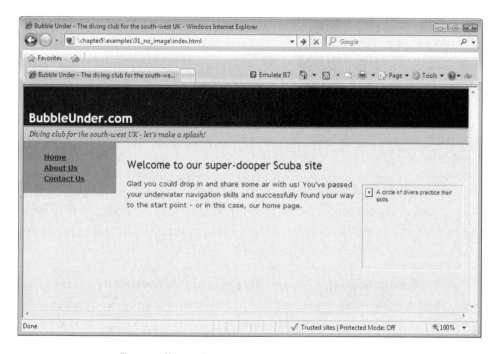

Figure 5.1. When a slow connection delays the image download

If a user was browsing the site over a very slow connection and was presented with the screen shown in Figure 5.1, he or she could read the text alternative and, based on that description, decide whether to wait until the image downloaded completely, or click on a link to go elsewhere. The `alt` attribute delivers a similar benefit to users who browse the site with images disabled: if the description seems interesting, the user might choose to switch on images (in IE go to the **Tools** menu, select **Internet Options**, go to the **Advanced** tab, and under **Multimedia** tick the box labeled **Show Pictures**). For a blind user, though, this so-called alternative is actually an *essential* feature of the image upon which they rely.

Web Accessibility

The practice of making sure that images have appropriate `alt` attributes comes under the general banner of **web accessibility**. This is a specialized area of web design and programming that create web sites with the specific aim that they can be accessed and used by everyone—including those who have disabilities.

Here are some examples:

- people who have poor eyesight (Are your font sizes too small? Can they be scaled up?)

- blind users (Do your `alt` attributes explain the visual elements on your page?)

- deaf users (If you use any sounds on the site—for example, an audio interview—do you have an alternative, text version?)

- mobility-impaired users (Can the user move a mouse around easily, if at all? If not, can your site be navigated using the keyboard alone?)

- people who have reading difficulties (Could text on the site be worded differently, so that it is more easily understood by a person who is dyslexic, or by people for whom English is a second language?)

This is most definitely an area beyond the scope of this book. I haven't provided any solutions for the above examples; I've just tried to encourage you to think about the issues. However, it's generally agreed that if you make an effort to make your `alt` attributes right, you're already helping to make your site more accessible.

If you'd like to learn more about web accessibility, a great introduction can be found at Dive Into Accessibility.[3]

---

[3] http://diveintoaccessibility.org/

Screen Readers: Hearing the Web

Once upon a time, blind users had to rely on Braille alternatives to printed content, or they had to ask a friend to read content aloud to them. However, using electronic media such as web pages, blind users now have a genuine alternative: the **screen reader**. A screen reader is software that provides a sound-based replication of a web page—it reads aloud the text that appears on screen. Some screen readers are used only to access web sites, while others provide audible feedback for the entire operating system and many other applications, including office productivity and email programs.

For the sake of these users, it's especially important that you take care with your `alt` attributes: the screen reader will read these aloud when it comes across images on your web pages. As Figure 5.2 shows, including a description of the image that doesn't provide any insight (for example, just writing the word IMAGE) isn't terribly helpful to anyone.

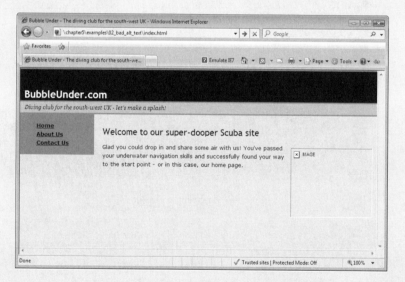

Figure 5.2. An `alt` attribute that leaves everyone in the dark

If you'd like to learn more about the way screen readers work, and in particular, how they handle images on your web pages, you could try the WebAIM screen reader simulation.[4] If you want to try a screen reader on your own web site, download a trial version of JAWS (for Windows).[5]

---

[4] http://www.webaim.org/simulations/screenreader/

[5] http://www.freedomscientific.com/products/fs/jaws-product-page.asp

What Makes a Good alt?

I could write a lot about the topic of `alt` attributes, as it can be quite a subjective field. What one person believes is an appropriate description of an image may not be seen that way by others. However, there are a few simple rules that you can use as guidelines:

■ If the image conveys useful information, describe the image as briefly but accurately as possible. This rule is exemplified in Figure 5.3 and the code that follows:

Figure 5.3. Describing the image you see

```
<img src="sydney.jpg" width="500" height="354"
    alt="Sydney Opera House, night-time shot with the
    Harbour Bridge in the background"/>
```

■ If the image is purely decorative, and provides no practical information, use an empty `alt` attribute (`alt=" "`). This informs screen readers that the image isn't relevant, and that they needn't read it out. Note that this is *not* the same as omitting the `alt` attribute; that's a real no-no!

■ If the image is being used as a link, do not describe the image as it appears; instead, describe the *function* of that image. So, if you're using an image of the

Sydney Harbour Bridge as a call to action, the `alt` attribute should reflect just that. See below the `alt` text that's used to describe the function of Figure 5.4:

Figure 5.4. Using an image as a link

```
<a href="win-holiday.html"><img src="win-a-trip.jpg"
    width="500" height="354" alt="Win a trip to
    Sydney!"/></a>
```

There are many other aspects of web accessibility—the discipline of making your web pages accessible to a wide range of people with disabilities—and you might like to learn more about these in due course. For our purposes, though, taking care of the `alt` attributes used with images will be of great benefit.

GIF vs JPG vs PNG

You may have wondered why some images have a **.gif** file extension while others use **.jpg**. I'm now going to explain the difference, because it's extremely important.

The image formats that are most commonly used on the Web are GIF, JPEG, and PNG. Each have their advantages, but here's a summary of how they can be best used:

- **JPEG** images, or JPEGs, are great for photographic images. JPEG images achieve small file sizes by using "lossy compression," which means that there is a loss of detail from the original image during the compression process. In photographs, the effect of this lossy compression is minimal, but in images using clear, crisp lines (such as illustrations or logos, for example), this compression can make the image appear blurred.

- **GIF** images, on the other hand, are great for illustrations and logos, as well as images that have large areas of a single color. They're not great for photographs, though, because GIFs can only show 256 colors. This might sound like a lot, but a colorful photograph can contain millions of different colors. GIFs also offer transparency, the ability to make part of the image see-through (see below).

- The **PNG** format combines the best aspects of both image formats mentioned above (millions of colors, transparency), even adding more. There is one (admittedly decreasing) problem: IE6 does not fully support the PNG format. Given that the current version of IE is version 8, this is not as big an issue as it once was.

Transparency

When you save an image, it will most likely be rectangular and fill the entire space. But imagine that you have an image that's not a regular shape—for instance, an oval-shaped company logo. The straight edges of image files don't really lend themselves to placing that image on a background. The GIF format, however, allows you to specify the transparent portions of an image. Of the 256 colors that make up a GIF, just one can be set to transparent, as illustrated in Figure 5.5.

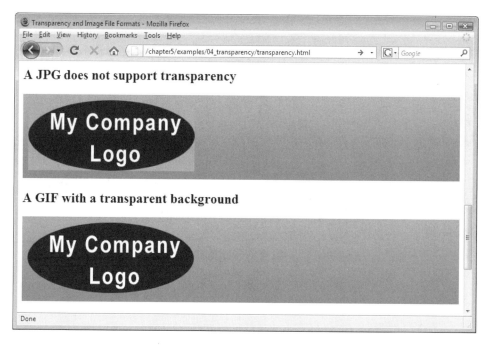

Figure 5.5. The differences between JPEG and GIF support for transparency

PNG: King of Transparency

Undoubtedly, the best image format for using transparent images is PNG, because it is capable of handling **alpha channel** transparency. This means that PNG can handle different levels of transparency—it doesn't just turn transparency on or off the way a GIF does.

A good example is demonstrated on the 2008 web site for the Future of Web Applications conference[6] (FOWA). It uses numerous PNG images that have drop-shadow effects, requiring full alpha transparency for it to look and behave as the designer intended—as you scroll up and down the page, the shadows blend smoothly over whatever part of the background is showing through.

---

[6] http://london2008.futureofwebapps.com/

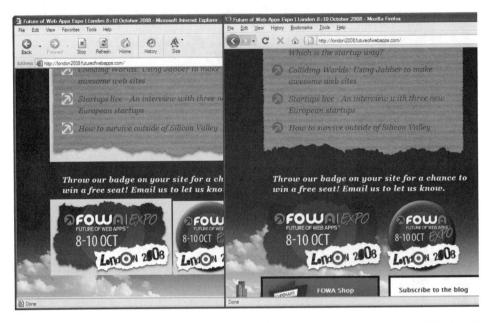

Figure 5.6. IE6 handling PNG transparency poorly on the left, Firefox 3 rendering correctly on the right (note: both browsers shown here are running on Windows XP)

Figure 5.7 demonstrates the drop-shadow effect of the torn paper over a background of clouds. (The browser shown is Firefox 3 but the same goes for all other current browser versions.)

Figure 5.7. A drop-shadow demonstrating that different levels of transparency are at play

Adding an Image Gallery to the Site

One of the great joys of diving is being amongst all the beautiful creatures that live in the sea. You can try to explain the wonder of all this to a non-diver but, usually, they just can't comprehend it. Our web site provides a great opportunity to show people how beautiful these underwater sights can be.

It's time to grow the project site a little by adding a new page: a simple image gallery. Before we start looking at the images themselves, we need to rejig the existing web site files slightly to accommodate the new page.

Updating the Navigation

- Open **index.html** in your text editor.

- Find the navigation section and add another link to your list of links, like so:

```
                                                    index.html (excerpt)

<div id="navigation">
  <ul>
    <li><a href="index.html">Home</a></li>
    <li><a href="about.html">About Us</a></li>
    <li><a href="contact.html">Contact Us</a></li>
    <li><a href="gallery.html">Image Gallery</a></li>
  </ul>
</div> <!-- end of navigation div -->
```

- Save the file, then look at it in the browser to make sure the link appears appropriately.

- Repeat the steps above for **about.html** and **contact.html**.

The navigation in all your pages should look like that shown in Figure 5.8.

Figure 5.8. Adding the Image Gallery to the navigation list

There's just one small problem: the gallery page doesn't exist! Let's rectify that now.

Adding the New Gallery Page

■ Create a copy of **contact.html** and rename it **gallery.html**, just as we did back in Chapter 2.

■ Open the newly-created gallery page in your text editor, and change the level 2 heading (h2) content to "Image Gallery."

■ Remove the single paragraph that appears below that heading, and replace it using the following:

gallery.html *(excerpt)*

```
<p>Below are some of the great views that club members have
    captured on film (or digital memory) on various dive
    trips.</p>
<p>Please do drop me a line (that's Bob) if you would like to
    <a href="mailto:bob@bubbleunder.com">submit an image</a> to
    this gallery.</p>
```

■ Change the `title` content to: Image Gallery—Underwater Photography from Bubble Under's members.

■ Finally, save the amendments and check the page in your browser.

Adding the First Image

Now, we're ready to add the first picture to our gallery: a picture of a turtle. But this is one tough turtle—it appears that a local shark has taken quite a chomp out of his side, as Figure 5.9 reveals.

Figure 5.9. Ouch! That must have hurt!

I've made a point of commenting on that image—after all, it's quite a sight, isn't it? Clearly the image deserves a descriptive `alt` attribute—better than `A picture of a turtle`, which doesn't really tell the full story. Here's the markup we'll use instead for this image:

```
<p><img src="gallery/turtle-bite.jpg" width="400" height="258"
    alt="A turtle swims comfortably among the coral, despite its
    old injury - a large shark bite on one side"/></p>
```

Get the Picture

You'll find this image—and all the others that we'll use in this chapter—in the code archive (see the preface for details about how to access it).

Note that the value of this `src` attribute is a little different than the others we've seen so far. That forward slash tells the browser that the image is inside a folder. In this case, `gallery/turtle-bite.jpg` tells the browser that the image file (**turtle-bite.jpg**) is inside a folder named **gallery**. So, before you add this image to the gallery, create the **gallery** folder inside your web site's folder. (We learned how to create a folder back in Chapter 1: in Windows, select **File > New > Folder**; on a Mac, select **File > New Folder**.) Then place the image inside it.

When you have saved the image inside the folder, add the previous markup (above) to **gallery.html**, like so:

gallery.html (excerpt)

```
<div id="bodycontent">
  <h2>Image Gallery</h2>
  <p>Below are some of the great views that club members have
      captured on film (or digital memory) on various dive
      trips.</p>
  <p>Please do drop me (that's Bob) a line if you would like to
      <a href="mailto:bob@bubbleunder.com">submit an image</a> to
      this gallery.</p>
  <p><img src="gallery/turtle-bite.jpg" width="400" height="258"
      alt="A turtle swims comfortably among the coral, despite its
      old injury - a large shark bite on one side"/></p>
</div> <!-- end of bodycontent div -->
```

Save the page and make sure it appears as expected in your browser—like Figure 5.10.

The size of the photo is sensible: at a width of 400 pixels, it fits quite well on the page without any further adjustment. Soon, I'll show you how to resize larger photos (as most of the photos you take on a digital camera will be far too large for the gallery page).

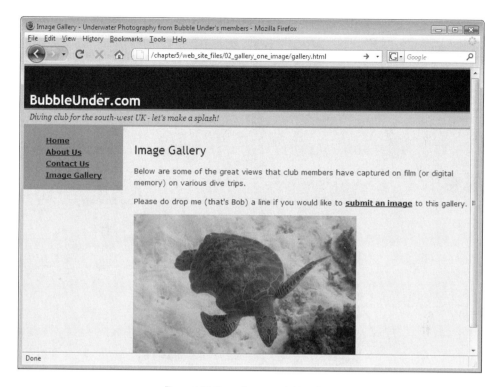

Figure 5.10. The gallery page taking shape

Formatting the Picture using CSS

A common mistake that many people make when building image galleries, is to use a graphics program to create borders around their images. As we saw in the previous chapter, we can use CSS for border effects; let's use this technique now. How about a reasonably thick, white border, reminiscent of Polaroid snaps?

■ Open **style1.css** and add a new rule for the `img` element, like so:

```
                                                            style1.css (excerpt)
img {
  border: 15px solid white;
}
```

■ Save the CSS file, then go back to your web page (**gallery.html**), and refresh it. You should be looking at a view like the one shown in Figure 5.11.

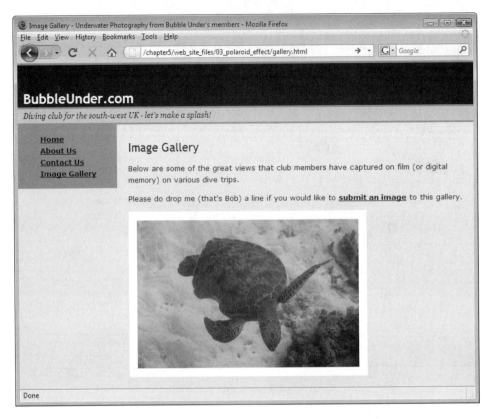

Figure 5.11. The white border gives the photo a Polaroid-like effect

Of course, you're free to try out any effect you like—perhaps you'll experiment using some of the effects we discussed in Chapter 4. For the purposes of this project site, I'm going to maintain the white borders. I know it's not very adventurous, but you *can* overdo it if you're not careful.

Beware of the Flow-on Effects

If you go to the homepage now, the image of the divers in a circle will also have a thick white border around it. Well, we did ask for *all* images to have a white border—the browser's just following orders! If you'd rather have the white borders just around the images on the gallery page, you'll have to get more specific with your selector so that the rule will only take effect on that page. Don't worry about it right now—but don't forget it, because we'll deal with the issue in the next section.

Captioning the Picture

Pick up any newspaper, flick through the pages, and you'll notice that the photos are accompanied by captions. It's a standard practice, and I'm going to show you how we can implement image captions here. First, let's think about what information might appear beneath this photo. You'll probably want a description of the photo, perhaps a location, and almost certainly a credit for the photographer. All these items could be styled in the same way, but I'm going to use two new styles.

When's a **caption** Not a Caption?

Strangely, a *picture* caption element does not exist in XHTML—which may seem like an oversight—but there is a `caption` element. However, that element is not used for this purpose; instead it is used for captioning tables, which we'll be looking at in Chapter 6.

In **gallery.html**, remove the opening and closing paragraph tags that surround the picture of the turtle, and replace them using `<div class="galleryphoto">` and `</div>` tags instead:

```
gallery.html (excerpt)

<div class="galleryphoto">
  <img src="gallery/turtle-bite.jpg" width="400"
      height="258" alt="A turtle swims comfortably among the
      coral, despite its old injury - a large shark bite on
      one side"/>
</div>
```

■ Next, add a paragraph after the image (but inside the containing div), like so:

gallery.html (excerpt)

```
<div class="galleryphoto">
  <img src="gallery/turtle-bite.jpg" width="400"
      height="258" alt="A turtle swims comfortably among the
      coral, despite its old injury - a large shark bite on
      one side"/>
  <p>This turtle was spotted swimming around the Great Barrier
      Reef (Queensland, Australia) quite gracefully, despite
      having had a large chunk taken out of its right side,
      presumably in a shark attack. [Photographer: Ian
      Lloyd]</p>
</div>
```

■ Finally, let's add a span element around the photo credit part of the caption, so that we can style it differently.

gallery.html (excerpt)

```
<p>This turtle was spotted swimming around the Great Barrier
    Reef (Queensland, Australia) quite gracefully, despite
    having had a large chunk taken out of its right side,
    presumably in a shark attack. <span
    class="photocredit">[Photographer: Ian Lloyd]</span></p>
```

■ Save **gallery.html** and take a look at the page in your browser. It should resemble Figure 5.12. You won't see any real stylistic changes, but it's important to look at the page first, so that you can understand why I suggest the changes I'm about to recommend.

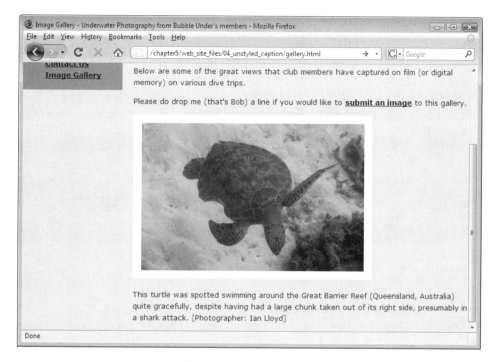

Figure 5.12. The picture now has a caption, not yet styled

It's common for a picture caption to be displayed in a different font to that of the document's main body text; this may also include a different font weight and size, too. That's the first aspect we'll change. Secondly, the gap between the text and the photo is a little too big; I'll show you how we can fix that using the `margin` property. Finally; I'm going to show you how we can add a stylistic touch beneath the caption that will help us once we add more photos to the gallery.

Open **style1.css** and add the following CSS:

```
                                            style1.css (excerpt)

.galleryphoto p {
  font-size: 65%;
  font-weight: bold;
  margin-top: 0;
  width: 430px;
  line-height: 1.4em;
}
```

This markup makes the necessary changes to the font, reduces the width of the caption to make it easier to read, removes the spacing immediately above the paragraph that describes the photo, and reduces the spaces between the lines to be more suitable.

Next, add a new rule for the `photocredit` class:

```
                                                    style1.css (excerpt)

.photocredit {
  font-weight: normal;
  color: gray;
}
```

This will affect the text contained in the `span` element only.

 An Alternative Approach

Incidentally, you could use some selector wizardry to achieve the same effect without having to use the `photocredit` class at all. It would look like this:

```
.galleryphoto p span {
  font-weight: normal;
  color: gray;
}
```

This contextual selector translates as "for every `span` that is inside a `p` which is inside an element using a class of galleryphoto, make it normal font and gray". If you opted for that approach, you could remove the **class** attribute from the `span` element. I've suggested using a class selector in this instance for future-proofing purposes: you might want to use a photo credit elsewhere in the site, outside the context of the photo gallery.

Save the CSS file, refresh the web page once more, and review your work. It should look like the page shown in Figure 5.13.

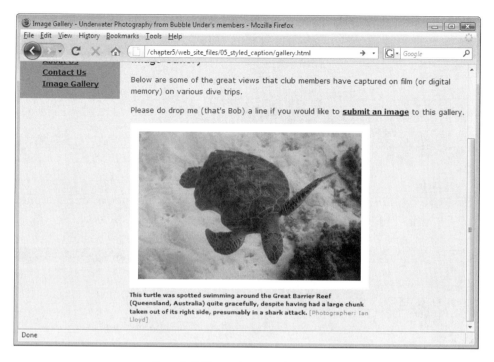

Figure 5.13. The caption now using style rules

Now, remember previously how our nice white gallery photo borders were being applied to all the images on the web site? We now have a very simple way to deal with this issue. The `<img>` tag for the gallery photo now resides within a `div` element with the `class galleryphoto`. Therefore, we can use that class name in the selector of the rule that applies the border, like so:

style1.css *(excerpt)*

```
.galleryphoto img {
  border: 15px solid white;
}
```

If you make the above change to the site style sheet, only the gallery photos will have the white border. Problem solved—isn't CSS great?

Lastly, we're going to add some style declarations to the `.galleryphoto` rule, in order to apply some layout adjustments to the `div` that contains the image and associated text. This class will be used to help separate the many different photos that this page will eventually display.

■ Add the following to **style1.css**:

```
                                              style1.css (excerpt)

.galleryphoto {
  padding-bottom: 20px;
  border-bottom: 1px solid navy;
  margin-bottom: 10px;
}
```

■ Save the CSS file, then refresh the view in your browser once more. It should look similar to Figure 5.14.

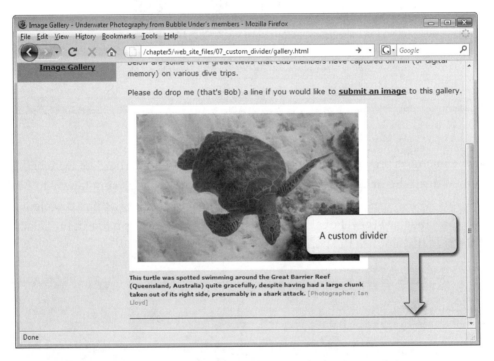

Figure 5.14. A custom divider provides a clean separation between our photos

Basic Image Editing

Image Cropping

An easy mistake to make when preparing images for display on web pages, is to *resize* the image to fit the available space without *cropping* the image in some way first (note that we'll discuss resizing shortly). It's all too easy to end up using small images that try to pack in far too much detail—detail that, ultimately, is lost. It's much better to crop first, then resize. In the image shown in Figure 5.15, the blue water around the fish isn't really required. We can make the image smaller—but keep the fish the same size—by cropping it.

Figure 5.15. Uncropped fish image

Picasa

In Chapter 1, I suggested that Windows users may want to download Picasa[7] for the purposes of managing photos (be they your own happy snaps, or photos used on the project site). Among other features, Picasa offers a range of special effects that you can apply at the touch of a button. Imagine that another two images have been added to our **gallery** folder—trebling the gallery size! Once you've downloaded Picasa, any image that is added to this folder will automatically appear in Picasa's library, as have the two shown in Figure 5.16.

---

[7] http://picasa.google.com/

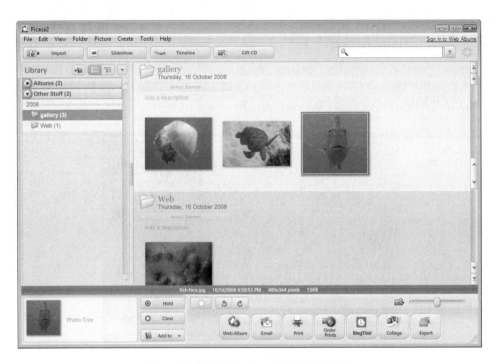

Figure 5.16. Picasa, booming with gallery images

If you double-click on one of the images, a range of new tools will appear on the left-hand side, as illustrated in Figure 5.17.

Perhaps the most important tool you'll use here is **Crop**: you can remove any extraneous clutter, and focus on the most important part of the image.

Just press the **Crop** button, then drag a rectangle around the area to which you want to crop the image, as shown in Figure 5.18. You can also choose to crop the image to a predetermined aspect ratio by selecting any of the dimension buttons: **10×15**, **13×18**, or **20×25**. Once you've selected the size, click the **Apply** button to crop the picture.

Figure 5.17. The range of basic photo fixes offered by Picasa

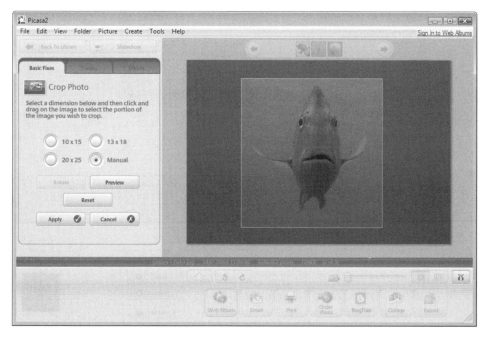

Figure 5.18. A fishy pic receives a good, solid cropping!

GraphicConverter

We mentioned this handy little program for Mac users back in Chapter 1. Despite its name, GraphicConverter[8] has more uses than simply converting pictures from one format to another. I didn't mention, though, that GraphicConverter is not the most intuitive program in the world. Powerful—yes—but finding some of these powerful features requires a bit of poking around, and quite often the problem is simply the terminology used. Let me explain.

Cropping an image in GraphicConverter is fairly straightforward. But if you go looking for a menu option called Crop, you'll be searching all day.

Figure 5.19. Cropping images using GraphicConverter

To crop an image, open your image and choose the **Selection** tool from the toolbox to the right of your image. Click and drag your mouse to mark where you wish to

---

[8] http://www.lemkesoft.com/

crop, then choose the **Edit** > **Trim Selection** option from the menu bar, as shown in Figure 5.19. Voila!

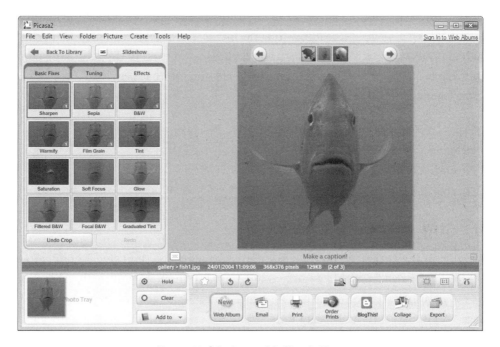

Figure 5.20. Selecting special effects in Picasa

Special Effects

Programs like Photoshop offer a wide range of special effects, and whole books are devoted to explaining the various techniques you can use. Needless to say, we don't have the space for such discussions, but the photo editing programs we've looked at do have some nifty tools you should explore.

Picasa

Figure 5.20 shows a screen shot featuring our recently cropped picture of a fish on the right-hand side; under the **Effects** tab to its left are a number of available effects, such as black and white, sepia tone, and soft focus.

I'm going to leave this image just as it is—but now that you know where to find the effects, why not go and experiment for yourself?

GraphicConverter

Some of the effects available in Picasa are also present in GraphicConverter. The tools included in GraphicConverter range from very useful to "not sure what I'd use *that* for." It's probably best just to experiment, so that you can gain an inkling of which tools you might use most. Try and guess what each of the following menu options does, then try the different effects on one of your images to see if they behave as you expected.

- **Picture > Simple Brightness/Contrast...**
- **Picture > Colors > Grayscale > 256 Grays**
- **Picture > Colors > Change To Sepia**
- **Effect > Red Eye**

Resizing Large Images

It's highly unlikely that everyone will submit images of the right size for our gallery. Let's take an image from this book's code archive (I know it's not really code, but let's not split hairs!) and resize it. The image you want is **jellyfish.jpg**. It's a giant image—1359 pixels in width—so it needs some serious knocking down in size! Here's how you can do the job using a couple of different programs (I've assumed you already have the file open).

Picasa

If you already have images somewhere on your hard drive, they'll automatically appear in the Picasa library. An easy way to use Picasa to create a web-page-friendly image from a larger photo is as follows:

- In the Picasa gallery, find the image you want to use and click on it.

- Select **File > Export Picture to Folder** from the menu.

- You will be presented with the dialog pictured in Figure 5.21, which allows you to choose from a series of preset widths. (Don't be fooled by the text box and slider control; you can choose widths of 320, 480, 640, 800, and 1024 pixels only—but these are all sensible sizes for web pages.) You can also select the amount of JPEG compression you want to use from the **Image Quality** control (the lower the number, the smaller the file size ... and the worse the photograph will look).

Figure 5.21. Exporting a large image for the Web using Picasa

Click the **Browse...** button and select your **Web** folder inside **Documents**. (Don't select the **gallery** folder; if you do, Picasa will create another folder named **gallery** inside your **gallery** folder!)

Under **Name of exported folder:**, enter the name of the folder to which you'd like the resized image saved. In this case, enter `gallery`.

Click **OK** and the resized picture will be saved.

GraphicConverter

From the menu, select **Picture > Size > Scale...**

In the drop-down list next to the **Width** textbox, select **Pixel** if it's not selected already, and enter **400**. Click **OK**.

Save the file by selecting **File > Save as...**

Select the format in which you want to save the file from the **Format** drop-down list (you'll probably want JPEG for a photo or GIF for a logo image) and click **Save**. If you save as a JPEG, GraphicConverter will pop up a dialog using an overwhelming array of options. The only one you're likely to need is the quality slider at the top of the window. As with Picasa, the lower this number, the lower the quality of the image.

Other Software

The instructions above cover Picasa (Windows) and GraphicConvertor (Mac) only, but most other graphics applications will perform similar functions. If you can't find the equivalent process in your image editor, try the built-in help files, or search the Web for tutorials (for example: resizing images in Photoshop)).

A Quick Search

A quick search on Google found these tutorials:

- Photoshop Tutorial: How to Resize an Image, a YouTube video (http://www.youtube.com/watch?v=qu5adJfxuhw)

- Rotating, Cropping and Resizing Photos for the Web using Jasc Paint Shop Pro at about.com (http://graphicssoft.about.com/od/digitalphotography/l/blpsp_prep.htm)

- Apple's excellent iPhoto Tutorial (http://www.apple.com/support/iphoto/tutorial/)

Filling up the Gallery

With the wave of a magic wand—not to mention the techniques we've been using (XHTML, CSS, and image editing)—we can easily finish off our gallery. You can see the results below in Figure 5.22. Of course, if you prefer you can retrieve this from the code archive:

```
<div class="galleryphoto">
  <img src="gallery/turtle-bite.jpg" width="400" height="258"
      alt="A turtle swims comfortably among the coral, despite
      its old injury - a large shark bite on one side"/>
  <p>This turtle was spotted swimming around the Great Barrier
      Reef (Queensland, Australia) quite gracefully, despite
      having had a large chunk taken out of its right side,
      presumably in a shark attack. <span
      class="photocredit">[Photographer: Ian Lloyd]</span></p>
</div>
<div class="galleryphoto">
  <img src="gallery/jellyfish.jpg" width="400" height="300"
      alt="A jellyfish flanked by smaller fish"/>
  <p>Jill was just snorkelling when she took this picture - the
      jellyfish was only a couple of feet under the surface,
      hence the light is excellent. Jill assures us that the
      jellyfish had no "nasty, stingy, dangly bits"!
      <span class="photocredit">[Photographer: Jill
      Smith]</span></p>
</div>
<div class="galleryphoto">
  <img src="gallery/turtle-face.jpg" width="400" height="300"
      alt="A close-up, straight-on shot of a turtle feeding on the
      coral"/>
  <p>"I was right next to him as he bit chunks of coral off for
      dinner - what a sound!" So describes club member Paul who
      took this shot in Fiji. <span
      class="photocredit">[Photographer: Paul Spencer]</span></p>
</div>
<div class="galleryphoto">
  <img src="gallery/what-a-star.jpg" width="400" height="318"
      alt="Black and white patterned starfish"/>
  <p>You're a star - and don't let anyone tell you any different!
      <span class="photocredit">[Photographer: Helen
      Cranfield]</span></p>
</div>
<div class="galleryphoto">
  <img src="gallery/reef2.jpg" width="400" height="285"
      alt="Another beautiful example of the Great Barrier Reef"/>
  <p>Another cracking shot of the reef from Mark.
      <span class="photocredit">[Photographer: Mark
      Willams]</span></p>
</div>
```

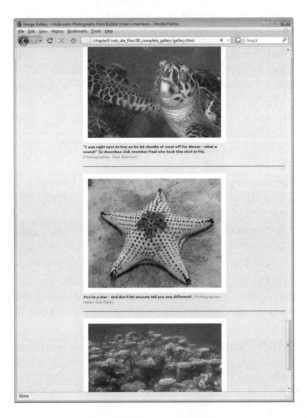

Figure 5.22. The complete gallery

Moving beyond a Simple Gallery

This is a simple example of an image gallery. As you add more images, the page will take longer and longer to download. For this reason, most people opt for a two-step design: a page containing **thumbnails**, which are small, thumbnail-sized copies of the image (well, approximately), linked to full-size versions. However, if you think that your site's image gallery has the potential to grow beyond all manageability, you might want to look into an automated system of some kind; many are available, and plenty just happen to be free services!

You can search for "free thumbnail gallery generator" or similar, to attract lots of results. A good collection is listed at http://freewarehome.com/Graphics/Graphic_Manipulation/Thumbnails_t.html. Mac users, if you have iPhoto, you can make use of the Export facility (Share in later versions) to create a thumbnail gallery. More info and tips are available at http://www.peachpit.com/articles/article.asp?p=30217.

Sourcing Images for Your Web Site

The creation of an online gallery is all well and good if you have a large collection of suitable photos at your disposal, but what if you need an image that isn't in your collection? There are numerous web sites that allow you to download and use images **royalty-free**, such as iStockphoto[9] and Fotosearch.[10] Note that royalty-free means that the image—once purchased—is free of royalty charges (ongoing payments to the owner based on sales or downloads made, usually a percentage of the sales price). It doesn't mean that the image itself is free to use. However, once you've paid the one-off fee, if it's a great image, you probably won't be all that worried about spending a dollar or two.

Another potential source of images is Flickr,[11] where you can search images based on how people have *tagged* them—a generally accepted term meaning keywords. For example, you could search for all photos tagged with the word "scuba"[12] and look for a suitable image in the search results.

 Using Images from Flickr

Flickr is a photo-sharing service, not a professional photo stock library, and every Flickr photographer has a different policy on how the photos can be used. The licensing details are clearly listed on each photo's page. But even if the photo is marked "All Rights Reserved," you could try dropping the photographer a line—many people will quite happily let you use one of their photos if it's not for personal financial gain (indeed, many people will actually be quite flattered to have been asked).

---

[9] http://www.istockphoto.com/
[10] http://www.fotosearch.com/
[11] http://www.flickr.com/
[12] http://www.flickr.com/photos/tags/scuba/

Background Images in CSS

So far, we've purely used inline images. Inline images constitute an integral part of a page's content, but there's another way that you might use images in a web site: as decorative backgrounds.

In the last chapter, we learned how to specify background colors for any block element. We can assign background images in a similar way. In practice, we can do both: provide a background image for those who are browsing using a well performing web connection, and an alternative background color for those using a slower one. In fact, this background color can be displayed for the first group of users while the background image is loading. Let's take a look at a simple example:

Repeated Patterns

```
#repeatedclouds {
  border: 1px solid black;
  padding: 20px;
  background-color: #aebbdb;
  background-image: url(clouds.jpg);
}
```

Here's the XHTML that refers to this CSS:

```
<div id="repeatedclouds">
  <p>Content of some kind goes here.</p>
  <p>Some more content goes here.</p>
</div>
```

Using the additional code above, the browser will simply repeat the selected background image, filling the available space (I've added a `border` and `padding` to make it easier to see the shape of the box and the white page background peeking through around the edges). Figure 5.23 shows how the effect displays on the screen (remember that you can obtain this example from the code archive).

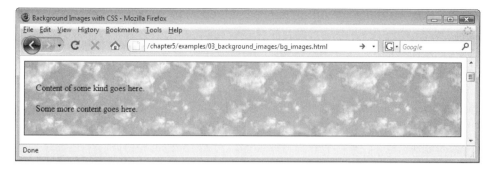

Figure 5.23. A background image of a cloud pattern, repeated to fill the space

Notice that this rule also includes a background color. Whenever you choose a background image, you should also choose a suitable color alternative in case images are not downloaded with your page for some reason. If the browser finds the image you've referred to, it will use it, but if not, it will display the specified background color—like the page shown in Figure 5.24. This is an important point. Imagine that, in one section of your page, you had a dark background image with white text displayed on it. If the user disables images, or the background image does not download for some reason, you'll need to have a dark background color in place. Otherwise, the user may be presented with white text on a white background, rendering that section of the page unreadable.

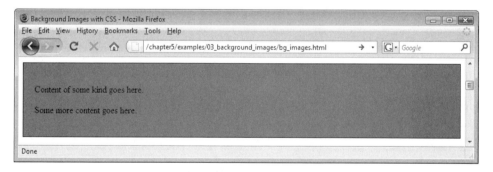

Figure 5.24. Displaying a plain-colored background in place of an image

Horizontal Repeats

It is possible to set a background so that it repeats only in one direction—for example, from left to right. You may remember the process of plotting graphs along the x-axis (the horizontal axis) or the y-axis (the vertical axis) in math class from your school days. We use the same x and y notations to specify direction in CSS. For example, you could use the following code to repeat an image along the horizontal axis:

```
#verticalfade {
  border: 1px solid black;
  padding: 20px;
  padding-top: 300px;
  background-color: #e3e3e3;
  background-image: url(vert-fade.gif);
  background-repeat: repeat-x;
}
```

The effect is depicted in Figure 5.25.

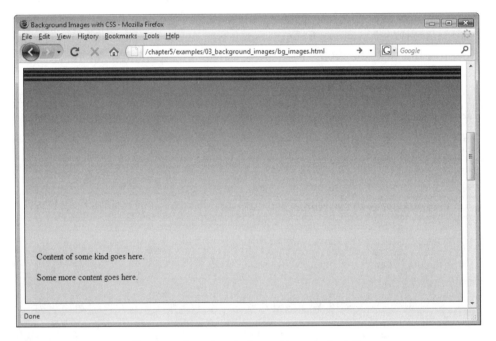

Figure 5.25. Repeating a background image horizontally

Ironically, an image that you want to repeat horizontally will usually be taller than it is wide. Such images provide an efficient way to create interesting effects using what are, generally, small image sizes (in terms of download size). The image used to create the effect we saw in Figure 5.25 is shown in Figure 5.26.

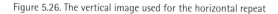

Figure 5.26. The vertical image used for the horizontal repeat

When background images are repeated in one direction only, setting the background color becomes even more important. For instance, consider what would happen if we removed the background color from the previous example—Figure 5.27 reveals the result. If you don't set a background color, the background will be set to the browser's default background color. Usually this is white, but it can be changed by the user in their browser settings. As you can see, once the background image ends, the background color is displayed, so it's important to make sure the colors complement each other.

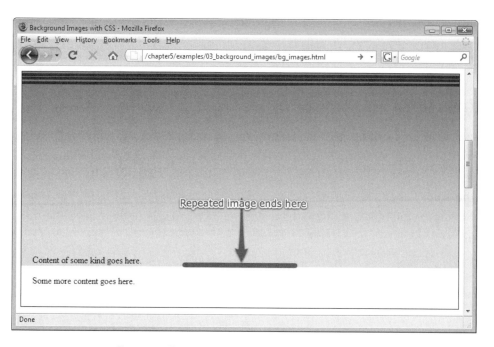

Figure 5.27. The horizontal repeat without a background color

Vertical Repeats

You shouldn't be too surprised to learn that it's just as easy to create the same repeat effect vertically:

```
#horizontalfade {
  border: 1px solid black;
  background-color: white;
  background-image: url(hori-fade.gif);
  background-repeat: repeat-y;
  padding: 20px;
  padding-left: 180px;
}
```

Figure 5.28 displays the result.

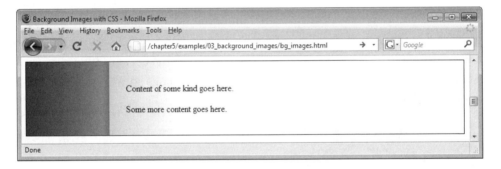

Figure 5.28. Repeating a background image vertically

Non-repeating Images

You may simply want to display a background image once, and once only; for example, to drop a company logo behind text, like a watermark effect. Whatever your plans, the CSS that displays a background image once is simple and very similar to the examples above. In such cases, you need to use no-repeat to tell the browser not to repeat the image at all, and specify the location where the image should appear.

Here's the CSS to use:

```
#palmtree {
  border: 1px solid black;
  background-color: white;
  background-image: url(palm-trees.jpg);
  background-repeat: no-repeat;
  background-position: top right;
  padding: 60px;
  padding-right: 210px;
}
```

Figure 5.29 shows the effect.

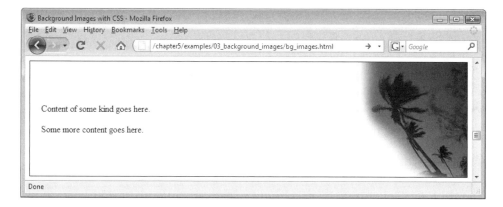

Figure 5.29. Palm trees as a non-repeating background image

The background-position property requires two values: the vertical position (top, center, or bottom) and the horizontal position (left, center, or right). If you use no-repeat without a background-position, the browser defaults to placing the image in the top-left corner.

Shorthand Backgrounds

In the same way that we can set the color, style, and thickness of a border using the border shorthand property, we can set a background image and color using the background shorthand property:

```
#repeatedclouds {
  border: 1px solid black;
  padding: 20px;
  background: #aebbdb url(clouds.jpg);
}

#palmtree {
  border: 1px solid black;
  background: white url(palm-trees.jpg) no-repeat top right;
  padding: 60px;
  padding-right: 210px;
}
```

Fixed Heights and Widths

One final example remains before we start to apply some of these visual techniques to our project site: artistic effects using fixed dimensions. In Chapter 4, we saw how we can fix a block-level element to a certain size. Here, I'll show how you can achieve the same end using a background image rather than a solid background color. When this is combined using a contrasting text color, you can create an interesting and artistic text overlay effect. (Note that in this example, I've used padding to move the line of text away from the top of the containing div element.). Here's the CSS:

```
.sunset {
  border: 1px solid black;
  color: white;
  font-weight: bold;
  font-size: 300%;
  background: black url(sunset.jpg);
  width: 650px;
  height: 125px;
  padding-left: 50px;
  padding-top: 400px;
}
```

The XHTML for this effect couldn't be simpler!

```
<div class="sunset">Sunsets are a gift of nature.</div>
```

The effect of the XHTML and CSS working in harmony produces the display shown in Figure 5.30.

Figure 5.30. A sized `div` using a background image

The effect looks good, though I have to agree that the sunset is rather spectacular, too.

I think we're done using the theory here. Let's roll up our sleeves and integrate these techniques into the project site!

Setting a Background for Our Navigation

The evolution of our site continues apace! The first thing that I'd like to make look a little prettier is the navigation area. The image I want to use is shown in Figure 5.31 (and is available from the code archive, of course).

Figure 5.31. Decorative background for the navigation

I know what you're thinking: this image is the correct width, but it's far too tall for our current navigation area. Don't worry: the size of the navigation area can easily be set within the CSS to match the height of our new background image. Here's the modified markup:

```
#navigation {
  width: 180px;
  height: 484px;
  background: #7da5d8 url(backgrounds/nav-bg.jpg) no-repeat;

}
```

Figure 5.32 shows the effect in context.

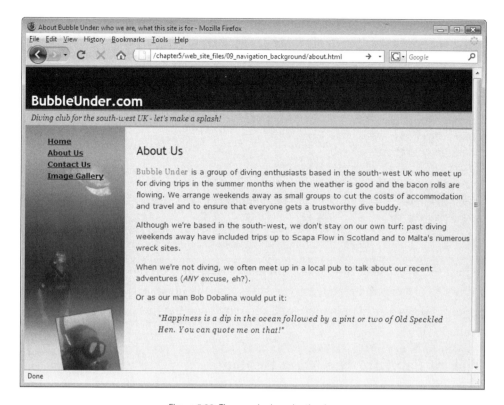

Figure 5.32. The new-look navigation bar

Applying a Fade to the Tag Line

The tag line under the main heading performs its task efficiently, but is a little simple and, perhaps, too blocky. One way to reduce this chunky look is to apply a background image using a smoothing effect. Let's use the graduated fade shown in Figure 5.33.

Figure 5.33. The tag line background image

For the effect we're after, the image should be locked to the right-hand edge of the tag line paragraph. This can be achieved easily using CSS:

```
                                                    style1.css (excerpt)

#tagline p {
  font-style: italic;
  font-family: Georgia, Times, serif;
  border-top: 3px solid #7da5d8;
  border-bottom: 3px solid #7da5d8;
  padding-top: .2em;
  padding-bottom: .2em;
  padding-left: .8em;
  margin: 0;
  background: #bed8f3 url(backgrounds/tagline-fade.jpg) repeat-y
    right;
}
```

The position keyword `right` is all you need to use to keep the image hugging the
tag line's right-hand side; `repeat-y` ensures that the image will repeat downwards
(vertically) if the font size is increased, thereby boosting the size of the tag line
overall.

A Lick of Paint for the Main Heading

I'm now going to show you how the main header (h1) can be livened up a little,
using the previous technique. Once again, I've opted for an image that's going to be
attached to the right-hand side. This time, though, it's not a fade, and it can't be
repeated. Instead, it's the image shown in Figure 5.34, but only a part of it will be
visible in the header.

Figure 5.34. The background image for our main heading

The image is tonally dark (ensuring that the BubbleUnder.com white text will be
legible on top) and the left edge fades out nicely to match the navy background
color that the h1 headings use. We discussed this technique when we applied the

graduated fade to the tag line—and the best way to appreciate the technique is try it out. Type the example out or extract it from the code archive. I'd recommend resizing your browser window, so that you can see the effect such changes have on the background image.

We've used an image that's taller than the main page heading; this ensures that the page displays well if users resize their fonts, causing the height of the container to grow. Yes, you *do* need to think about these things!

Let's look at the CSS for this effect. Make sure that the code below appears after the grouped h1, h2, h3 rule; we want to redefine the simple blue background that was applied in Chapter 4 using this more stylish version:

```
                                                        style1.css (excerpt)

h1 {
    font-size: x-large;
    color: white;
    padding-top: 2em;
    padding-bottom: .2em;
    padding-left: .4em;
    margin: 0;
    background: navy url(backgrounds/header-bg.jpg) repeat-y right;
}
```

The effect is shown in Figure 5.35.

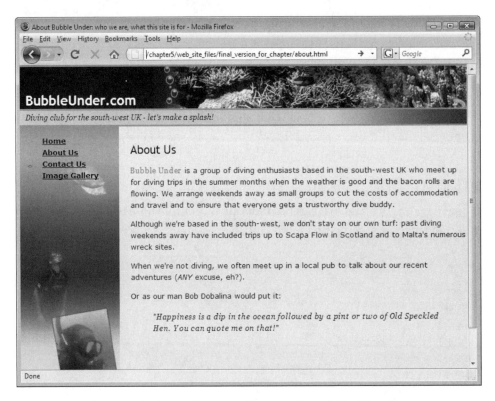

Figure 5.35. A selection of background images applied to finish off the effect

Summary

In this chapter, we've seen how you can source free images from the Web, or use your own photos, to compile an image gallery for your site. We've discussed the processes of resizing images to suit your site's specific needs and how to apply various effects. I've also explained how you can use CSS to add creative effects to your images (for instance, defining colored borders in a style sheet, rather than producing them in image editing software), and how you can apply images as decorative backgrounds that can be used once on a page or repeated.

It's amazing how much a web site can be improved by a liberal sprinkling of imagery. Just a couple of chapters back, our project site was a fairly dull-looking collection of documents; now it's starting to look more like a proper web site—one that we could very easily re-style by making a few changes in our CSS file.

In the next chapter, we'll learn all about **tables**, as I show you how you can use these to display data in a clean, easy-to-understand format.

Chapter 6

Tables: Tools for Organizing Data

The title of this book is Build Your Own Web Site *The Right Way*. It's important to emphasize this point as we begin this chapter because in the "Bad Old Days," the content of this chapter—concerning tables—would have been right up near the front of the book as the author taught you how to use tables to create exciting page layouts! This approach has since been recognized as bad, bad, *bad*! But, you know what? There are still books that teach you to use tables for layout. Thankfully, you didn't pick up one of those books: bonus points to you!

As the name suggests, tables are designed to present *tabular data*; this could include information displayed as a calendar of events, or perhaps a spreadsheet showing how pitiful your bank balance is this month (or am I just speaking for myself?). There are many different circumstances in which tables are a sensible choice—but laying out an entire web page is definitely not among them.

What is a Table?

Several times in the preceding chapters, I compared web techniques to tools that you might use in Microsoft Word, and in the case of tables there's another direct correlation. If you've used this Microsoft Office program, you've probably inserted a table before, using the toolbar icon shown in Figure 6.1.

Figure 6.1. The **Insert Table** icon in Microsoft Word

You can use this tool to create a table like the one in Table 6.1 very easily.

Table 6.1. An example of a table

Name	Contact (Home)	Contact (Work)	Location
Jane Bradley	02380 123123	02380 577566	Southampton
Fred Bradley	01273 177166	01273 946376	Brighton
Lionel Rundel	01793 641207	01793 626696	Swindon

A table is the most sensible, tidy way to organize this kind of data. You can easily scan down a column, or along a row, and see what's what. The exact same effect can be achieved on a web page.

Before we embark on table creation, though, let's make a couple of essential changes to our project site—that way we have an appropriate place to use tables. What sort of data would warrant the use of tables on a diving web site? How about a table of forthcoming club events? That'll do nicely!

■ First, we need to add some links to *all* of the web site's files. We need to make one addition to the navigation on the left of the page. I think this new navigation item should appear between the About Us and Contact Us page navigation links. Be sure to add it to all of the files in the web site, as shown here:

```
<div id="navigation">
  <ul>
    <li><a href="index.html">Home</a></li>
    <li><a href="about.html">About Us</a></li>
    <li><a href="events.html">Club Events</a></li>
    <li><a href="contact.html">Contact Us</a></li>
    <li><a href="gallery.html">Image Gallery</a></li>
  </ul>
</div> <!-- end of navigation div -->
```

- Next, take a copy of **index.html**, and rename it in Windows Explorer (or Finder, if you're using a Mac) to **events.html**.

Open **events.html** and make the following changes:

- Change the content between the opening `<title>` and closing `</title>` tags to read: "Forthcoming club diving events and trips with Bubble Under."

- Change the page heading (the `h2` element) to read: "Forthcoming Club Events."

- Delete everything except the heading inside the `div` whose `id` is `bodycontent`.

- Beneath that heading, add a new paragraph that reads:

> Bubble Under members love meeting up for dive trips around the country. Below are all the dive trips that we currently have planned. For more information about any of them, please get in contact with that event's organizer.

If you've completed all those steps, your code should look like this:

```
<!DOCTYPE html PUBLIC "-//W3C//DTD XHTML 1.0 Strict//EN"
    "http://www.w3.org/TR/xhtml1/DTD/xhtml1-strict.dtd">
<html xmlns="http://www.w3.org/1999/xhtml">
  <head>
    <title>Forthcoming club diving events and trips with Bubble
        Under</title>
    <meta http-equiv="Content-Type"
        content="text/html; charset=utf-8"/>
    <link href="style1.css" rel="stylesheet" type="text/css"/>
  </head>
  <body>
    <div id="header">
      <div id="sitebranding">
        <h1>BubbleUnder.com</h1>
      </div>
      <div id="tagline">
        <p>Diving club for the south-west UK - let's make a
            splash!</p>
      </div>
    </div> <!-- end of header div -->
    <div id="navigation">
      <ul>
        <li><a href="index.html">Home</a></li>
        <li><a href="about.html">About Us</a></li>
        <li><a href="events.html">Club Events</a></li>
        <li><a href="contact.html">Contact Us</a></li>
        <li><a href="gallery.html">Image Gallery</a></li>
      </ul>
    </div>
    <div id="bodycontent">
      <h2>Forthcoming Club Events</h2>
      <p>Bubble Under members love meeting up for dive trips
          around the country. Below are all the dive trips that we
          currently have planned. For more information about any
          of them, please get in contact with that event's
          organizer.</p>
    </div> <!-- end of bodycontent div -->
  </body>
</html>
```

Why Tables Are Bad (but *Only* for Layout!) and CSS Rocks

It's time for a very short history lesson.

The reason why web designers used to use tables for layout was quite simple: in the early days of web development, tables were the only way to achieve a layout that resembled a magazine- or newspaper-like grid. Designers wanted to have a heading at the top of the page, a column on the left for navigation, a column in the middle for content, and a third column on the right for more links. The problem was that using tables to achieve such effects was an abuse of the markup—a hack—but it worked at the time, and people didn't see anything wrong with it.

Today, CSS is so well-supported that there really is no excuse for using tables for layout, and CSS is definitely the better tool for the job. Nevertheless, many web sites still use table-based layouts. This doesn't mean that this approach is right: it's simply an old habit that refuses to die quietly in the corner as it should—although you can play your part to help redress the situation. But just what are the advantages of using CSS instead of tables? Here are a few for you to consider:

Design and Redesign Flexibility

A CSS-based layout ensures that you place all your styles (from cosmetic touches such as font styling, to the major structural rules) in one location. Change the layout rules you set in that style sheet, and you affect every page that refers to it. Using a table-based layout locks your page design in at page-level, so changing a layout becomes a major problem—one that cannot be resolved simply by changing the style sheet.

Better Accessibility

A table is supposed to be used for tabular data only. For this reason, some **assistive devices** (such as screen readers, which we discussed in the section called "Web Accessibility" in Chapter 5) are a bit confused when the content is not presented as expected. In other words, these kinds of devices expect to access tabular data inside a table; if the table is being used for a purpose for which it was never intended, all bets are off, and accessibility may be the first casualty. If you use a table for the purposes of layout, content that may appear to be located logically on the screen may not be logical at all when read out by a screen reader. This is a phenomenon known as table linearization, which we'll explore in detail shortly.

Quicker Downloads (or Perception of Download)

A table-based page layout often renders more slowly than an equivalent CSS-based layout; this is especially true of pages that have a lot of content. There are a couple of reasons for this. The first is that a table-based layout will generally require much more markup to hold the page together—acting like a scaffold, if you like. Using a table-based layout, it's not just a matter of marking up sections of the page with `div` elements. This extra markup adds to the page file size, and therefore, the amount of time it takes to download the file.

The second reason is related to the user's *perception* of download speed. Browsers don't download entire web pages in one go: when they ask for a web page, they receive it as a trickle of information. And the browser tries to render that information as it arrives. In the case of our site, the browser would render the header, then the navigation, and finally the body content. If the trickle of information is so slow that there's a pause halfway through the body content, the browser is still able to display the first half of the body content without any trouble. This isn't the case using table-based layouts. In a table-based layout, the browser needs to have downloaded *all* the content in the table before it knows how to accurately render that information on the screen. As such, a CSS-based page layout will usually appear on the screen faster than a table-based layout.

If there's one point I hope you remember from this chapter, it's this: despite what anyone tells you, using tables is not a sin. They should not be used for page layout (that's where they gain their bad reputation from), but it is *perfectly okay to use tables for their originally intended purpose*: the presentation of data in a grid.

Anatomy of a Table

Before we start adding the table to our Events page, let's take a step back and look at the general example we saw in Table 6.1: the simple table of telephone contact details. At a glance, we can identify some specific areas of the table, namely the headers, rows, columns, and table data cells. Figure 6.2 explains this diagrammatically.

Although I mentioned columns, you do not need to indicate these in the XHTML. At its most basic level, a table is put together using commands that tell the browser where to start a new row, or a new cell within any given row; as the columns are a natural by-product of this approach, you don't need to declare each new column.

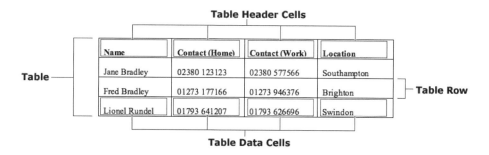

Figure 6.2. The anatomy of a table

The areas marked in Figure 6.2 have the following direct equivalents in XHTML:

table[1]   contains the entire table

tr[2]   contains an entire row of a table (hence **t**able **r**ow)

th[3]   signifies a **t**able **h**eader cell

td[4]   a general **t**able **d**ata cell

Let's see how the example table looks in XHTML:

```
<table>
  <tr>
    <th>Name</th>
    <th>Contact (Home)</th>
    <th>Contact (Work)</th>
    <th>Location</th>
  </tr>
  <tr>
    <td>Jane Bradley</td>
    <td>02380 123123</td>
    <td>02380 577566</td>
    <td>Southampton</td>
  </tr>
  <tr>
    <td>Fred Bradley</td>
```

---

[1] http://reference.sitepoint.com/html/table/

[2] http://reference.sitepoint.com/html/tr/

[3] http://reference.sitepoint.com/html/th/

[4] http://reference.sitepoint.com/html/td/

```
      <td>01273 177166</td>
      <td>01273 946376</td>
      <td>Brighton</td>
    </tr>
    <tr>
      <td>Lionel Rundel</td>
      <td>01793 641207</td>
      <td>01793 626696</td>
      <td>Swindon</td>
    </tr>
  </table>
```

Can you see how the two marry up? The various elements that make up a table can seem a little daunting when you first encounter them, but like so many XHTML elements, their names are quite easy to remember.

Styling the Table

The `table` element is pretty simple: it's the element that contains all of the data that makes up the table ... though, as Figure 6.3 shows, it *is* fairly ugly.

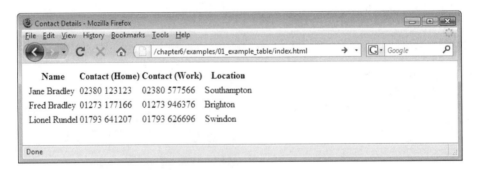

Figure 6.3. The uninspiring default appearance of a table

How can we jazz this up? If you're thinking CSS, give yourself a pat on the back: CSS is definitely the way to go!

Borders, Spacing, and Alignment

Let's start by putting some borders around these cells. Figure 6.4 shows the impact of the following CSS code:

```
td {
  border: 1px solid black;
}
```

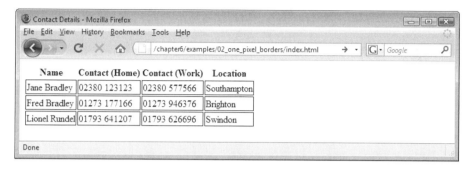

Figure 6.4. One-pixel borders placed around each cell

Perhaps this is not quite what you expected. That space between each of the cell's borders is called **cell spacing**, and you can turn it off by applying the `border-collapse: collapse;` declaration to the `table` element.

Let's turn off the cell spacing, and add a little more decoration to our table. We'll also set the table headings to align to the left of the cell. By default, the content inside table headings (`th`) is aligned to the center, which can be confusing. Figure 6.5 shows the results of the suggested changes (and a few other enhancements too):

```
table {
  border-collapse: collapse;
  border: 1px solid black;
}

th {
  text-align: left;
  background: gray;
  color: white;
  padding: 0.2em;
}

td {
  border: 1px solid black;
  padding: 0.2em;
}
```

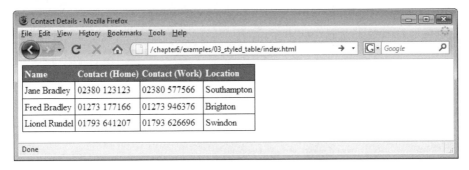

Figure 6.5. Style rules applied to the table

It's looking a lot sharper, isn't it?

class-ifying Your Tables

Tables can be used for a variety of purposes, and each type of table may warrant a different look. For this reason, it may be a good idea to use classes in your CSS selectors for tables.

For example, imagine your site includes the following types of tables:

- rates
- schedule
- events

You could set different style rules for each table type in your CSS:

```
table.rates {
  /* declarations for rates tables */
}

table.schedule {
  /* declarations for schedule tables */
}

table.events {
  /* declarations for events tables */
}
```

Then, when you added a `table` to your XHTML, all you'd need to do would be to give it the appropriate `class` attribute:

```
<table class="rates">
```

A little forethought goes a long way!

Making Your Tables Accessible

I introduced the idea of web accessibility in the section called "Web Accessibility" in Chapter 5 to emphasize the importance of the `img` element's `alt` attribute. It's important to think about accessibility when it comes to tables, too. The question that all web designers ask themselves at some point in their careers is, "How on earth does a screen reader read out a table?"

Linearization

In reading out the content of a table, a screen reader **linearizes** that content. Linearization simply means that the screen reader reads the content in the order in which it appears in the table's markup. As an example, consider Table 6.2, which displays TV listings. Visually, it's easy to associate a time-slot with the associated program.

Table 6.2. An example of TV listings set out in a table

9:30 p.m.–10:00 p.m.	10:00 p.m.–11:00 p.m.	11:00 p.m.–11:45 p.m.
Regional News	Lost	Big Brother

Using a visual scan, we can quickly and easily see when each program starts and ends. Let's take a look at the markup:

```
<table>
  <tr>
    <td>9:30 p.m.-10:00 p.m.</td>
    <td>10:00 p.m.-11:00 p.m.</td>
    <td>11:00 p.m.-11:45 p.m.</td>
  </tr>
  <tr>
    <td>Regional News</td>
    <td>Lost</td>
    <td>Big Brother</td>
  </tr>
</table>
```

The linearized interpretation of this would be: "9:30 p.m.–10:00 p.m., 10:00 p.m.–11:00 p.m., 11:00 p.m.–11:45 p.m., Regional News, Lost, Big Brother." That's not the most comprehensible piece of content! We can fix this problem either by changing the orientation of the table (i.e., making the program names run down the left and the time slots run down the right), or by marking up the cells that contain the names of the programs using th instead of td, and adding a scope[5] attribute to each of the th elements. We'll take a look into this second solution later in the chapter, when we discuss some advanced table concepts.

summary

No, I'm not about to summarize what we've just discussed in this chapter just yet! Instead, it's time to introduce the table's summary[6] attribute. This is an invisible attribute (it doesn't render on the screen or, for that matter, when you print the web page) that can be used to provide extra information about the table to assistive devices. Here's an example of a summary:

```
<table summary="Area representatives, and their home and work
    telephone numbers">
```

When you add a summary, be brief but descriptive. This attribute is a bit like the alt attribute we use for images: brief, but not so as to beg more questions.

Captioning your Table

If you think the summary attribute seems like a bit of a wasted opportunity because it doesn't appear in the table's on-screen display, don't worry. You can use the caption[7] element for this purpose. Many people would insert a heading (e.g., h2, h3) in the XHTML above a table, but the caption element is really the right element for the job. Also, you can use CSS to style it, just as you style headings:

```
<table summary="Area representatives, and their home and work
    telephone numbers">
  <caption>Contact details</caption>
  <tr>
    <th>Name</th>
```

---

[5] http://reference.sitepoint.com/html/th/scope/

[6] http://reference.sitepoint.com/html/table/summary/

[7] http://reference.sitepoint.com/html/caption/

```
    <th>Contact (Home)</th>
    <th>Contact (Work)</th>
    <th>Location</th>
  </tr>
```

Recap

So far, we've looked at some of the basics of tables, and discussed some examples that demonstrate the key concepts. I've shown you how to use CSS to style the table content, and how to make the table content accessible, but it's best to see this in practice. So, let's move along to our project site and see how we can apply some of this knowledge.

Adding an Events Table

You've learned about the various elements that make up a table. Now, you're going to build one of your own.

- Open up **events.html** in your text editor.
- Type the following code beneath the paragraph you added earlier:

events.html *(excerpt)*

```
<table class="events" summary="Details of upcoming club events and
    dive trips">
  <caption>Club events/dive trips for the next six
      months</caption>
  <tr>
    <th>Date</th>
    <th>Event Description</th>
    <th>Approximate Cost</th>
    <th>Contact</th>
  </tr>
  <tr>
    <td>12 July</td>
    <td>Committee meeting, deciding on next year's trips</td>
    <td>N/A</td>
    <td>Bob Dobalina</td>
  </tr>
  <tr>
    <td>19 July</td>
    <td>7-day trip to Hurghada (package deal) - limited
        spaces</td>
```

```
      <td>&pound;260 pp (all inclusive), departing Luton</td>
      <td>Bob Dobalina</td>
    </tr>
    <tr>
      <td>5 August</td>
      <td>Ocean &amp; Sports Diver Theory Course</td>
      <td>Call for details</td>
      <td>Jeff Edgely</td>
    </tr>
    <tr>
      <td>12 August</td>
      <td>Murder Mystery Weekend, Cotswolds (no diving!)</td>
      <td>&pound;65 pp (accommodation included)</td>
      <td>Jill Smith</td>
    </tr>
</table>
```

Remember that you don't *have* to type this all out yourself—you can grab the markup from the code archive instead.

Note that all the features we've covered in the chapter are present here: the table summary attribute, the caption element, table headers (th), and the basic items of construction that you need for every table: the table, tr, and td elements. But, never mind the markup; how does it look in the browser? Figure 6.6 illustrates:

Well, in my mind this display can be summed up in one word: yuck! Like the unstyled table we saw earlier, this one doesn't look too appealing, nor is it very easy to interpret. Fortunately, it's CSS to the rescue once again. The first task we should perform to make our table more legible is add some borders to it.

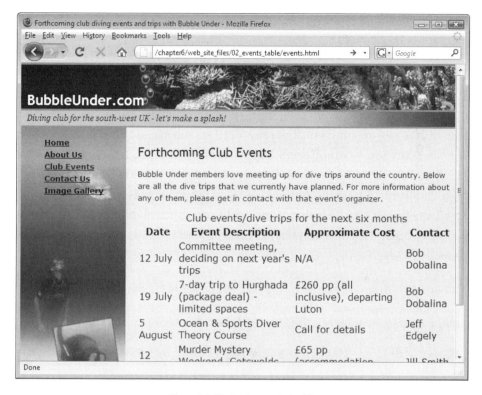

Figure 6.6. The basic, unstyled table

Open **style1.css** and add a new rule for the th and td elements. Here's the CSS you need:

```
                                                    style1.css (excerpt)

table.events {
  border-collapse: collapse;
}


table.events th, table.events td {
  padding: 4px;
  border: 1px solid #000066;
}


table.events th {
  font-size: x-small;
}
```

```
table.events td {
  font-size: small;
}
```

Here, we've created four rules. The first affects all `table` elements that have a `class` attribute set to `events`. The rule uses the `border-collapse` property to turn off the cell spacing effect we saw earlier. The second rule uses a selector that's slightly more complicated: `table.events th, table.events td` affects all `th` and `td` elements between the `<table class="events">` and `</table>` tags. Unfortunately, a simpler-looking declaration such as `table.events th, td` affects the `th` elements inside our table and *all* `td` elements. We're killing a couple of birds with one stone here, those proverbial birds being the `border` and `padding` for each cell.

The last two rules take care of the `font-size` for our cells and headers.

Figure 6.7 shows the effect of the above CSS on our web page.

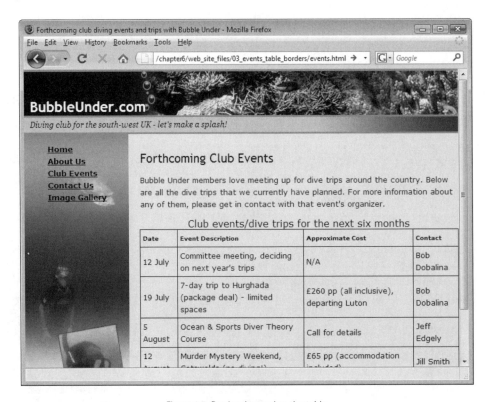

Figure 6.7. Borders improving the table

Next, we'll improve the alignment of the table header text. As I mentioned before, the default setting for th centers the header text, which prevents the majority of your content from lining up with that header. It's crazy, I know. Let's fix it quickly and easily.

In **style1.css**, modify the declaration for the table header (th) element, like so:

style1.css (excerpt)

```
table.events th {
    font-size: x-small;
    text-align: left;
}
```

That should solve the problem, but let's go a little further to make the table header look more attractive.

Add some more declarations to the `table.events th` rule: one to change the foreground (or text) color to white, one to add a background image, and a few padding rules:

style1.css (excerpt)

```
table.events th {
    font-size: x-small;
    text-align: left;
    background: #241374 url(backgrounds/header-bg.jpg);
    color: #ffffff;
    padding-top: 0;
    padding-bottom: 0;
    padding-left: 2px;
    padding-right: 2px;
}
```

■ While we're here, we might as well spruce up the table's caption:

```
                                                    style1.css (excerpt)

table.events caption {
  color: #000066;
  font-size: small;
  text-align: left;
  padding-bottom: 5px;
  font-weight: bold;
}
```

■ Save the style sheet and refresh the browser one more time to see how it looks. Compare your work with Figure 6.8.

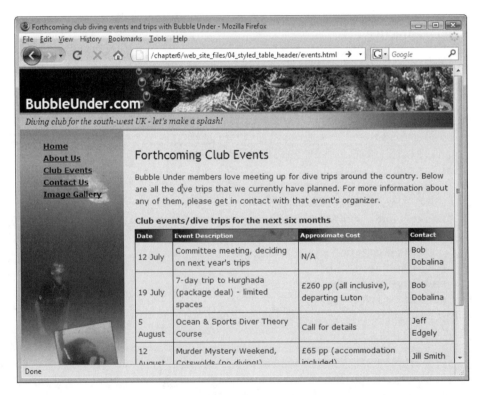

Figure 6.8. A much improved table header

I want to draw your attention to two points in that last addition. First, the background image is actually the same as the one we used in the page header (beneath the BubbleUnder.com text at the top), but it looks very different here. Why? In the page header, we positioned the image so that it hugs the bottom right-hand edges; in the `th` declaration, we haven't specified any positioning, so the image starts at the top left, and that portion of the image is quite different. Utilizing an image that's already used elsewhere in the web site can save ourselves a little download time (because the image will already have downloaded, the computer does not have to request a different image file for this background).

The second point I want to make is about the text color. Here, I've specified a color of `#ffffff`. This is the hexadecimal color specification for white, and although it may be easier to remember the word "white" than an obscure hex value, it's important to be familiar with a handful of hex values so you don't get confused the next time you see one. Another hex value that you'll come across often is `#000000`, which means black (the red, green, and blue values are 0, 0, and 0—in other words, there's no light at all—so `#000000` represents black).

Stylish Table Cells

I have just one more suggestion for our Events table. While it looks fine now, I'd like to give it that extra bit of polish. Once again, I'm going to suggest using a background image for this effect: a very subtle, faded background that will be positioned at the top of each table cell. Here's the markup:

```
                                                    style1.css (excerpt)
table.events td {
  font-size: small;
  background: #e2edff url(backgrounds/td.jpg) repeat-x top;
}
```

That background color—yet another obscure-looking hex value—is a very light blue that matches the blue that appears in the top of the image. The background image repeats horizontally (as demonstrated in Chapter 5) and is positioned along the top of the cell, giving our data table the very polished look depicted in Figure 6.9.

It's up to you to decide how far you want to take your table styling—you are limited only by your imagination (or, in my case, skill using graphics applications!). If you're interested in this area, have a look at Veerle Pieters' example of a CSS-styled table,[8] for starters.

---

[8] http://veerle.duoh.com/?id=P315

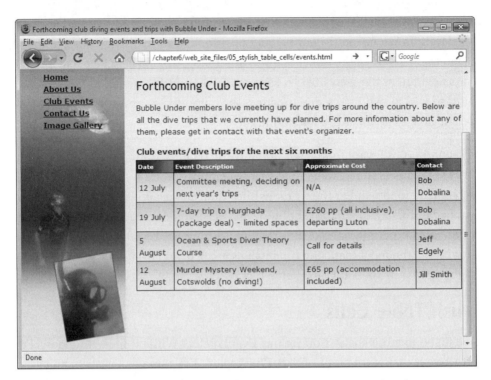

Figure 6.9. The final presentation of the data table

Advanced Tables

In the examples we saw earlier in the chapter, and in the table we've created in the project web site, the tables' structures have been quite simple: we have straight columns and rows, and no complications. What kinds of complications *could* we encounter?

Merging Table Cells

The complication that you're most likely to encounter as you work with tables arises within merged table cells. Let's consider the table from the project site again, and imagine it has the slightly different layout shown in Table 6.3 (I've removed the formatting to make it a little clearer).

Table 6.3. A more complicated table construction

Date	Event Details		Contact
	Event Description	Approximate Cost	
12 July	Committee meeting, deciding on next year's trips	N/A	Bob Dobalina
19 July	7-day trip to Hurghada (package deal) – limited spaces	£260 pp (all inclusive), departing Luton	Bob Dobalina
5 August	Ocean & Sports Diver Theory Course	Call for details	Jeff Edgely
12 August	Murder Mystery Weekend, Cotswolds (no diving!)	£65 pp (accommodation included)	Jill Smith

rowspan and colspan

In the example above, the headings of the first and last columns (Date and Contact) span across two rows of the table. Along the top, the table header that has the text "Event Details" takes up the space of two columns. To achieve this effect, we use the following XHTML attributes:

- rowspan[9]
- colspan[10]

The example above would be marked up as follows (the code is partly abbreviated):

```
<table>
  <tr>
    <th rowspan="2">Date</th>
    <th colspan="2">Event Details</th>
    <th rowspan="2">Contact</th>
  </tr>
  <tr>
    <th>Event Description</th>
    <th>Approximate Cost</th>
  </tr>
  <tr>
    <td>12 July</td>
    <td>Committee meeting, deciding on next year's trips</td>
```

---

[9] http://reference.sitepoint.com/html/td/rowspan/
[10] http://reference.sitepoint.com/html/td/colspan/

```
    <td>N/A</td>
    <td>Bob Dobalina</td>
  </tr>
```

Note that the first row appears to have three cells (1 column + 2 columns + 1 column = 4); the second row has only two table headers, but because the left- and right-most cells in the previous row have been set with a rowspan of 2, everything adds up quite nicely.

Are you feeling confused? If so, you're not the first person to find rowspan and colspan tricky; many a web designer has tripped over this in the past. If you get your rowspan and colspan mathematics wrong, your table constructions can do some *very* weird (and not so wonderful) things! That's why I placed this exercise in the advanced section of this chapter. If you want to merge table cells, there are two ways that you can approach it:

- Use a dedicated web development tool that's capable of handling and creating tables visually (such as Dreamweaver).[11]

- Rough it out on paper! Start using a simple table that has no merges, and simply cross out the lines you don't need. As you do so, make a note of the increased numbers of rows or columns that these cells span. Only when you're finished with your paper layout should you start translating this back to XHTML.

Advanced Accessibility

Badly constructed tables cause some of the biggest accessibility headaches. While it's beyond the scope of this book to tell you everything about web accessibility, there is a feature you can easily add to your tables to improve access to tabular content for assistive technology, like screen readers.

The scope Attribute

When you look at a table of data on the screen, it's very easy to glance at a header, then scan down the column and see the data that relates to that header. For a blind user who relies on a screen reader to interpret that table data and read it back, it can be tricky to associate data stored deep within a table with its appropriate header. The scope attribute can make this easier.

---

[11] http://www.adobe.com/products/dreamweaver/

The scope[12] attribute is applied to a header and has two possible values: row and col. Essentially, the scope attribute says to the browser (and any other piece of technology that needs to make use of it), "Hey, see this header cell? Well, everything below it is related to this cell, and don't you forget it!" The code below puts this a little more formally:

```
<tr>
  <th scope="col">Date</th>
  <th scope="col">Event Description</th>
  <th scope="col">Approximate Cost</th>
  <th scope="col">Contact</th>
</tr>
```

The table we're using on our project web site has headers at the tops of the columns only, but you might use tables that have headers down the left-hand side as well, like the one shown in Figure 6.10.

Figure 6.10. Applying scope="row" and scope="col" to table headers

Here's the XHTML for the above example:

```
<table>
  <caption>Train times and departures</caption>
  <tr>
    <td></td> <!-- empty cell in the top-left corner -->
    <th scope="col">Departure Time</th>
    <th scope="col">Platform</th>
    <th scope="col">Buffet Coach</th>
  </tr>
  <tr>
    <th scope="row">Southampton</th>
    <td>13:03</td>
    <td>12</td>
```

---

[12] http://reference.sitepoint.com/html/th/scope/

```
      <td>Yes</td>
    </tr>
    <tr>
      <th scope="row">Edinburgh</th>
      <td>14:47</td>
      <td>4</td>
      <td>Yes</td>
    </tr>
    <tr>
      <th scope="row">Newcastle</th>
      <td>15:55</td>
      <td>7</td>
      <td>No</td>
    </tr>
  </table>
```

If you start to merge cells (using the aforementioned colspan and rowspan), it gets incredibly tricky to mark the table up in a way that ensures its accessibility. Tools are available to help, though—namely the headers and id attributes, which are explained in the article *Bring on the Tables*, by Roger Johansson.[13] At this point, I'll simply say that it's far better to keep your tables simple. When using complicated tables (with rowspan, colspan, headers, and id attributes), it's still difficult to ensure that it'll be understood by assistive technology such as screen readers. Even for those readers that *do* fully support complex tables, there is a high cognitive load on the user to recall the various methods and keystrokes required to access the information. This really is a topic that you can leave for now!

Summary

When you need to present information in a tidy, organized fashion, tables really are the right technique for the job, and using XHTML, you have all the necessary tools at your disposal. In this chapter, we've seen how you can use combinations of simple XHTML elements to provide the necessary order, and employ CSS to style tables in such a way that they can be visually appealing. We've also covered some of the basic considerations that you need to take in order to make tabular information accessible to a much wider audience.

---

[13] http://www.456bereastreet.com/archive/200410/bring_on_the_tables/

Now that we've given tables their due attention, we can move on to another topic that's essential to grasp if you're going to have people interact with one another—not to mention your good self— on your web site. That topic is forms. If you're done here, the next chapter will "fill you in" on the details!

7

Forms: Interacting with Your Audience

One of the great things about the Internet is the apparently never-ending wealth of information it puts at your disposal. The term *web surfing* came about because, like real-world surfers, users never know which path they'll end up: if a topic piques their interest, that's the direction they'll take. But the process of simply reading, clicking on a link, and reading some more is very passive—users aren't really becoming involved. They're simply on the receiving end of all that information. At some point, users need to interact in some way with the web site, changing that one-way flow of information.

Imagine this scenario: you're looking to book a holiday—perhaps a surfing trip or a diving holiday—and the first steps you take are to search for information about resorts, read other people's reviews, and look at some stunning pictures. You make a decision fairly quickly about which resort you'd like to visit, then you decide to find a site through which you can book a trip, arrange your flights, and so on. As you book the holiday, you'll need to enter details, such as your name and address; you may have to select travel dates from a drop-down list; you might also need to specify certain features that you want to include in your holiday using checkboxes. To make these kinds of selections, you use HTML forms.

In this chapter, you'll learn about the various elements that make up a form, the tasks for which those elements should and should not be used, and how you can make sense of information submitted through forms. As part of the practical work of this chapter, we're going to add a simple form to the diving project site; it will allow users to notify the webmaster of forthcoming diving events. But, to start, let's investigate the different parts of a form.

Anatomy of a Form

It might not surprise you to learn that a form begins with an opening `<form>` tag and ends with a closing `</form>` tag. Inside that `form`[1] element, the browser can expect to find some special XHTML elements that can capture data in some way. Though the `form` element doesn't have any visual characteristics to speak of, it's a block-level element, and as such, will cause the browser to create breaks before and after its opening and closing tags.

Before we move any further into a description of what a `form` does, it's probably a good idea to review an example of a `form` as we'd see it in the browser. Take a look at the example in Figure 7.1.

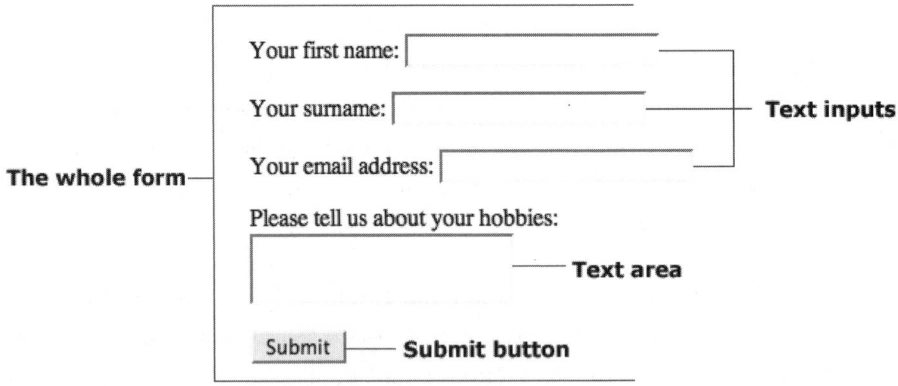

Figure 7.1. The basic anatomy of a form

The `form` element is a special kind of container. It contains a variety of XHTML elements that can exist only inside the `form` element, including:

---

[1] http://reference.sitepoint.com/html/form/

- fieldset
- legend
- input
- textarea
- select

I'll explain all of these elements through the course of this chapter, but let's start at the beginning with a very simple form that you can build for yourself. Then, we'll start to talk about all the different elements we might want to use in our forms.

A Simple Form

Let's get a feel for what a form does. Open your text editor and enter the following markup:

simpleform.html

```html
<!DOCTYPE html PUBLIC "-//W3C//DTD XHTML 1.0 Strict//EN"
    "http://www.w3.org/TR/xhtml1/DTD/xhtml1-strict.dtd">
<html xmlns="http://www.w3.org/1999/xhtml">
  <head>
    <title>A Simple Form</title>
    <meta http-equiv="Content-Type"
        content="text/html; charset=utf-8"/>
  </head>
  <body>
    <h1>A Simple Form</h1>
    <form method="get" action="simpleform.html">
      <p>
        <label for="yourname">Enter your name:</label>
        <input type="text" name="yourname" id="yourname"/>
      </p>
      <p><input type="submit"/></p>
    </form>
  </body>
</html>
```

Save the page as **simpleform.html**, then open it in your browser. You should see a very simple example of a form, like the one shown in Figure 7.2, which has:

- one text input in which you can enter your name
- a submit button that sends the details that were entered into the form

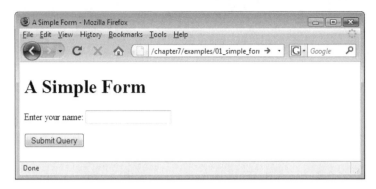

Figure 7.2. A very simple form

Now, enter your name in the text input and click on the submit button (it's usually labeled **Submit Query** or just **Submit**). The page should reload, your name should disappear from the text box, and if you look in the address bar, you'll see that the data you entered has been appended to the address for that page. It should look similar to this:

```
file:///C:/Documents%20and%20Settings/Bob%20Dobalina/My%20Document
s/Web/simpleform.html?yourname=Bob
```

We haven't done anything with the data yet, but you can appreciate that even with this basic example, the entered data is there for the taking (and manipulating).

Let's start looking at the different elements you can place in a form, and their uses.

The Building Blocks of a Form

The `form` Element

As we've already seen, a form begins with the `form` element. You'll see a few important attributes in an opening `<form>` tag, and these are:

method[2]

> This tells the browser *how* to send the data in the form when the user clicks the submit button. The options are `get` and `post`. The option you use will depend on what you're doing with the data (see the tip below, "Get It or Post It?" for

---

[2] http://reference.sitepoint.com/html/form/method/

more on this). For now, don't worry too much about `method`; we'll use `get` for our simple examples.

`action`[3]

This attribute tells the browser *where* to send the data that was collected in the form. Normally, this will specify another web page that can read and interpret the data entered.

Get It or Post It?

The decision about whether to use `get` or `post` in the `method` attribute of your `form` normally won't be yours if you want to avoid writing the form processing code. As you'll see later on, we'll use a third-party form processor to make our form useful, and that will dictate which method we use. However, there are a couple of points about these different methods that are useful to know:

▪ If you specify a `get` method, your form data will appear in the address bar of the page to which you submit that form. This can be useful: if you want to, you can bookmark that page[4] with those pieces of information included. For example, because Google's search form includes `method="get"`, you can bookmark a search for "cake shops Southampton." Then, every time you call up that bookmark, Google will give you its up-to-date list of cake shops in Southampton.

▪ Sometimes, you won't want users to be able to bookmark the results of their form usage; nor will you want the information in the form to be visible to a passerby. A good example that meets both these criteria is the log-in form for an Internet banking site. You'd want to make sure that only the actual bank account holder (not another family member, for example) can access the details for the account in question; you certainly wouldn't want people to see the user's password, either. In cases like these, we use the `post` method.

It's also worth noting that if you're sending a large amount of data, `post` is the preferred method.

As usual, there's more to this topic if you're interested,[5] but we won't need to concern ourselves with it anymore in this chapter.

---

[3] http://reference.sitepoint.com/html/form/action/
[4] Or, if you use IE, "add to favorites".
[5] A good place to start is *Methods GET and POST in HTML forms—what's the difference?* by Jukka Korpela [http://www.cs.tut.fi/~jkorpela/forms/methods.html].

The `fieldset` and `legend` Elements

These two elements really do go hand in hand; the `fieldset`[6] element groups related elements within a form together (by drawing a box around them), while the `legend`[7] element lets you caption that group of elements appropriately. Here's the XHTML for using this dynamic duo:

```
<form method="get" action="simpleform.html">
  <fieldset>
    <legend>All About You</legend>
    <p>
      <label for="yourname">Enter your name:</label>
      <input type="text" name="yourname" id="yourname"/>
    </p>
    <p><input type="submit"/></p>
  </fieldset>
</form>
```

Figure 7.3 shows how the form looks with these elements added.

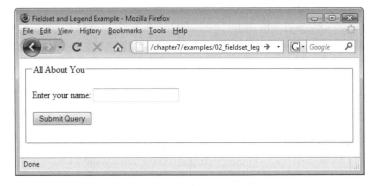

Figure 7.3. A form to which a `fieldset` and `legend` have been applied

Nesting `fieldsets`

You're not limited to using just one `fieldset` and `legend`. On more complex forms, you can nest these elements to provide more clarity within form sections, as Figure 7.4 shows.

---

[6] http://reference.sitepoint.com/html/fieldset/
[7] http://reference.sitepoint.com/html/legend/

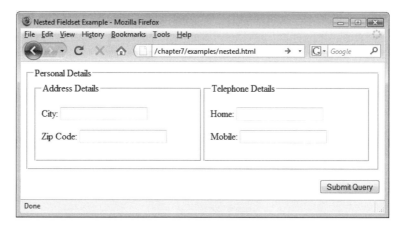

Figure 7.4. Nested `fieldsets` help to organize form inputs

The `label` Element

Form **controls** (e.g. text inputs) are the bits of the form the user interacts with to enter their data. The `label`[8] element is used to tell the user what kind of data they should enter in each control.

The `label` element is linked directly to the `input` to which it relates, using the `for`[9] attribute. The value of the `for` attribute should be the same as the `id` attribute of the `input` element.

The `label` element also enables the user to activate a `radio input` or `checkbox input`, or place the focus on a `text input` or `select` element.

The `input` Element

With the preamble out of the way, we can go to the nuts and bolts of the form: the section in which we actually capture data from users. The first element that you'll learn to use is the `input`[10] element; this is used to insert controls into the form that the user can interact with.

---

[8] http://reference.sitepoint.com/html/label/

[9] http://reference.sitepoint.com/html/label/for

[10] http://reference.sitepoint.com/html/input/

The input element is very versatile; its appearance and behavior can be changed dramatically using the type[11] attribute. Some of the most common values of the type attribute are:

- text
- password
- checkbox
- radio
- hidden
- submit

Each of these values causes a dramatically different control to be placed on your page. Let's start by looking at the most commonly-used one: the **text input** control.

Text Input

You've seen this control countless times on web pages. The text input, depicted in Figure 7.5, is the most basic type of form data users can enter.

Enter your name:

Figure 7.5. A simple text input

The XHTML for this control is very simple:

```
<p>
  <label for="yourname">Enter your name:</label>
  <input type="text" name="yourname" id="yourname"/>
</p>
```

Let's look at each of these components in turn:

the label element

The label is used to label a control, so that users know what kind of data they should enter.

---

[11] http://reference.sitepoint.com/html/input/type/

the `type` attribute

We can set the `input` element as a simple text input control by setting the `type` attribute to `text`.

the `name`[12] attribute

Remember in our very first form, the name we entered appeared at the end of the address bar when the form was submitted? The code is below:

```
file:///C:/Documents%20and%20Settings/Bob%20Dobalina/My%20Docum
ents/Web/simpleform.html?yourname=Bob
```

The `yourname` part came from the `name` attribute of the `input` element, which can be used to identify which piece of data came from a given control.

the `id`[13] attribute

At first glance, the `id` attribute seems identical to the `name` attribute, and for some types of controls, it is. However, as we'll see later, some controls can share the same `name`, and it is in these cases that the `id` is used to distinguish between various controls on the page.

The `id` attribute is referred to by the `label` element's `for` attribute. An `id` attribute can be used for many different purposes (you've already seen it used in this book to aid the styling of layouts created with CSS). However, in this example, its purpose is to give the `label` a referral point.

You might also want to add a couple of optional attributes to a text input:

`size`[14]

tells the browser how many characters the text box should display (alternatively, you could set a width with CSS)

`maxlength`[15]

places an upper limit on how many characters the user can enter into the text box

---

[12] http://reference.sitepoint.com/html/input/name/
[13] http://reference.sitepoint.com/html/core-attributes/id/
[14] http://reference.sitepoint.com/html/input/size/
[15] http://reference.sitepoint.com/html/input/maxlength/

Setting the Value of a Text Box

If you'd like to set the initial value of a text box, you can use the `value` attribute to do so. Load the following markup into a form, and a text box with the value "Bob" (without the quotation marks, of course) will be displayed:

```
<p>
  <label for="yourname">Enter your name:</label>
  <input type="text" name="yourname" id="yourname" value="Bob"/>
</p>
```

Password Input

The **password input** control is almost identical to the text input control, with one notable exception: the characters typed into the control are not displayed on the screen. Instead, they're replaced by asterisks or dots, as shown in Figure 7.6:

```
<p>
  <label for="password">Your password:</label>
  <input type="password" id="password" name="password"/>
</p>
```

Your password: ⁕⁕⁕⁕⁕⁕⁕⁕⁕

Figure 7.6. A password input control displays entered characters as asterisks

A Password INPUT Does Not Make a Secure Form

Although the password input control stops potential fraudsters from identifying a user's password as they're typing it in, it does not make the form any more secure during the actual data submission. For that, you'd need to consider security a little more seriously. To ensure that form data is sent securely, you'll need to use a protocol called HTTPS. Although you may not know it, HTTPS is used when you fill in a form on an ecommerce web site such as Amazon or eBay—it's this that causes the little padlock icon to display in the status bar on your browser (usually at the bottom).

Hidden Inputs

As the name suggests, a **hidden** input is one that doesn't appear in the page at all. Hidden fields are typically used to send additional data to the form processor; these have been input by the creator of the form (or through an automated application), rather than by the user. An automated application could insert the time and date into a hidden field (rather than ask the user what the current time is), but tricky scripting like that is beyond the scope of this book.

Later in the chapter we'll use hidden fields to identify ourselves to a third-party form processor. For now, all you need to understand is that the following markup won't cause anything to appear on the screen:

```
<input type="hidden" name="peekaboo" value="hereiam"/>
```

However, it will be passed to the form processor (along with all the other data inputted) when the user submits the form:

```
file:///C:/Documents%20and%20Settings/Bob%20Dobalina/My%20Document
s/Web/hidden.html?peekaboo=hereiam
```

Checkboxes

Checkboxes are an excellent tool for gathering answers to *yes* or *no* questions. A text input is completely free and open, but with a checkbox, the user has a direct choice of yes or no, as the example in Figure 7.7 demonstrates.

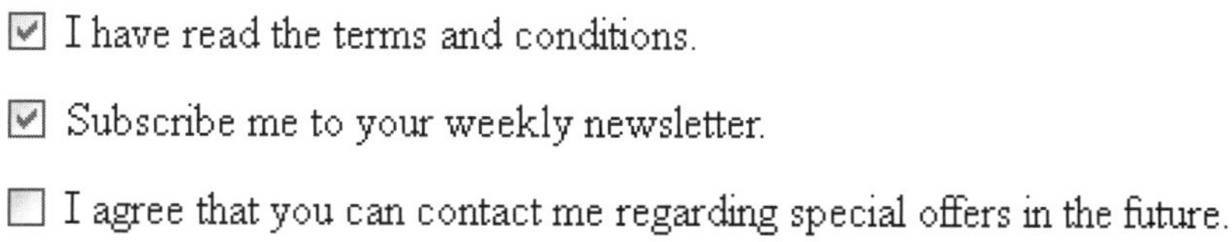

☑ I have read the terms and conditions.

☑ Subscribe me to your weekly newsletter.

☐ I agree that you can contact me regarding special offers in the future.

Figure 7.7. Using checkboxes in a form

Here's how you can achieve that effect in XHTML:

```
<p>
  <input type="checkbox" name="terms" id="terms"/>
  <label for="terms">I have read the terms and conditions.<label>
</p>
<p>
  <input type="checkbox" name="newsletter" id="newsletter"/>
  <label for="terms">Subscribe me to your weekly newsletter.<label>
</p>
<p>
  <input type="checkbox" name="offers" id="offers"/>
  <label for="offers">I agree that you can contact me regarding
      special offers in the future.</label>
</p>
```

Preselecting Checkboxes

Often, when you're working with checkboxes, you might want them to be already checked (or selected) when the page loads, with the onus being on users to uncheck them as they see fit. To achieve this, we use the `checked` attribute. Oddly enough, the value you need to use for `checked` is `checked` (rather than `checked="yes"` or `checked="true"`):

```
<p>
  <input type="checkbox" name="terms" id="terms"/>
  <label for="terms">I have read the terms and conditions</label>
</p>
<p>
  <input type="checkbox" name="newsletter" id="newsletter"/>
  <label for="terms">Subscribe me to your weekly newsletter.<label>
</p>
<p>
  <input type="checkbox" name="offers" id="offers"
      checked="checked"/>
  <label for="offers">I agree that you can contact me regarding
      special offers in the future</label>
</p>
```

Radio Buttons

Checkboxes are handy when you may require the respondent to tick more than one option. However, what would you do if you wanted the user to select only one option? For this scenario, we use **radio buttons**, as shown in Figure 7.8.

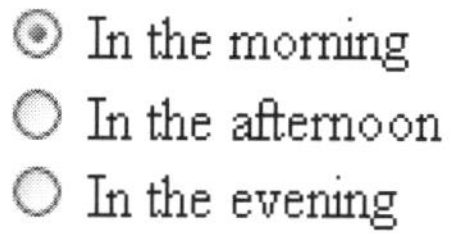

⦿ In the morning
◯ In the afternoon
◯ In the evening

Figure 7.8. Radio buttons as they may appear in a form

This code creates the radio buttons:

```
<p>
  <input type="radio" name="timeslot" id="morning"
      value="morning"/>
  <label for="morning">In the morning</label>
  <br/>
  <input type="radio" name="timeslot" id="afternoon"
      value="afternoon"/>
  <label for="afternoon">In the afternoon</label>
  <br/>
  <input type="radio" name="timeslot" id="evening"
      value="evening"/>
  <label for="evening ">In the evening</label>
</p>
```

The key difference between this and the checkbox example is that, in this case, we have three different options, *yet the* `name` *attribute is the same for all three inputs.* This is essential: it's having the same value in the `name` attribute that binds the three inputs together. They share the same `name`, but each `input` has a different `value` attribute. As a user selects an option and submits the form, the appropriate value is sent to the server.

It's also worth pointing out that each `input` has a different `id`. In fact, *any* `id` that is assigned to an element in the document *must* be unique, whether it is a `form` element, an image, or another XHTML element. In this case, it also benefits the `label` elements, which must refer to unique identifiers.

"Hey, these don't look like buttons! And what have they got to do with radios?"

The earlier radios featured push-buttons that listeners would use to select a station. You could only press one button in at a time, and when you did, the previously selected button would pop up again. This is where the name radio button name originates. Younger readers will just have to take my word on the subject!

Preselecting Radio Buttons

The technique we use to preselect a given radio button is exactly the same as that used for checkboxes:

```
<p>
  <input type="radio" name="timeslot" id="morning" value="morning"
      checked="checked"/>
  <label for="morning">In the morning</label>
  <br/>
  <input type="radio" name="timeslot" id="afternoon"
      value="afternoon"/>
  <label for="afternoon">In the afternoon</label>
  <br/>
  <input type="radio" name="timeslot" id="evening"
      value="evening"/>
  <label for="evening ">In the evening</label>
</p>
```

The `select` Element

Radio buttons allow you to choose only one item from a range of options, which is useful ... up to a point. But what would happen if you had 20 or more options? Do you really want to display them all on the screen when only one will be selected? Probably not. A better option might be to use the `select`[16] element. This control lets users choose from a range of options, but takes up less space on your web page; initially taking up a single line, users view the options by clicking on the drop-down arrow (using a mouse or keyboard). You've probably used this form control countless times, illustrated in Figure 7.9.

---

[16] http://reference.sitepoint.com/html/select/

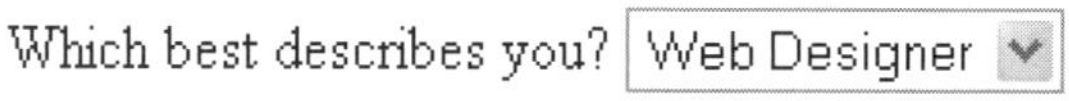

Which best describes you? | Web Designer ▼ |

Figure 7.9. The `select` element produces a drop-down list control for forms

The `select` element contains an array of `option` elements. Each `option` correlates to an option in the drop-down list. Here's the XHTML for this type of form control:

```
<p>
  <label for="role">Which best describes you?</label>
  <select name="role" id="role">
    <option>Secretary</option>
    <option>Web Designer</option>
    <option>Manager</option>
    <option>Cleaner</option>
    <option>Other</option>
  </select>
</p>
```

Preselecting Options

Like checkboxes and radio buttons, it's possible to preselect one of the options in a drop-down menu. To preselect an option for a drop-down list, we need to use a `selected` attribute with a value of `selected`.

Here is the `select` element once again, this time with the "Web Designer" option preselected:

```
<p>
  <label for="role">Which best describes you?</label>
  <select name="role" id="role">
    <option>Secretary</option>
    <option selected="selected">Web Designer</option>
    <option>Manager</option>
    <option>Cleaner</option>
    <option>Other</option>
  </select>
</p>
```

Making Multiple Selections

It's actually possible to create a list that allows several items to be selected, but this technique is frowned upon by most usability experts. This is because it requires the user to hold down the **Ctrl** key and click on the items required—not exactly obvious and awkward if only using a keyboard, let alone if the user has to scroll as well. In many cases, checkboxes are the better option over multiple select lists.

The `textarea` Element

A text input control is good for capturing short pieces of information, but is not effective for longer amounts of text. As the viewable area can only show minimal text, you've probably experienced these limitations first-hand when inputting chunks of text into a search engine—the words start to disappear from view. The better choice for collecting larger amounts of text is the `textarea`[17] element shown in Figure 7.10.

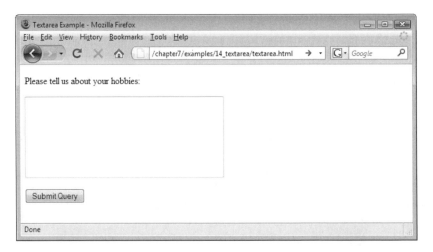

Figure 7.10. Using a `textarea` element for collecting larger amounts of text

Here's some code that displays a `textarea`:

```
<p><label for="hobbies">Please tell us about your
    hobbies:</label></p>
<p><textarea name="hobbies" rows="7" cols="40"
    id="hobbies"></textarea></p>
```

---

[17] http://reference.sitepoint.com/html/textarea/

Submit Buttons

Users must click on the submit button to send the data they've entered into the form. Strangely, it's also a type of `input` element, even though you can't really put anything *into* it at all! All you can do is activate it by clicking on it.

Although submit buttons also use an `input` tag, I left this one until last—rather than grouping it with the text box, password, radio button, and checkbox controls. This is simply because the submit button will almost always be the last element in your form.

Inserting a submit button is easy. The code below produces the display shown in Figure 7.11:

```
<p><input type="submit"/></p>
```

Submit Query

Figure 7.11. The humble submit button

The wording on this button is a little bland, isn't it? The reason for this is that we haven't set a `value` attribute, so the browser uses its default. Adding in a `value` helps to make the button a little more friendly and intuitive, as Figure 7.12 illustrates:

```
<p><input type="submit" value="Send Your Feedback"/></p>
```

Send Your Feedback

Figure 7.12. A more friendly-looking button

 No Mouse Required!

You may not realize this, but you don't have to use a mouse to submit a form; it's not always necessary to click that button. Usually, you can fill in the form data and simply hit **Enter**.

The Default Control Appearance

It's worth noting that forms can look quite different when displayed on different browsers and operating systems. Throughout this book, we've used Firefox for Windows for most of our screen shots, but it's important to be aware of how users of other systems will see your forms. Imagine that we combined all of the different form elements into one form; let's see how it looks in different browsers.

Figure 7.13 shows a form displayed in Firefox on Windows.

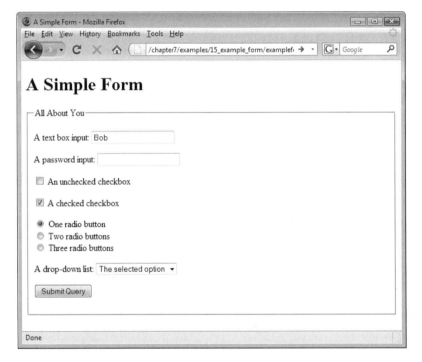

Figure 7.13. Firefox for Windows displays our combined form elements

This is very similar to the world's most used browser, Internet Explorer. Subtle differences include a blue/grey `fieldset` border with rounded corners and a slightly larger submit button. Figure 7.14 shows IE7 on Windows Vista; however, it's worth mentioning that there's variation between IE6, IE7, and IE8.

Firefox on Mac OS X isn't too different from its Windows cousin. Naturally, however, it inherits a bit more of a Mac OS X flavor. The selected checkboxes and radio buttons are blue as Figure 7.15 illustrates.

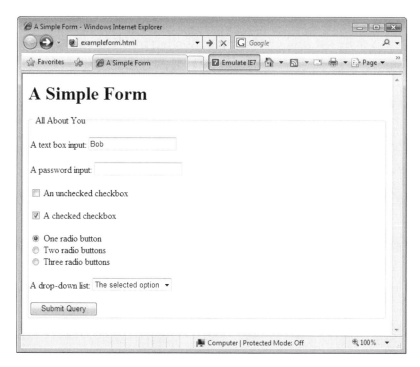

Figure 7.14. IE7 has subtle differences with rounded corners and a larger submit button

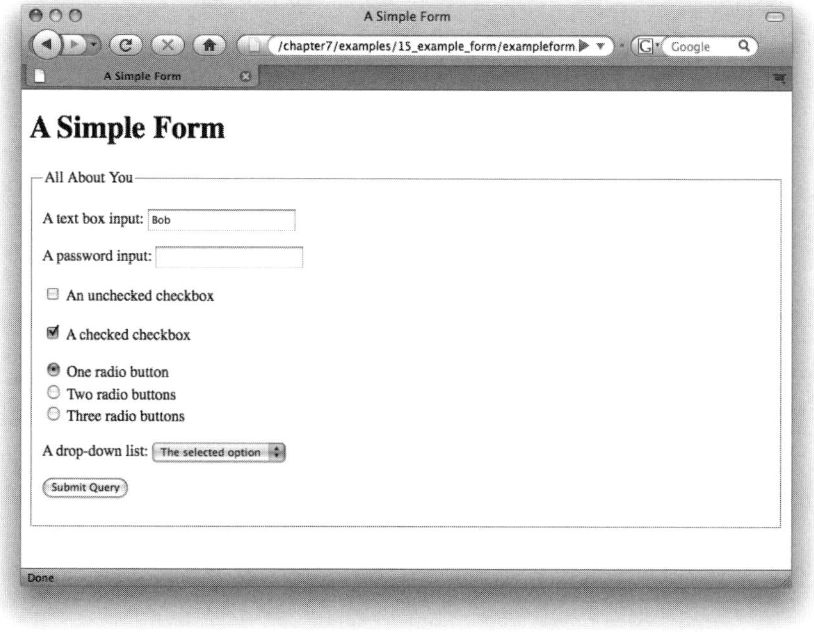

Figure 7.15. Firefox on Mac OS X—naturally with Mac OS X controls

Safari, is almost identical to Firefox on Mac OS X. The drop-down has also changed to a Mac OS X-style list, and our submit button has nicely rounded ends, as Figure 7.16 shows.

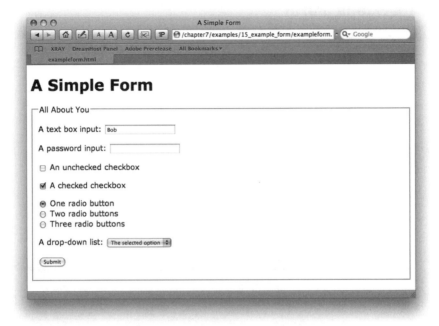

Figure 7.16. Safari is almost identical to Firefox on Mac OS X

As you can see, there's a subtle degree of variation between the controls that different browsers display. We can customize the appearance of many of these controls with CSS. However, the appearance of radio buttons, checkboxes, and drop-down lists is largely determined by the user's operating system.

Building a Contact Page

Let's apply some of our newfound knowledge by adding a contact form to the project site. In the process, I'll show you again how CSS can spruce up the plain default styling of these XHTML elements. This time around, we won't need to add any new pages to the project site; instead, we'll expand on the existing *Contact Us* page.

Processing the Data: it's Coming!

A problem I've had with many web design and development books in the past, was the lack of explanation on how you might *use* the form data entered by the user. I would merrily build a form, click the submit button, then ask, "Now what?"

Processing form data is not a minor task: it requires programming know-how or, at the very least, web hosting with support resources that can explain to the beginner how to set up form handling. As you're reading an HTML beginners' book, the chances are that your programming skills have yet to develop, but don't despair. By the end of the chapter, I will have demonstrated an easy method for receiving the form data submitted by your users. This form-building exercise will *not* be a purely cosmetic affair that leaves you wanting to know more about the black art of handling form data!

Editing the Contact Us Page

In your text editor, open **contact.html**.

We need to edit the wording that exists in the body of the page. It's useful to have an email address or telephone number on the page, just in case the visitor prefers to contact you via those means. With this in mind, let's replace the paragraph in the page with the following:

contact.html (excerpt)

```
<p>To let us know about a forthcoming dive event, please use
    the form below.</p>
<p>If you need to get in touch urgently, please call Bob
    Dobalina on 01793 641207. For anything else, please <a
    href="mailto:bob@bubbleunder.com">drop us a line by
    email</a>.</p>
```

Adding a `form` and a `fieldset` Element

Next, let's set up the basics for the form, using the `form`, `fieldset`, and `legend` elements.

- In **contact.html**, add an opening `<form>` tag and a closing `</form>` tag in between the two paragraphs that you just added (above) to the page.

- In the opening `<form>` tag, add the following attributes:

  - `action=""` (We'll be filling in the blanks later.)

  - `method="post"` (We're using post because we intend to submit a fair bit of data through this form.)

  - `class="contact"` (We'll use this when it comes to applying styles to our form.)

- Next, add a `fieldset` and a `legend` element. Remember that the `fieldset` is contained inside the `form` element, and the `legend` immediately follows the opening `fieldset` tag.

- For the `legend` element, use the phrase, "Tell us About a Dive Event."

Hopefully your XHTML should look like this:

```
                                                    contact.html (excerpt)

<p>To let us know about a forthcoming dive event, please use the
    form below.</p>
<form action="" method="post" class="contact">
  <fieldset>
    <legend>Tell us About a Dive Event</legend>
  </fieldset>
</form>
<p>If you need to get in touch urgently, please call Bob Dobalina
    on 01793 641207. For anything else, please <a
    href="mailto:bob@bubbleunder.com">drop us a line by
    email</a>.</p>
```

If so, save **contact.html**, then take a look at it in the browser. It should appear similarly to Figure 7.17.

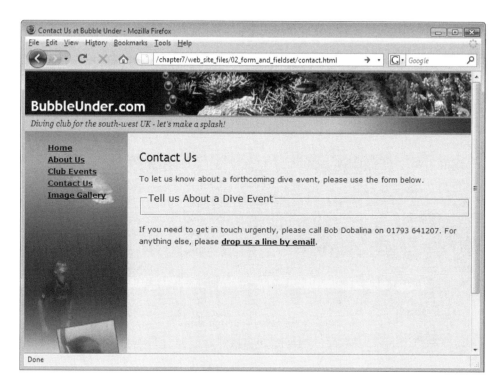

Figure 7.17. An empty form

IE and Empty `fieldsets`

If you're using a version of IE *earlier* than IE8, don't worry if you don't see the `fieldset` border. In IE7 and previous versions, the `fieldset`'s border won't display if there's nothing (apart from the `legend` element) inside the `fieldset`; other browsers will show the border even when `fieldset` doesn't contain any content.

If you're using IE7 (or earlier), add some temporary content so you can see the border. Then, we can start to play around with it:

contact.html *(excerpt)*

```
<form action="" method="post" class="contact">
  <fieldset>
    <legend>Tell Us About a Dive Event</legend>
    <!-- some temporary content -->
```

```
    <p>Form elements go here</p>
  </fieldset>
</form>
```

Figure 7.18 now shows the unstyled `fieldset` border as it appears in IE on Windows Vista.

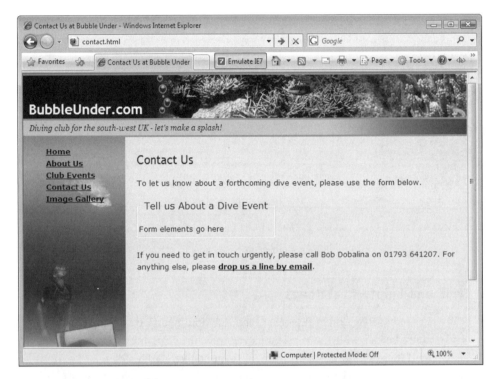

Figure 7.18. An unstyled `fieldset` displayed in IE

Styling `fieldset` and `legend` with CSS

If you wish, you can leave the styling of form controls until later (i.e., after you've built the actual form and have all the controls in place). However, I prefer to jump right in there and apply CSS to forms as I go, mainly because I use CSS to set the widths of text boxes and so on, and I like to make sure each part looks right before I move to the next.

While the default appearance of the `fieldset` doesn't look all that bad in Figure 7.18, other browsers don't display the curved border that IE provides, and as a result, it can look a little bland. With CSS, though, it is possible to apply some styles that improve the look of our form and help to standardize the page's appearance across different browsers. Let's sort out the `fieldset` and `legend` elements in one hit. Open **style1.css** in your text editor and add the following style rules:

```
                                                    style1.css (excerpt)

form.contact fieldset {
  border: 2px solid navy;
  padding: 10px;
}

form.contact legend {
  font-weight: bold;
  font-size: small;
  color: navy;
  padding: 5px;
}
```

Save **style1.css**, then take a look at the Contact Us page in your browser. The result should look like Figure 7.19.

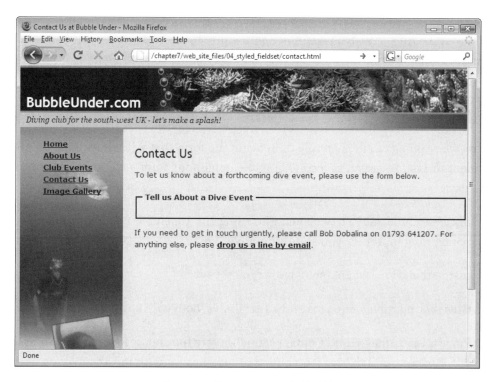

Figure 7.19. The `fieldset` styled in CSS

class-ified Forms

Note that we're using the `contact` class to style the elements in this form in the same way that we used the `events` class to style our table in Chapter 6. We're doing this in case we decide to add other kinds of forms to the site later on. For example, we may add a search form in the future, and we may wish that form to have a very different appearance from this one.

The only problem I can see with this page is that there seems to be a little too much space between the first paragraph and the form. This can be fixed with a negative margin, which we apply to the `form` element like so:

```
                                                              style1.css (excerpt)

form.contact {
  padding: 0;
  margin: 0;
  margin-top: -15px;
  line-height: 150%;
}
```

In the above rule, I've also taken the opportunity to remove any default `padding` or `margin` values that the browser might want to set on the `form` element. Additionally, I've increased the default line height.

Adding Text Input Controls

Now we're going to add a couple of items to the form that will allow us to obtain some information—such as a contact name, telephone number, and so on—from the user.

▪ In **contact.html**, add a `div` element just after the `legend`. If you added some temporary content for IE, you should remove it now.

▪ Inside that `div`, add an `input` with `type="text"`.

▪ Give the `input` element `name` and `id` attributes, both with a value of `contactname`.

▪ Place a `label` that reads "Contact Name" before the `input`. Remember to add the `for` attribute, and to give it a value that matches up with the `id` attribute of the `input` element.

Save the web page, then take a look at it in your browser.

How does it look? Does it resemble a text input? If not, check your XHTML to see if you got it right:

contact.html *(excerpt)*

```
<form action="" method="post" class="contact">
  <fieldset>
    <legend>Tell Us About a Dive Event</legend>
    <div>
      <label for="contactname">Contact Name</label>
      <input type="text" name="contactname" id="contactname"/>
    </div>
  </fieldset>
</form>
```

The div element will keep those items together and cause line breaks to appear before and after them; we'll be using this approach on all the form elements on this page.

<div> or <p> Elements to Layout Your Form?

I'm sure some people have a passionate opinion on this matter but in the quest for semantic purity there are arguments for either case. Some developers like to use lists to mark up their forms. Use what ever works for you. Sometimes it makes sense to inherit the styles from a p like font color or margin; at other times, it will be preferable to start with the blank canvas that a div offers.

We'll use <div>s on the Bubble Under web site.

Next, I'm going to address the styling of the text that sits inside the label element. Just a couple of minor tweaks are required:

style1.css *(excerpt)*

```
form.contact label {
  font-weight: bold;
  font-size: small;
  color: blue;
}
```

Figure 7.20 shows our progress so far.

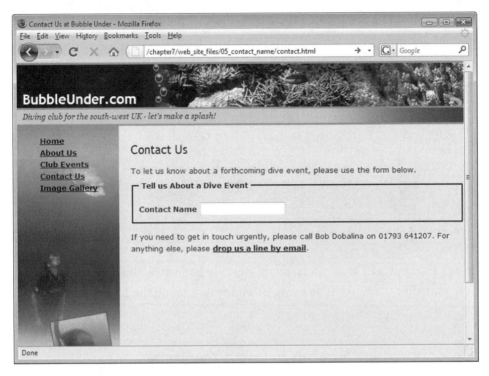

Figure 7.20. Adding a contact name text input control to the form

Okay, let's add a bunch of other text input controls in one fell swoop. Here's the XHTML you need (new parts are shown in bold):

```
contact.html (excerpt)

<form action="" method="post" class="contact">
  <fieldset>
    <legend>Tell us About a Dive Event</legend>
    <div>
      <label for="contactname">Contact Name</label>
      <input type="text" name="contactname" id="contactname"/>
    </div>
    <div>
      <label for="telephone">Telephone Number</label>
      <input type="text" name="telephone" id="telephone"/>
    </div>
    <div>
      <label for="email">Email Address</label>
```

```
      <input type="text" name="email" id="email"/>
    </div>
    <div>
      <label for="eventname">What's the event called?</label>
      <input type="text" name="eventname" id="eventname"/>
    </div>
    <div>
      <label for="eventdate">When's the event happening?</label>
      <input type="text" name="eventdate" id="eventdate"/>
    </div>
  </fieldset>
</form>
```

Figure 7.21 shows how it looks.

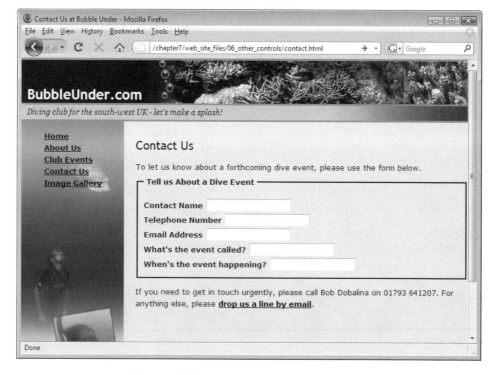

Figure 7.21. Building up the form with several text inputs

Tidying up `label` Elements with CSS

That form might work well, but the misalignment of the text input controls is not attractive. Thankfully, you can correct this issue using CSS. Rather than apply the style to *all* `label` elements inside the form, we'll add a `class` attribute to all of the `label` elements so that we can style only these `labels` (we'll need to add some different style rules to other `labels` later on). Add the following code to **style1.css**, just after the previous `label` selector:

style1.css (excerpt)

```css
form.contact label.fixedwidth {
  display: block;
  width: 240px;
  float: left;
}
```

Next, add the `class` attribute to the `labels` that you have in **contact.html**. Your XHTML should now look like this:

contact.html (excerpt)

```html
<form action="" method="post" class="contact">
  <fieldset>
    <legend>Tell us About a Dive Event</legend>
    <div>
      <label for="contactname" class="fixedwidth">Contact
          Name</label>
      <input type="text" name="contactname" id="contactname"/>
    </div>
    <div>
      <label for="telephone" class="fixedwidth">Telephone
          Number</label>
      <input type="text" name="telephone" id="telephone"/>
    </div>
    <div>
      <label for="email" class="fixedwidth">Email Address</label>
      <input type="text" name="email" id="email"/>
    </div>
    <div>
      <label for="eventname" class="fixedwidth">What's the event
          called?</label>
      <input type="text" name="eventname" id="eventname"/>
```

```
    </div>
    <div>
      <label for="eventdate" class="fixedwidth">When's the event
          happening?</label>
      <input type="text" name="eventdate" id="eventdate"/>
    </div>
  </fieldset>
</form>
```

Refresh the page of your browser, and it should look like Figure 7.22.

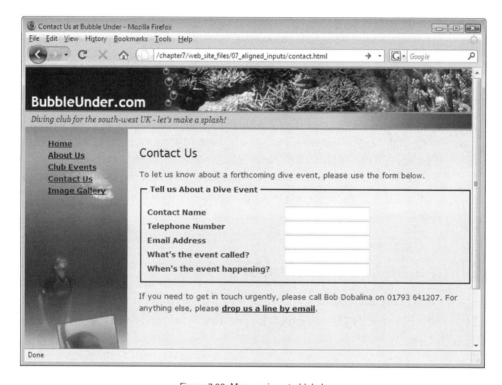

Figure 7.22. More regimented labels

What Just Happened There?

Sorry—I glossed over that CSS a bit! What we did above was a little clever (even if I do say so myself, ahem)—it veers into *advanced* CSS territory. Essentially, the declarations we used told the browser to display the following:

display: block

> This declaration converts an inline element (such as a `label` element) into a block-level element. Once it's treated as a block-level element, we can start doing a little more to it, for instance, setting a `width`.

width: 240px

> Ah, there we go! By setting the `width`, we've reserved a certain amount of space for the `label` text. Nothing's going to encroach upon that. However, normally a break appears before and after a block-level element.

float: left

> Remember this? We used it on the home page to move the feature image over to the right. In this case, we'll use it to place the `label` on the left; the content that immediately follows (the form input) aligns to the right of it, in much the same way text in a newspaper wraps around photos in the page layout. Without this declaration, the text input control would appear beneath the `label` text.

Adding a `select` Element

Now, let's add a `select` element. Where could we use this on our page? We could make a control to specify the region of the country in which the diving event or trip will take place.

- Add another `div` at the end of your `form` in `contact.html`.
- Insert a `select` element into the `div` element you just added.
- Give the `select` element `id` and `name` attributes with the value `region`.
- Add a `label` that has some appropriate text.
- Add an `option` element inside the `select` element for each of these following regions:
  - South-west
  - South-east
  - Midlands

- Central
- London
- East
- North
- Scotland
- Northern Ireland
- Wales
- International (see details below)

Your XHTML should now look like this:

```
                                                      contact.html (excerpt)

<div>
  <label for="region" class="fixedwidth">What region is the event
     in?</label>
  <select name="region" id="region">
    <option>South-west</option>
    <option>South-east</option>
    <option>Midlands</option>
    <option>Central</option>
    <option>London</option>
    <option>East</option>
    <option>North</option>
    <option>Scotland</option>
    <option>Northern Ireland</option>
    <option>Wales</option>
    <option>International (see details below)</option>
  </select>
</div>
```

And, of course, Figure 7.23 shows the obligatory screenshot.

Figure 7.23. Activating the drop-down list (or `select` element)

Adding a `textarea` Element

We've got the basics. Now it's time to let the user go a bit wild! Let's move beyond the somewhat restrictive inputs we've created so far. The `textarea` will let the user enter as much text as they like, so we'll need to create a little extra space for this element.

Because a `textarea` is an "anything goes" kind of input, you might like to insert some guideline text before it, just to let people know what they should enter:

> "Please provide any other details you think will be useful to us in the text area below (it may save us calling or emailing you, and help avoid delays)."

Now, let's add a `textarea` to the form:

■ In **contact.html**, add an opening `<textarea>` tag and a closing `</textarea>` tag. Be sure to leave *no space between them*, as any spaces or carriage returns in the source code will appear inside the `textarea`, which can be annoying.

■ Add the following attributes with the values indicated:

  ■ `id="details"`

  ■ `name="details"`

  ■ `cols="30"`

  ■ `rows="7"`

■ As before, add a `label` element just before the `textarea` and tie that in with the `id` and `name` attributes in the `textarea` element (use the value `details`).

■ Give the label a `class` attribute with the value `fixedwidth`.

■ Save your work, then take a look at the web page in your browser.

The XHTML for this text area is as follows:

```
                                              contact.html (excerpt)
<div>
  <p>Please provide any other details you think will be useful to
      us in the text area below (it may save us calling or
      emailing you, and help avoid delays).</p>
  <label for="details" class="fixedwidth">More details (as much as
      you think we'll need!)</label>
  <textarea id="details" name="details" cols="30"
      rows="7"></textarea>
</div>
```

Figure 7.24 shows the intended result.

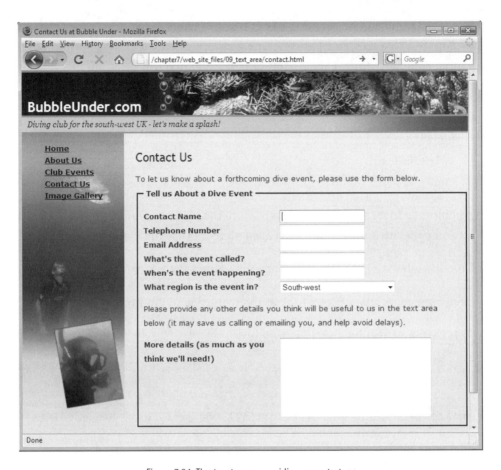

Figure 7.24. The `textarea` providing room to type

Our form's nearly complete. Truth be known, it's probably detailed enough in its current state, but it's better to see a working example of *all* the input controls that you're likely to want to use, than to stop now. So, let's fast-track through the last task: adding checkboxes and radio buttons.

Adding Radio Buttons and Checkboxes

As you know, we use radio buttons to allow users to choose one only from a group of options. With checkboxes, each option is independent of the others, so, if you have ten checkboxes, your users may check:

- all of them
- none of them
- any number of them

We're going to utilize radio buttons to allow users to choose a convenient time for a call-back (just in case the information they supplied in the form is not clear). A checkbox will be employed to let the user confirm whether the information entered in the form can be shared—a very common use of checkboxes.

As I mentioned a moment ago, I'm going to fast-track through this section. Here's the XHTML you need to add for the radio buttons:

contact.html *(excerpt)*

```
<div>
  <p>If we need to call you back for any more info, what would be
     the best time to call you on the number supplied?</p>
  <input type="radio" name="timetocall" id="morning"
     value="Morning"/>
  <label for="morning">In the morning</label>
  <br/>
  <input type="radio" name="timetocall" id="afternoon"
     value="Afternoon"/>
  <label for="afternoon">In the afternoon</label>
  <br/>
  <input type="radio" name="timetocall" id="evening"
     value="Evening"/>
  <label for="evening">In the evening</label>
  <br/>
  <input type="radio" name="timetocall" id="never" value="Never"
     checked="checked"/>
  <label for="never">No calls please</label>
</div>
```

Here's the final part of the code, which deals with the checkbox:

contact.html *(excerpt)*

```
<div>
  <p>Bubble Under may share information you give us here with
     other like-minded people or web sites to promote the event.
     Please confirm if you are happy for us to do this.</p>
  <input type="checkbox" name="publicize" id="publicize"
     checked="checked"/>
  <label for="publicize">I am happy for this event to be
     publicized outside of and beyond BubbleUnder.com, where
     possible</label>
</div>
```

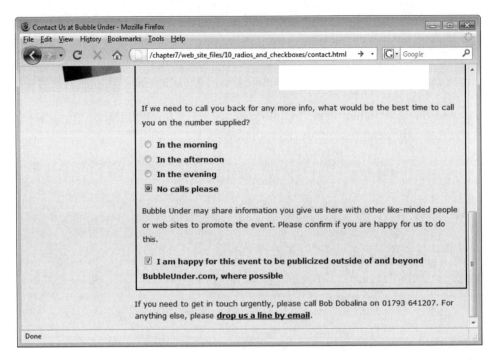

Figure 7.25. Radio buttons and checkboxes in the form

Now, go type that lot in! Seriously, though, there's only one aspect here that you haven't already seen: when you use a checkbox or a radio button, the control comes *before* the text that's associated with it. This is common practice with forms; please don't break the convention by putting your text first, before the form control—no matter how much you might be tempted. You'll see that we have deliberately not included the `fixedwidth class` on the labels we want to appear after the `input` elements, as we don't want them to float or display as a block.[18]

Let's take a look at how the form displays in Firefox: Figure 7.25 shows its appearance.

Completing the Form: a Submit Button

This really is the last step, and it will take but a moment. Simply add the following markup before the closing `</fieldset>` tag:

---

[18] Read more on how the order of a control's text affects form accessibility at http://webstandards.org/learn/tutorials/accessible-forms/01-accessible-forms.html.

```
<div class="buttonarea">
  <input type="submit" value="Send Us the Info"/>
</div>
```

I've added a `class` attribute to the `div` element that contains the submit button, and I've given it the appropriate value: `buttonarea`. I've done this because I want to be able to style the button area (the button and its containing `div`) in CSS. In most browsers, buttons look a little bland by default (as we saw when we looked at a few examples earlier in this chapter).

- In **style1.css**, add a new contextual selector for the button. We want it to affect an `input` that's contained in an element that has a `class` of `buttonarea`.
- Set the background color to navy.
- Set the text color to white.
- Make the font bold.
- Add a little padding around the button—five pixels should do it.
- Finally, add a one-pixel border on the button to make the border solid and white.

The CSS for these steps is shown here:

style1.css (excerpt)

```
form.contact .buttonarea input {
    background: navy;
    color: white;
    font-weight: bold;
    padding: 5px;
    border: 1px solid white;
}
```

Check the effect of this markup by saving **style1.css**, then refreshing the view in your browser. Are you looking at a blue button instead of a gray one? If you're still looking at a gray button, are you using an older version of Safari or Camino? Remember, not all browsers support styling of all form controls. IE and Firefox should render the colors as requested, though.

Our button looks a little lost, though. I like to create a special area for buttons like this. After all, they're special: they're the final part of the form—besides, a special area helps to draw attention that they're there to be clicked. Let's add a class selector for the button area:

```
form.contact .buttonarea {
  text-align: center;
  padding: 4px;
  background-color: #0066ff;
}
```

The button now sits in the middle of an eye-catching blue strip, rather than display-ing at the bottom of the form all alone. Figure 7.26 shows the final product: our form from start to finish.

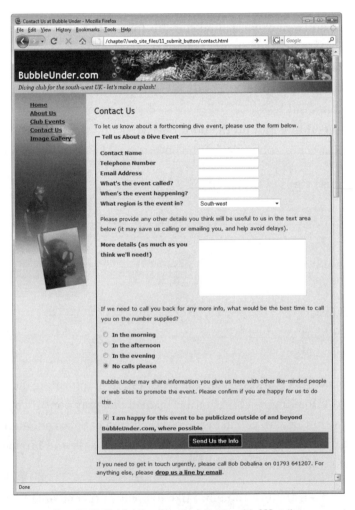

Figure 7.26. Highlighting the submit button with CSS styling

What Have We Achieved?

In this chapter, you've learned what different form elements are used for, and which types of controls are suitable for particular purposes. Together, we've stepped through the process of building a form, and we've styled it with CSS along the way. But, what now? Where's this data going?

For the last part of this chapter, I'll walk you through the process involved in signing up for a free form processing service that will handle your data for you.

Processing the Form

Handling form data is a skill that requires programming. I mentioned this earlier, and I'm unable to teach you how to program in PHP, Perl, or some other server-side language that can manipulate this data as it would take another book to explain it. Fortunately, others have acknowledged the need for a simple form-processing service that doesn't cost much, or is free.

There are a number of services you could sign up for, but the one I'm going to walk you through now is provided by Freedback.com . I have chosen this one as it offers a free service (hence the name, "free feedback") with few limitations and, at the time of writing, a very easy-to-use web site that guides you through the process. You may only use one form for free—if you wanted to add another form later for a different purpose, you would need to upgrade from the free service. There are numerous services out there, so if the features below don't match your needs, your best bet is to head to your search engine of choice and try searching "free form email service" or similar.

Signing Up for Form Processing

The steps below explain the process of setting up a form for our project site. Naturally, you'll provide your own sign-on details for your site.

Head on over to the Freedback web site[19] and register an account—it takes just a few moments—then click the *Get Started Now* button, as shown in Figure 7.27. You'll need to provide a valid email address to verify the new account.

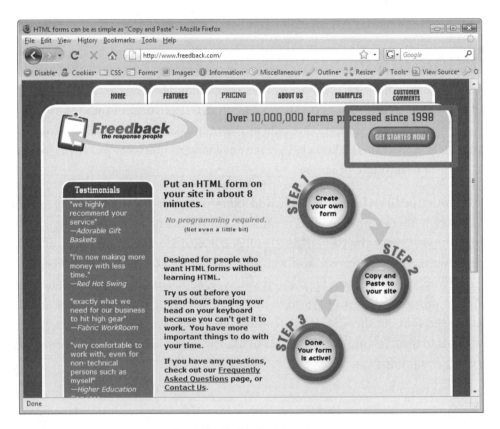

Figure 7.27. The Freedback home page

Once you've dealt with that, you'll be logged in to the service and can start to build your form. The system should take you straight there, otherwise click on the **Create a Form** link. (If you've previously started building a form and return to the site, you should have a form showing at the bottom of the screen, as shown in Figure 7.28. In that case, select **Edit** and continue.)

---

[19] http://www.freedback.com/

Figure 7.28. The Freedback interface for creating a form

The service automatically sets up a name and email address field, marking them both as "required." Then simply add other fields (e.g. telephone number, date of event etc), as shown in Figure 7.29. Don't worry if you make a mistake—you can re-order, delete, and amend any fields later. Work your way through, making sure to add all the fields that we want to capture in our form.

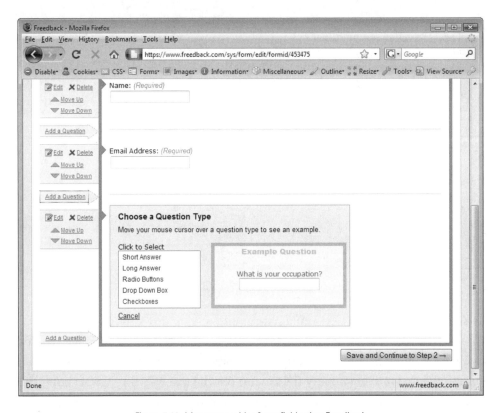

Figure 7.29. It's easy to add a form field using Freedback

After adding the form fields, you'll have some further options to complete. Choose the option to show Freedback's *Thank you* page. Alternatively, you can send the user to your own customized thank you page, which can be done at a later date if you prefer. You will also need to select the option to **Email a copy of each form submission to you**, as shown in Figure 7.30—otherwise there's little point to this service!

Figure 7.30. Directing the form your way

Once you've worked your way through all the fields, Freedback will present the markup that it *thinks* you'll need for your form, shown in Figure 7.31. I say *thinks*, because we'll need to adapt it a little to suit our needs (to make sure that it meets our high markup standards!).

Figure 7.31. The form HTML that Freedback provides

In the figure, you'll notice that below the HTML that you need to copy is a warning not to edit it. Guess what? We're going to ignore that warning! There are a few reasons why: it has produced the markup in a `table` layout (bad), it's missing `label` elements (also bad) and it commits the most heinous crime of using `<font>` tags! Rather than attempting to kick the Freedback markup into shape, we'll simply take what we need from it and apply it to the form that we built earlier in this chapter.

Inserting the Form Code

Freedback provides the following complete markup (note that I've removed some spacing and indents to save space here). We need to pluck out the parts that we'll copy and then paste into our own form. The parts you need have been marked in bold:

```
                                    Freedback-generated markup (excerpt)

<!-- Begin Freedback Form -->
<!-- DO NOT EDIT YOUR FORM HERE, PLEASE LOG IN AND
  EDIT AT FREEDBACK.COM -->
<form enctype="multipart/form-data" method="post"
  action="http://www.freedback.com/mail.php" accept-charset="UTF-8">
```

```
<div>
<input type="hidden" name="acctid" id="acctid"
  value="4784f33t1rcqsOic"/>
<input type="hidden" name="formid" id="formid" value="453475"/>
<input type="hidden" name="required_vars" id="required_vars"
  value="name,email,field-36062fa488a2705"/>
</div>
<table cellspacing="5" cellpadding="5" border="0">
<tr>
<td valign="top">
<strong>Contact Name</strong>
</td>
<td valign="top">
<input type="text" name="name" id="name" size="40" value=""/>
</td>
</tr>
<tr>
<td valign="top">
<strong>Telephone Number</strong>
</td>
<td valign="top">
<input type="text" name="field-33312ecfc9046ef"
  id="field-33312ecfc9046ef" size="40" value=""/>
</td>
</tr>
<tr>
<td valign="top">
<strong>Email Address</strong>
</td>
<td valign="top">
<input type="text" name="email" id="email" size="40" value=""/>
</td>
</tr>
<tr>
<td valign="top">
<strong>What&#39;s the event called?</strong>
</td>
<td valign="top">
<input type="text" name="field-2ab4a4f7753db57"
  id="field-2ab4a4f7753db57" size="40" value=""/>
</td>
</tr>
<tr>
<td valign="top">
<strong>When&#39;s the event happening?</strong>
```

```
</td>
<td valign="top">
<input type="text" name="field-566e6c3b82f311e"
  id="field-566e6c3b82f311e" size="40" value=""/>
</td>
</tr>
<tr>
<td valign="top">
<strong>What region is the event in?</strong>
</td>
<td valign="top">
<select name="field-36062fa488a2705"
  id="field-36062fa488a2705">
  <option value="South-west">South-west</option>
  <option value="South-east">South-east</option>
  <option value="Midlands">Midlands</option>
  <option value="Central">Central</option>
  <option value="London">London</option>
  <option value="East">East</option>
  <option value="North">North</option>
  <option value="Scotland">Scotland</option>
  <option value="Northern Ireland">Northern Ireland</option>
  <option value="International (see details below)">International
    (see details below)</option>
</select>
</td>
</tr>
<tr>
<td valign="top">
<strong>More details (as much as you think
  we&#39;ll need)</strong>
</td>
<td valign="top">
<textarea name="field-7867bb0ac63527e"
  id="field-7867bb0ac63527e" rows="6" cols="40"></textarea>
</td>
</tr>
<tr>
<td valign="top">
<strong>If we need to call you back for any more info,
  what would be the best time to call you on the number supplied?
</strong>
</td>
<td valign="top">
<input type="radio" name="field-cb22229510659c0"
```

```
    id="field-cb22229510659c0_0" value="In the morning"/>
    In the morning<br/>
<input type="radio" name="field-cb22229510659c0"
    id="field-cb22229510659c0_1" value="In the afternoon"/>
    In the afternoon<br/>
<input type="radio" name="field-cb22229510659c0"
    id="field-cb22229510659c0_2" value="In the evening"/>
    In the evening<br/>
<input type="radio" name="field-cb22229510659c0"
    id="field-cb22229510659c0_3" value="No calls please"/>
    No calls please<br/>
</td>
</tr>
<tr>
<td valign="top">
<strong>Bubble Under may share information you give us here
    with other like-minded people or web sites to promote the event.
    Please confirm if you are happy for us to do this.</strong>
</td>
<td valign="top">
<input type="checkbox" name="field-e958308eb4304cf[]"
    id="field-e958308eb4304cf_0" value="I am happy for this event to
    be publicised outside of and beyond BubbleUnder.com where
    possible"/> I am happy for this event to be publicised outside
    of and beyond BubbleUnder.com where possible<br/>
</td>
</tr>
<tr>
<td colspan="2" align="center">
<input type="submit" value=" Submit Form "/>
</td>
</tr>
</table>
</form>
<br><center><font face="Arial, Helvetica" size="1"><b>
<a href="http://www.freedback.com">create web form</a>
</b></font></center>
<!-- End Freedback Form -->
```

Well, let's get cracking! Open **contact.html** in your text editor.

First take Freedback's opening form tag and paste it over the opening <form> tag in **contact.html**. Take all of the hidden inputs just after Freedback's opening <form> tag and paste them inside a div element, just after the opening form tag in **con-**

tact.html. It should look similar to the following markup (although the `acctid`, `formid` and `required_vars` values will be unique to you … so don't copy the values below):

```
contact.html (excerpt)

<form enctype="multipart/form-data" method="post"
action="http://www.freedback.com/mail.php" accept-charset="UTF-8">
  <div>
   <input type="hidden" name="acctid"
   id="acctid" value="4784f33t1rcqsOic"/>
   <input type="hidden" name="formid" id="formid" value="453475"/>
   <input type="hidden" name="required_vars" id="required_vars"
   value="name,email,field-36062fa488a2705"/>
  </div>
  <fieldset>
  ⋮
```

Now go through each of the form fields—e.g. telephone number, best time to call, and so on—taking the parts of the markup that I previously drew your attention to. You'll need to copy each of these pieces of information and paste them over the equivalent section on the contact form. You need not concern yourself with the text that appears next to each form control, just copy and paste the respective `input`, `select`, and `textarea` elements. Once you've completed all the steps, your contact form should look something like this (again, I say *something* because the `id` attributes' values will be unique to your account):

```
contact.html (excerpt)

<form enctype="multipart/form-data" method="post"
   action="http://www.freedback.com/mail.php" accept-charset="UTF-8">
<div>
<input type="hidden" name="acctid"id="acctid"
   value="4784f33t1rcqsOic"/>
<input type="hidden" name="formid" id="formid" value="453475"/>
<input type="hidden" name="required_vars"
   id="required_vars" value="name,email,field-36062fa488a2705"/>
</div>
<fieldset>
<legend>Tell us About a Dive Event</legend>
<div>
<label for="contactname" class="fixedwidth">Contact Name</label>
<input type="text" name="name" id="name" size="40" value=""/>
```

```
</div>
<div>
<label for="telephone" class="fixedwidth">Telephone Number</label>
<input type="text" name="field-33312ecfc9046ef"
  id="field-33312ecfc9046ef" size="40" value=""/>
</div>
<div>
<label for="email" class="fixedwidth">Email Address</label>
<input type="text" name="email" id="email" size="40" value=""/>
</div>
<div>
<label for="eventname" class="fixedwidth">What's the
  event called?</label>
<input type="text" name="field-2ab4a4f7753db57"
  id="field-2ab4a4f7753db57" size="40" value=""/>
</div>
<div>
<label for="eventdate" class="fixedwidth">When's the event
  happening?</label>
<input type="text" name="field-566e6c3b82f311e"
  id="field-566e6c3b82f311e" size="40" value=""/>
</div>
<div>
<label for="region" class="fixedwidth">What region is
  the event in?</label>
<select name="field-36062fa488a2705" id="field-36062fa488a2705">
  <option value="South-west">South-west</option>
  <option value="South-east">South-east</option>
  <option value="Midlands">Midlands</option>
  <option value="Central">Central</option>
  <option value="London">London</option>
  <option value="East">East</option>
  <option value="North">North</option>
  <option value="Scotland">Scotland</option>
  <option value="Northern Ireland">Northern Ireland</option>
  <option value="International (see details below)">International
    (see details below)</option>
</select>
</div>
<div>
<p>Please provide any other details you think will be useful to us
  in the text area below (it may save us calling or emailing you,
  and help avoid delays).</p>
<label for="details" class="fixedwidth">
  More details (as much as you think we'll need!)</label>
```

```
<textarea name="field-7867bb0ac63527e"
  id="field-7867bb0ac63527e" rows="6" cols="40"></textarea>
</div>
<div>
<p>If we need to call you back for any more info, what would be
  the best time to call you on the number supplied?</p>
<input type="radio" name="field-cb22229510659c0"
  id="field-cb22229510659c0_0" value="In the morning"/>
<label for="morning">In the morning</label>
<br/>
<input type="radio" name="field-cb22229510659c0"
  id="field-cb22229510659c0_1" value="In the afternoon"/>
<label for="afternoon">In the afternoon</label>
<br/>
<input type="radio" name="field-cb22229510659c0"
  id="field-cb22229510659c0_2" value="In the evening"/>
<label for="evening">In the evening</label>
<br/>
<input type="radio" name="field-cb22229510659c0"
  id="field-cb22229510659c0_3" value="No calls please"/>
<label for="never">No calls please</label>
</div>
<div>
<p>Bubble Under may share information you give us here with
  other like-minded people or web sites to promote the event.
  Please confirm if you are happy for us to do this.</p>
<input type="checkbox" name="field-e958308eb4304cf[]"
  id="field-e958308eb4304cf_0" value="I am happy for this
  event to be publicised outside of and beyond
  BubbleUnder.com where possible"/>
<label for="publicize">I am happy for this event to be
  publicized outside of and
beyond BubbleUnder.com, where possible</label>
</div>
<div class="buttonarea">
<input type="submit" value="Send Us the Info"/>
</div>
</fieldset>
</form>
```

We're almost done, but if you're looking at the markup above and thinking "There's something wrong with that," then give yourself a well-deserved pat on the back! What's the problem with the previous block of markup? Earlier in the chapter I pointed out that each form control needs to have an associated label element. The `label` element is linked to the related form control with a `for` attribute that matches the form control's `id` attribute. By originating the form on Freedback.com, some unique `id` attributes have been created to manage the form handling, and these are completely different to those we set earlier. There's no working around this, so we'll have to accommodate these values by amending the `for` attribute for each control. In the markup below, I've highlighted the parts that have changed (again, the values will be unique to you, not *exactly* as shown below):

contact.html *(excerpt)*

```
<form enctype="multipart/form-data" method="post"
  action="http://www.freedback.com/mail.php" accept-charset="UTF-8">
<div>
<input type="hidden" name="acctid"
  id="acctid" value="4784f33t1rcqs0ic"/>
<input type="hidden" name="formid"
  id="formid" value="453475"/>
<input type="hidden" name="required_vars"
  id="required_vars" value="name,email,field-36062fa488a2705"/>
</div>
<fieldset>
<legend>Tell us About a Dive Event</legend>
<div>
<label for="name" class="fixedwidth">Contact Name</label>
<input type="text" name="name" id="name" size="40" value=""/>
</div>
<div>
<label for="field-33312ecfc9046ef"
  class="fixedwidth">Telephone Number</label>
<input type="text" name="field-33312ecfc9046ef"
  id="field-33312ecfc9046ef" size="40" value=""/>
</div>
<div>
<label for="email" class="fixedwidth">Email Address</label>
<input type="text" name="email" id="email" size="40" value=""/>
</div>
<div>
<label for="field-2ab4a4f7753db57"
  class="fixedwidth">What's the event called?</label>
<input type="text" name="field-2ab4a4f7753db57"
  id="field-2ab4a4f7753db57" size="40" value=""/>
</div>
<div>
<label for="field-566e6c3b82f311e"
```

```
      class="fixedwidth">When's the event happening?</label>
<input type="text" name="field-566e6c3b82f311e"
  id="field-566e6c3b82f311e" size="40" value=""/>
</div>
<div>
<label for="field-36062fa488a2705"
  class="fixedwidth">What region is the event in?</label>
<select name="field-36062fa488a2705" id="field-36062fa488a2705">
  <option value="South-west">South-west</option>
  <option value="South-east">South-east</option>
  <option value="Midlands">Midlands</option>
  <option value="Central">Central</option>
  <option value="London">London</option>
  <option value="East">East</option>
  <option value="North">North</option>
  <option value="Scotland">Scotland</option>
  <option value="Northern Ireland">Northern Ireland</option>
  <option value="International (see details below)">International
    (see details below)</option>
</select>
</div>
<div>
<p>Please provide any other details you think will be useful to us
in the text area below (it may save us calling or emailing you,
and help avoid delays).</p>
<label for="field-7867bb0ac63527e" class="fixedwidth">
  More details (as much as you think we'll need!)</label>
<textarea name="field-7867bb0ac63527e" id="field-7867bb0ac63527e"
  rows="6" cols="40"></textarea>
</div>
<div>
<p>If we need to call you back for any more info, what would be the
  best time to call you on the number supplied?</p>
<input type="radio" name="field-cb22229510659c0"
  id="field-cb22229510659c0_0" value="In the morning"/>
<label for="field-cb22229510659c0_0">
  In the morning</label><br/>
<input type="radio" name="field-cb22229510659c0"
  id="field-cb22229510659c0_1" value="In the afternoon"/>
<label for="field-cb22229510659c0_1">
  In the afternoon</label><br/>
<input type="radio" name="field-cb22229510659c0"
  id="field-cb22229510659c0_2" value="In the evening"/>
<label for="field-cb22229510659c0_2">
  In the evening</label><br/>
```

```
<input type="radio" name="field-cb22229510659c0"
  id="field-cb22229510659c0_3" value="No calls please"/>
<label for="field-cb22229510659c0_3">
  No calls please</label>
</div>
<div>
<p>Bubble Under may share information you give us here with other
  like-minded people or web sites to promote the event. Please
  confirm if you are happy for us to do this.</p>
<input type="checkbox" name="field-e958308eb4304cf[]"
  id="field-e958308eb4304cf_0" value="I am happy for this event to
  be publicised outside of and beyond BubbleUnder.com where
  possible"/>
<label for="field-e958308eb4304cf_0">I am happy for this
  event to be publicized outside of and beyond BubbleUnder.com,
  where possible</label>
</div>
<div class="buttonarea">
<input type="submit" value="Send Us the Info"/>
</div>
</fieldset>
</form>
```

You may have also noticed that Freedback has applied a `size` attribute to the text inputs of `size="40"`. It's not *critical* that you remove this, but I'd recommend it's better to set widths of text inputs using CSS than the `size` attribute.

Save the page, then try it out in your browser—and this time, *really* try it out! Enter data and then submit the form (assuming that you're online, of course!). If you've done it correctly, you should be sent to a confirmation page as shown in Figure 7.32.

Figure 7.32. Freedback reports that the form has been sent

Feedback by Email

You've built your form and submitted some data. Now all you have to do is open up your mail client and wait for the post to arrive! Based on the form that we've built in this chapter, and using the form processing service, this is what you can expect to receive:

```
Contact Name: Jill Smith

Telephone Number: 01793 654834

Email Address: jsmith@someisp.net

What's the event called? Murder Mystery Weekend

When's the event happening? 12th August

What region is the event in? South-west

More details (as much as you think we'll need): Murder mystery
weekend, Cotswolds (no diving!) £65 per person, accom. included

Best time to call: In the afternoon

Bubble Under may share information you give us here with other
```

```
like-minded people or web sites to promote the event. Please
confirm if you are happy for us to do this. I am happy for this
event to be publicised outside of and beyond BubbleUnder.com
where possible


--
Date/Time: 2008-08-09 11:40:09 PDT
Sender IP: 81.109.255.237 [United Kingdom] | 4784f33t1rcqs0ic
Referrer:
```

So that's basically all that's required to direct your form data into your inbox. You might still want to change some settings, though. For example, that last part where the user has accepted the terms and conditions? One little checkbox on the web page seems to create an awful lot of blurb in the email that's sent through! Just look at all this:

```
Bubble Under may share information you give us here with other
like-minded people or web sites to promote the event. Please
confirm if you are happy for us to do this. I am happy for this
event to be publicised outside of and beyond BubbleUnder.com
where possible
```

Wouldn't it better to have this?

```
T&Cs accepted: yes
```

You can adapt the form markup so that it doesn't output this great big long wordy response by changing the `value` attribute. Compare the checkbox markup below with the previous version:

contact.html (excerpt)

```
<input type="checkbox" name="field-e958308eb4304cf[]"
id="field-e958308eb4304cf_0" value="yes"/> <label
for="field-e958308eb4304cf_0">I am happy for this event to be
publicized outside of and beyond BubbleUnder.com, where possible
</label>
```

Similarly, you can edit the questions in Freedback.com afterwards to generate less wordy text in the final email sent through; what's displayed to the person filling in the feedback form is not affected. So, if we wanted the checkbox answer to come through as "T&Cs accepted: yes", we'd have to amend the question, as shown in Figure 7.33.

Figure 7.33. Amending existing questions for brevity

Once the form handler's set up and you've taken the essential values that we previously identified and put them into your form markup, you can continue fine-tuning the questions in Freedback until it produces just the right email. Don't be shy—feel free to experiment.

Finally, one more handy feature that's worth mentioning with Freedback: if you have email issues and lose some of your messages (it happens to the best of us!), you can log in to Freedback and retrieve previous form submissions, as they are stored for six months. You can even view the form submissions in graph form, if you'd like to see the information statistically (amount per month, breakdown per country, and more).

Summary

In this chapter, we've explored the different types of form input controls, discussed what we'd use them for, and understood their limitations. You've stepped through the process of building a practical form, before styling it with CSS to make it more attractive. Finally, you've discovered that you don't need to be a programming whiz to be able to deal with form data. But if you *do* want to have more control over how form data is handled—for example, you might want it stored in a database somewhere—you could consider learning a language like PHP. SitePoint published a book on that very topic, *Build Your Own Database Driven Website Using PHP & MySQL,*[20] written by Kevin Yank—you might want to check it out.

For now, though, the bulk of the work on our project site is done. We've got some content, some pretty pictures, some tabular information, a working form, and it's all styled in CSS, offering great flexibility for future redesigns. All that's left is to make these files live, so that the world at large can see our web site. Let's set those wheels in motion right now!

8

Launching Your Web Site

Creating web pages can be great fun. It's relatively easy to learn (compared to brain surgery and rocket science, at least)—and you can experiment until your heart's content with little more than a standard computer and some fiendishly good typing fingers. Spend as little or as much time as you like building and viewing web pages, but remember: in the end you'll have to make these babies "live" on the Internet. How you achieve this—including the tools you'll need to make it happen—is the subject of this chapter. Let's begin by reminding ourselves of some of the basics of the Internet and how it's possible to see all these lovely web pages.

The Client–Server Model

The –relationship between the browser that you use and the web sites you visit is known in technical circles as the "Client–Server Model." This is depicted in Figure 8.1.

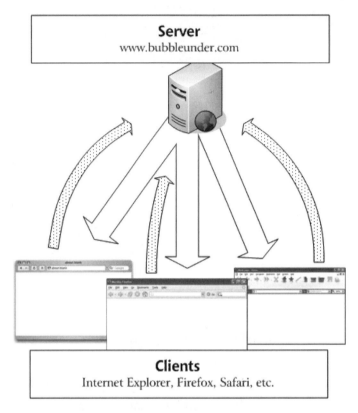

Figure 8.1. The Client–Server Model

The Client   That's you. You're the client (or rather, your browser is) and you want web pages. You send these requests for web pages via your ISP (Internet Service Provider), which provides the connection between you and the server.

The Server   That's the other party. Okay, it's another computer (and probably a hugely complicated, big fat beastie of a computer, at that) and its job is to meet all your requests for web pages.

That's the basics of the relationship. You and many others can ask that server for lots of different web pages and files at the same time—it's a very busy machine! The busier the web site, the greater the demands placed on the server—and the more expensive it can be, but your web site would need to receive *a lot* of visitors for this to become a problem. But that's not for you to worry about now—after all, we're trying to do this on the cheap!

Web Hosting Jargon

To start with, here are a few words of jargon that will help you up-front. (I'll expand on each of them further on in the chapter):

Bandwidth This is the size of the metaphorical pipe that runs between the client and the server, along which all the data travels. The wider the pipe, the more data can fit through it. The size of the pipe is usually measured in megabytes or gigabytes per month. You can now see where the term *broadband* evolved from—it's a big fat data pipe!

FTP This is the method used for transferring files from the client to the server and vice versa—and it's very useful for putting your web site onto the server in the first place! FTP stands for **File Transfer Protocol**.

Domain Name This is the "bubbleunder.com" part in the web address http://www.bubbleunder.com. You can buy the rights to use a domain name for a fixed period—usually one or two years at a time, as it's not yours to own forever. This is referred to as **registering** the domain.

Hosting Hosting refers to the storage of your web site files on an Internet-connected server. Hosting is entirely separate from the registering of your domain name, although many hosting companies offer both services. Site owners use web hosts to eliminate exposing their own hard drives to potentially malicious web surfers. Oh, and it beats having to maintain running their own computers so that their site can be accessed!

Hosting Your Web Site—Finding Server Space

The expression that there's no such thing as a free lunch is mostly true. Mostly. However, you can acquire many services for free on the Web, including hosting. Okay, you can pick up hosting almost for free. We have to be realistic about this!

The cost for web hosting can vary from around US$10, to hundreds or even thousands of dollars, each month. You get what you pay for, it has to be said.

- A cheap hosting plan is likely to have a limited monthly bandwidth allowance and may not offer advanced features. For example, web site statistics that allow you to see how many visitors your web site has attracted, and so on).

- A more expensive hosting plan will offer all the basics and should give you more advanced features, like those statistics. Usually it will allow you to do more with your web site as it grows or when your web programming skills improve.

However, it's folly to spend lots of money on features or bandwidth that you won't use—especially a small web site that you don't expect will attract masses of visitors. It's a bit like buying a double-decker coach to drive your auntie to work each day. I'll point out the web hosting features you'll need to consider shortly.

Free Hosting—with a Catch!

A sensible approach for beginners is to sign up for a free hosting service. Conditions will still apply to the service—perhaps you'll have popup ads forced upon your users, or be asked to include a link to the hosting company on your web site. However, these shouldn't be big obstacles, but be sure to check out the conditions thoroughly before you sign up: a service that causes a popup ad to appear on every page of your site might well deter visitors from returning. Regardless, free hosting can at least help at the start, letting you share your web site with others.

Of course, it pays to shop around. The best advice would be to conduct a search for the phrase **free hosting "no ads"** (be sure to wrap the "no ads" part in quotation marks) and check out the options available. But bear in mind these change quite frequently; many companies that offer free hosting close their virtual doors after they've had enough sign-ups. The best deals don't always last long!

 Beware of Ugly Addresses

> If you do decide to go for free hosting, you may find that the web site address for your files is a little on the ugly side, for example: **http://www.freespacefor-all.net/users/~bubbleunder/**. However, there are ways to mask this ugliness—as I'll explain later in the section Web Forwarding—so don't let this rule you out of using free hosting.

Free Hosting with Your ISP

If you already have a web connection, the chances are that your Internet Service Provider already offers you some free web space. Again, one could argue that this is not truly "free," but if you're already happily paying for the connection, having the hosting thrown in will at least mean you can host your web site at no extra cost. Well, almost—you will still have the issue of an ugly domain name to deal with, but that issue can be resolved using a web forwarding service.

 Try the Forums

Make use of the expertise already out there and be sure to pay a visit to SitePoint's online forums where you'll find a forum dedicated to web hosting.[1]

Free Hosting—with a Domain Name at Cost

Another option is to use a service that provides free hosting on the condition that you first register a domain name with them. This may be an economical option, as you'll have to pay for a proper domain name at some point; that's unavoidable, unless you're happy using one of the longer and less professional domain names offered through the free-with-a-catch services mentioned above.

Be a little wary, though: a service may claim to offer free hosting if you register the domain name with them, but the cost of registering may be higher than usual to offset the lack of hosting charges. In short, *free* may not be anything of the sort!

What is Web Forwarding?

If you opt for free or low-cost hosting, you'll probably gain a user-*un*friendly web address (like the fictional **http://www.freespaceforall.net/users/~bubbleunder/** address I mentioned earlier). That hardly rolls off the tongue, does it?

What web forwarding allows you to do is register a sensible domain name—there's no hosting to be paid for—that points to the address where your web pages are *really* hosted. You can then reassuringly tell people that your web site is at an address that's easy to remember (e.g. www.bubbleunder.com), and your pages will be delivered successfully.

---

[1] http://www.sitepoint.com/launch/webhostingforum/

Many small businesses (particularly family businesses) use web forwarding when setting up their first company site. Cheap (or free) hosting combined with a paid-for domain name keeps the costs down and provides an outwardly professional appearance. However, while this seems like a good solution for a new venture, there are some caveats of which you should be aware.

The Downsides of Web Forwarding

Often, web forwarding will make use of an older feature of HTML called **frames.**[2] These are normally used so that you can split the browser display into more than one area, a bit like cutting up a cake. It's a technique that is used less and less frequently though, and is not even covered in this book (most sensible people agree that frames are generally a bad idea, for a number of different reasons).[3] If you use web forwarding services, your web site—regardless of how many pages it has—will be displayed in a single frame. On the surface, this is okay to the casual observer, as Figure 8.2 illustrates. But really, your site's hiding a few little secrets.

There are a couple of anomalies in Figure 8.2 that, if you've a keen eye, you might have noticed. The first is the URL: normally, the filename of each page of a web site appears at the end of the domain name. For example, the address of the Club Events page (**events.html**) would be http://www.bubbleunder.com/events.html. However, as Figure 8.2 shows, web forwarding with frames means that all of our pages will appear to have the same address: **http://www.bubbleunder.com/**. This causes a number of problems:

1. When a user attempts to bookmark a certain page from the web site, they are actually only bookmarking the homepage.

2. It makes it tricky for other sites to link directly to a specific page in your site.

3. When a user clicks the **Refresh** button, the homepage reloads—regardless of which page the user was viewing.

---

[2] http://reference.sitepoint.com/html/frame

[3] A good discussion of why frames are bad can be found in the article "Who framed the web: Frames and usability" by Roger Johansson
[http://www.456bereastreet.com/archive/200411/who_framed_the_web_frames_and_usability/].

Figure 8.2. A web site that uses a web forwarding service— notice the subtle problems?

The second anomaly is the `title` that we so carefully crafted for every page of our site. Using this web forwarding service, no matter which page of our site the users visit, they'll see the same title—and we aren't able to change that! Some forwarding services may even take the liberty of using your title to advertise themselves—as our example does.

Finally, as if there were not enough reasons to think again about using web forwarding, there's one last reason to consider—and this could be the deal-breaker. Some search engines may not index content on your web site if it is referenced using a frameset in this way. So if you want your site to be found easily, it's a consideration you need to bear in mind.

Just as well paid-for web hosting can be relatively inexpensive.

Paying for Web Hosting

If you're willing to put your hand in your pocket and pay for hosting, your options increase immensely. You will not be hobbled by restrictions, such as forced links to the hosting provider's site, weird address behavior, or compulsory domain registration. And don't be fooled into thinking that hosting fees are financially crippling or only big businesses can afford them. These days, there are many excellent hosting plans to be had, and for a relatively small amount (less than US$10 per month) you can obtain a good package. Naturally, the more you pay, the more features there'll be—most of which probably seem like gobbledygook if you're new to this arena. However, as we mentioned before, there's no need to pay for masses of features that you'll never use (think people carrier, not double-decker coach!).

Based on what you've learned so far in this book, and what our project site will require, I'll outline briefly the features you'll need to look for when researching hosting providers.

Hosting Essentials

If you want to launch your web site online quickly and easily, you're going to need the following:

FTP Access to Your Server

As I mentioned earlier, FTP stands for File Transfer Protocol, but nobody ever says it in full. It's a bit like saying Automated Teller Machine instead of ATM. Stick to FTP and you won't stand out like a sore thumb! But what is FTP?

FTP is a method of transferring data over a network, and it's the primary method of transferring files between a server (where a web site is hosted) and a personal computer. Using an **FTP Client**—a program that helps manage these transfers—you can drag and drop files to your server as easily as if you were moving files within your hard drive (albeit a little more slowly). In this chapter, I'll show how you can use a selection of FTP clients to upload your files to the Web. You may also come across the term **SFTP**—this is still FTP, only a more secure version of it, hence Secure FTP.

Given a choice between the two, the latter is the better one to use but you may not have that choice: some web hosts won't let you use SFTP, and similarly, some FTP clients don't support SFTP. But if you are lucky on both those counts, SFTP is the way to go.

Adequate Storage Space

Once you've finished building your site, it's a good idea to work out the total size of all your site files. You can find this out quite easily:

Windows

Right-click on the folder you created back in Chapter 1 on your hard drive that contains all of your web site's files (that's the **Web** folder inside **My Documents**), then choose **Properties**. You will be presented with a dialog like the one depicted in Figure 8.3.

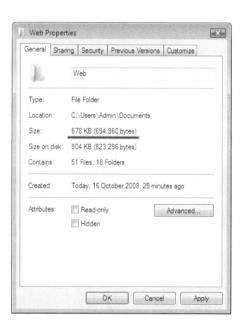

Figure 8.3. Windows' file properties dialog

Look for the number next to **Size** (not **Size on disk**—that will give you a skewed figure indicating how efficiently the file has been saved on your hard drive!)

Mac OS X

Figure 8.4. File properties in Mac OS X

In Finder, select the folder containing your web site files and select **File** > **Get Info**. Figure 8.4 displays the **Get Info** dialog on the Mac, showing files that add up to almost 700KB.

Armed with this knowledge, you can consider how many files you have in your completed web site, and try to work out how much your site is likely to grow. I know that this is not an exact science. Let's try a simple exercise to see how this might work in practice.

Multiply the total size of your existing web site files by ten, then add a little extra for luck. Make sure that your host will allow you that amount of storage space. These days, most hosts will give you more than you need for your first web site. A free host may provide 30MB, while a low-cost paid-for service may offer hundreds of megabytes.

Calculating File Sizes

In the examples above, the combined size of the files used in the web site was a measly 690 kilobytes (KB). No hosting company will tell you how many kilobytes they will offer—it will be referred to in megabytes (MB) or gigabytes (GB). As you perform your calculations, bear these figures in mind:

- 1 kilobyte = 1,024 bytes
- 1 megabyte = 1,024 kilobytes
- 1 gigabyte = 1,024 megabytes

A Reasonable Bandwidth Allowance

This is trickier to assess—it's the proverbial "how long's a piece of string" scenario. If you have 20MB of files on your web site and you access each of them once a month, then you'd need a 20MB monthly bandwidth allowance. Well, that's about as unlikely a figure as you'll ever find—after all, you'll want others to be able to view the web site as well. But how many? Ten? 100? 1,000? What happens if another web site links to your site and you suddenly have thousands of people visiting in a single day? Your bandwidth usage shoots up, that's what!

You should aim for a monthly bandwidth allowance of at least 5GB; this should be a comfortable allowance for your first web site, unless people are downloading large photos or video files from your pages.

You need to be careful about exceeding your monthly bandwidth allowance (although, arguably, it's beyond your control—others visiting your web site pushes your bandwidth usage up). Some hosting companies won't warn you if you've exceeded your bandwidth allowance: they'll simply block any further traffic to your site until the next calendar month or billing period starts. Others will allow the excess traffic, but they'll charge you a premium for their *flexibility*. It pays to check the fine print in your hosting agreement. Most hosts will notify you if you exceed your bandwidth allowance though—allowing some leeway to buy extra bandwidth to cope with your new-found popularity!

Hosting Nice-to-haves

Email Accounts

A free hosting service is likely to offer some free email facilities but, like the domain name that such hosts provide, the email addresses are not often very professional. For example, which of these looks better?

- `bob.bubbleunder@freespaceforall.net`
- `bob@bubbleunder.com`

It's amazing, but even the email address you provide to others can suggest a lot about the operation you run. This may be reason enough to shell out for hosting.

When you're assessing the host provider's email services, make sure they offer the following features:

POP3/IMAP   If the hosts offer either of these services (and they should), you will be able to download email to your computer using an **email client** such as Outlook Express, Thunderbird, or Mail.

Webmail   If you think you may need to keep in touch with others about the site while you're away from your personal computer, check to see whether the host offers a **webmail** facility. This facility allows you to log in to a web site and check your email from any computer, just as you might with a Yahoo! or Hotmail account.

Email Forwarding   If you already have an email address, you may want to have any mail for your new web site sent directly to your existing email address. This is called **email forwarding**. It's a bit like an electronic version of the mail redirection service you can use when you move house, but it has no expiry date.

The advantage of this service is obvious—you don't have to check multiple email addresses. The downside is that a person who emails you at your web site email address (`bob@bubbleunder.com`, for example) will receive a reply from your usual email address. This might make you look a little unprofessional, or confuse the recipient.

Server Side Includes (SSIs)

You'll already be aware that building a project site involves a lot of copying and pasting—as a change to the navigation in one file necessitates a change in all of them. That may be manageable for sites with a handful of pages, but if you have more than that—or can foresee your web site growing—it will become increasingly difficult to maintain these site-wide changes.

One solution is to use **Server Side Includes** (SSI), which let you create a file that's included automatically in all of your web pages; so a change to that one file will be reflected on every page of your site. This is a very useful feature that will save you time in the long term, but it does require you to learn about setting up your own computer to act as a personal web server. This is not the most straightforward of tasks, so this is one topic you'll have to investigate in your own time. A good place for Windows users to start would be to download the Apache web server software.[4] Apache is an open source product used for running web servers that serve web sites of all sizes. Mac OS X users will already have Apache installed; if that's you, you'll need to start **Personal Web Sharing**, which is accessible from the **Sharing** screen of **System Preferences**.

Support for Scripting Languages and Databases

If you want to make your web site more dynamic, you may want to make use of a **server-side scripting** language such as PHP (not covered in this book). Server-side scripting enables you to apply some logic within your pages so that content can display differently depending on particular circumstances. For example (and this is not real code, I should point out, just *pseudo* code):

```
If time is between 8pm and 6am then
  Show the night-time image
Else
  Show the day-time image
End
```

---

[4] http://httpd.apache.org/

If you can, sign up with a host that supports a scripting language. Even if it's not something that you're currently using, it will make life easier later on should you decide to dabble in server-side scripting and add dynamic content.

Often, database support goes hand in hand with support for a scripting language. If you start experimenting with a scripting language, you'll probably find that you need somewhere to store and read data—most likely a database. A database is a collection of data that you can access and present in many ways. For example, a database of customers could be listed alphabetically on one web page, by location on another, and who owes you money on another—particularly useful information to have! By updating your database, you then make it available to any of these web pages, and any new pages that you create can also tap into the stored information.

If you want to learn more about creating dynamic web sites, SitePoint has it all covered for you—you can learn online from the various dedicated forum communities (PHP[5] and MySQL[6]—a database technology), or pick it all up in one book—Kevin Yank's *Build Your Own Database Driven Website Using PHP & MySQL*[7] is a great place to start.

It's fair to say that the very cheapest hosting services (and most free ones) will not provide database access or allow you to use a scripting language.

 What if My Hosting Requirements Change?

The features that I've suggested here will almost certainly suit the requirements of your first web site. However, if later you find that you outgrow your hosting plan, don't worry—you won't be locked in with that company forever. You can transfer your domain name between different hosts as your needs change. Bear in mind though you may incur a small transfer or exit fee, depending on the terms of service.

Likewise, don't be fooled into thinking you should pay for services early on *in case* you need them later. For example, don't go paying for PHP and MySQL on the off-chance that you might need these technologies in eight months' time. Just make sure you're able to upgrade your current hosting plan when you actually need those facilities—preferable to moving to another hosting company.

---

[5] http://www.sitepoint.com/launch/phpforum
[6] http://www.sitepoint.com/launch/mysqlforum/
[7] http://www.sitepoint.com/books/phpmysql1/

Pre-flight Check—How Do Your Pages Look in Different Browsers?

If you build your web pages according to web standards (and if you've been following the advice in this book so far, you most definitely have), you should find that your web site works well on all or most browsers—no tweaks required! Still, you should check your page design as early as possible, just in case you spot anything. It's better to fix your prototype or template in as many browsers as possible before you create lots of web pages based on that first page. You should then check your entire site in a range of browsers before you put those files on a live web server for everyone else to see. Here are the browsers that I'd recommend you test against; the most important ones appear at the top of the list for each operating system. The version numbers stated were the most up-to-date at the time of writing, but if you spot a newer version for download, use that instead:

Windows
- Internet Explorer 8[8] (Bear in mind that there may be *a lot* of people still using IE7 and even IE6; it's well worth checking your pages in those browsers too.)
- Firefox 3[9]
- Opera 9.5[10]

Mac OS X
- Safari 3[11]
- Firefox 3[12] (You could try the Mac-only Camino,[13] which is based on the same open source code as Firefox.)
- Opera 9.5[14]

Uploading Files to Your Server

So, you've done your homework and settled on an affordable hosting plan that does everything you need. You've filled out countless forms and received just as many

---

[8] http://www.microsoft.com/windows/ie/

[9] http://www.mozilla.com/firefox/

[10] http://www.opera.com/

[11] http://www.apple.com/safari/

[12] http://www.mozilla.com/firefox/

[13] http://www.caminobrowser.org/

[14] http://www.opera.com/

confirmation emails—containing all kinds of gobbledygook—from your hosting service. Let's filter through that to focus on one specific piece of information: your FTP details.

FTP Settings

Your host will give you FTP details that look similar to those below. This example shows some *fictional* settings for the Bubble Under site (try as you might, entering these details won't lead to the live files—they're for demonstration purposes only).

```
Hello Bob Dobalina,

Your FTP account 'bubbleunder' has just been activated, and you
can begin uploading your web site's files to it.

When you have your software and are ready to connect, you will
need to provide it with a few settings: your username, password,
and where you want it to connect to.

        Hostname: ftp.bubbleunder.com
        Username: bobdobalina
        Password: fl1bbertyg1bbet
            Path: /home/bobdobalina
```

The host name, username, and password will always be required, but the path may not be necessary; in fact, it may not even be supplied. Carefully check the instructions provided by your host.

Now that we have these details handy, let's upload some files.

Uploading with FileZilla for Windows

You can download numerous free FTP clients for Windows, but one of the most popular is the open source program FileZilla Client (there is also a FileZilla Server, but we won't be using this). To download FileZilla, visit the FileZilla home page[15] and click on the **Download FileZilla Client** button to go to the Client Download page, as shown in Figure 8.5. We're only interested in the setup program. Click the link for the file named **FileZilla_x_y_z_setup.exe** (where *x*, *y*, and *z* make up the version number).

---

[15] http://filezilla.sourceforge.net/

Figure 8.5. The FileZilla download pages

Once you've downloaded this file, run it to install FileZilla. In most cases, the default settings should serve you fine. Once FileZilla has finished installing, start it by selecting **Start** > **All Programs** > **FileZilla** > **FileZilla**. The FileZilla window shown in Figure 8.6 should appear.

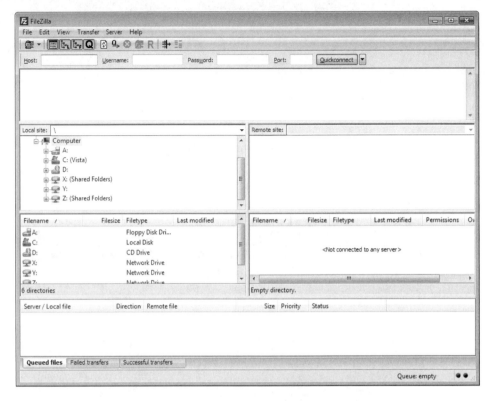

Figure 8.6. FileZilla FTP Client interface

To connect to your FTP server, enter the host name, username, and password into the **Host**, **Username**, and **Password** text boxes at the top of the FileZilla window, and click **Quickconnect**. The **Port** text box will be filled in automatically.

You should now be connected to your FTP server. The files that reside on your computer will appear on the left-hand side under **Local Site**; the files on the FTP server will be shown on the right, under **Remote Site**, as you can see in Figure 8.7.

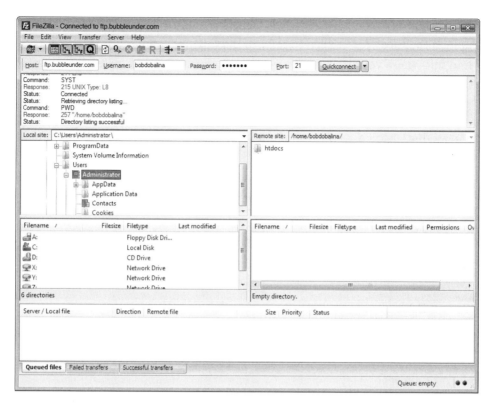

Figure 8.7. FileZilla, showing local files on the left, and server files on the right

To upload files, you need to follow three steps:

■ Locate the files that you want to upload using the left-hand pane.

Where's My Documents?

Unfortunately, FileZilla doesn't display the user's **Documents** folder in a location that's particularly easy to find—there's no shortcut to important folders like this or the desktop. Instead, you need to know where to find the folder. To reach **Documents** in Windows Vista, expand the **C:** icon (click the little plus sign to the left of the icon) to show the folders saved on your hard drive. Expand the **Users** folder the same way, then locate the folder that has your name (the example shows a folder inside an account in the name **Administrator**). Expand that folder and you'll see the **Documents** folder, which contains the **Web** folder you created back in Chapter 1.

■ In the right-hand panel, navigate to the folder on the server to which want to upload the files. You'll need to refer to the hosting company's instructions to find out where your files need to go, but if you see a folder named **web**, **htdocs**, or **public_html**, it's a safe bet that your web site files should go there.

■ To upload a file to the server, click and drag it from the left panel into the right panel, similar to how you would copy files in Windows Explorer. The progress of your upload will be displayed in the bottom of the FileZilla window, as shown in Figure 8.8. Also, you can drag an entire folder across; everything inside the folder will be copied over to the server.

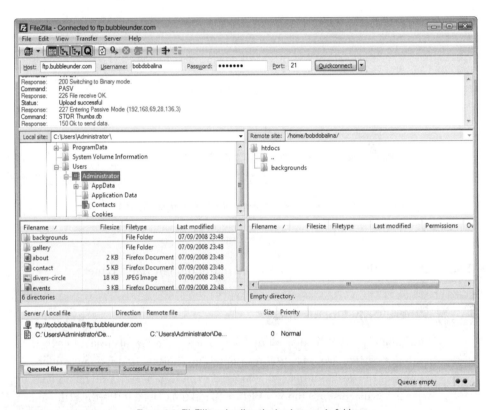

Figure 8.8. FileZilla uploading the **backgrounds** folder

Quickconnect Recent Servers List

A handy feature of FileZilla is the **Quickconnect recent servers list**. This remembers the usernames and passwords used for the last ten FTP servers you've connected to, so you don't need to re-enter those details every time you want to update your web site. To activate this list, simply click the little down-arrow next to the **Quickconnect** button, and select the appropriate option—in our case, it would be **bobdobalina@ftp.bubbleunder.com**.

Uploading with Cyberduck—Mac OS X

The Mac platform has fewer freely available FTP clients, but there is one nice tool (with an oh-so-cute icon) called Cyberduck.[16] Just like FileZilla (assuming you read the previous section, dear Mac user), Cyberduck will remember your login details, but you'll need to create an **FTP bookmark**. Here's how you do it:

- When you open Cyberduck, it should already show saved bookmarks—although if this is the first time you've used it, you won't have any bookmarks saved yet, as Figure 8.9 illustrates.

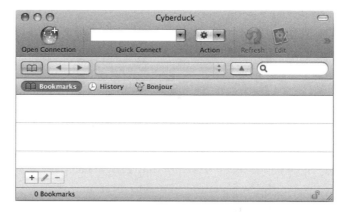

Figure 8.9. Cyberduck empty Bookmarks screen

- Next, add a bookmark. Click on the little + button at the bottom of that application, and you'll be presented with the dialog shown in Figure 8.10.

---

[16] http://cyberduck.ch/

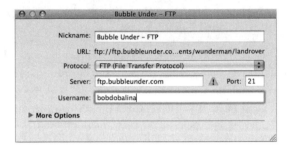

Figure 8.10. FTP server settings as seen in Cyberduck

Enter the FTP details (they're in the email from your hosting provider) into the **Server**, **Path** (under **More Options**), and **Username** text boxes. If you don't have a path, leave that field blank. Change the **Nickname** to anything you like—it's the name that will be displayed in the Bookmarks list. When you've done that, close the dialog and the bookmark will be saved for future use.

To connect to the server, simply double-click on the bookmark. You may receive a warning about the host being unknown. Don't worry about it if it does appear - just hit the **Allow** or **Always** button.

Figure 8.11. Cyberduck warning about unknown host key

The next message you'll receive is one saying **Login failed**—this is because you've yet to set a password. Here's your chance to do it, and if you want it to be re-membered for future reference, tick the **Add to Keychain** checkbox.

Figure 8.12. Cyberduck's password prompt

■ If all the details are correct, you should connect straight through to your server, and the main window of Cyberduck should have changed to display the files and folders stored on the server, as Figure 8.13 shows.

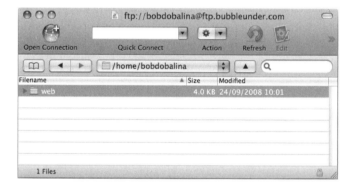

Figure 8.13. The 'web' folder on the live server, as displayed in Cyberduck

Uploading files to the server is now a simple case of dragging files or folders straight onto the Cyberduck window. If you treat the window above as a special Finder window, you won't go wrong.

Other Uploading Tools

As I mentioned previously, there are loads of stand-alone FTP clients that you could use (by stand-alone, I mean that's all their job is—FTP and FTP only). More fully-featured web development software packages like Dreamweaver include FTP facilities among their site management tools.[17] The procedure for uploading files using

---

[17] http://www.adobe.com/products/dreamweaver/

these services is exactly the same as the process I've outlined here—just make sure you enter the right details, as supplied by your web hosting company, into the correct boxes in the program's FTP dialogs.

Recap—Where's Your Site At?

Where's it at? It's on the Internet, that's where! If you've installed and run an FTP client, and uploaded your files, they should now be online for all to see. But your job's not done quite yet: you must make sure you don't have any broken links, and that your XHTML and CSS are up to scratch.

Checking Links

In our project site, there aren't too many web pages, nor images, to deal with. However, it only takes one careless typing error to break a link between your web pages or a reference to an image. Many web design and authoring programs include built-in link checkers, but you don't need to buy expensive software for this facility. Once again, there are oodles of free link checkers that you can download, or you can use an online service free of charge.

The first choice for checking your web pages is the W3C's Link Checker.[18] Simply enter the address for the web site in the box and press the **Check** button. I've used another web site in this example—my own supporting site for SitePoint's Ultimate HTML Reference,[19] (one that really should have zero errors or I'll be eating humble pie in large helpings)—as shown in Figure 8.14).

---

[18] http://validator.w3.org/checklink/
[19] http://htmlreferencebook.com/

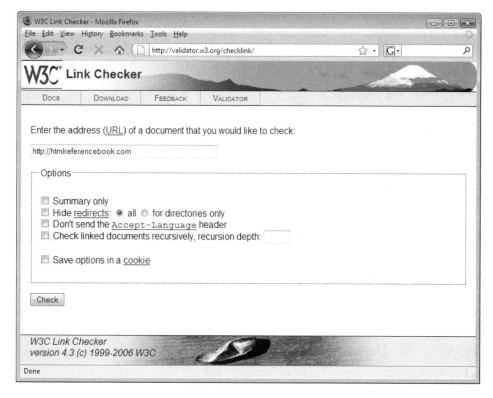

Figure 8.14. The W3C Link Checker service

The service will investigate all of your links, and provide you with a report of all the links it found. More importantly, it will report any links that were broken.

 Opt for a Summary Version

The report may be quite long if you have a lot of web pages, images, style sheets, or other dependencies linked to the page you submit. In such cases, you might like to check the *Summary only* option—then you'll only be told what's broken.

Validating Your Web Pages

Another important step before telling the masses to visit your new web site is to **validate** your web pages. This is the process of checking your markup to see if it conforms to the rules of the language you specified in the Document Type Declaration (otherwise known as the doctype).

As you'll recall back in Chapter 2, the Document Type Declaration is the first line of your file's XHTML:

```
<!DOCTYPE html PUBLIC "-//W3C//DTD XHTML 1.0 Strict//EN"
    "http://www.w3.org/TR/xhtml1/DTD/xhtml1-strict.dtd">
```

For the project site, we're using XHTML Strict. By validating your site, you're confirming that your pages follow the rules of XHTML Strict, and that you haven't made any errors that might cause your page to fail in any given browser. This is important to check, because although a web page may *appear* to be fine to you, if there's an error in the XHTML document, it may not appear correctly for a user of a different browser. Validation gives you a heads-up about anything that may be problematic in another browser on which you haven't checked your web site.

Another reason why it's important to validate your XHTML is that the associated CSS is intrinsically linked to it. An error in the XHTML can cause problems with the CSS that can range from the minor—like the wrong link color displaying—to the much more drastic, such as a broken page layout.

How to Validate Your Live Web Pages

Again, specialist web development software like Dreamweaver has this functionality built-in, but there's always the W3C Markup Validation Service[20] if you don't have access to other tools. As with the link checker, simply type into the **Address** text box the address of the live web page that you want to check, then click the **Check** button. If you've followed the instructions in this book, you should see a nice message like the one depicted in Figure 8.15.

---

[20] http://validator.w3.org/

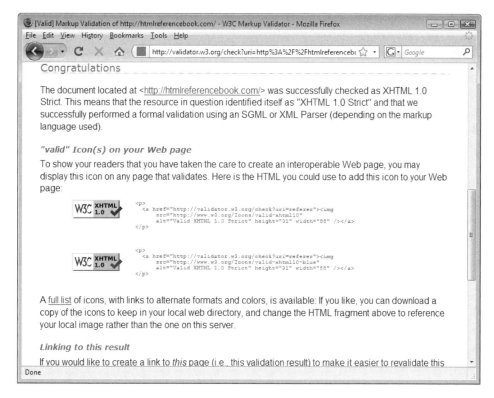

Figure 8.15. A pass mark for your markup!

If you aren't seeing this (try scrolling down a little, just in case it's off-screen), your web page probably has errors that need to be fixed. The good news is that the validator will point out the problem, providing some explanation about why it's wrong. A typical validation failure looks like the page shown in Figure 8.16.

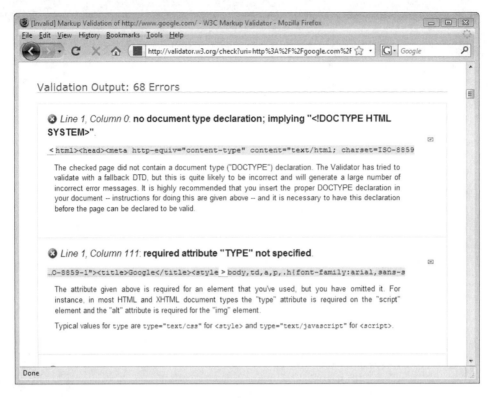

Figure 8.16. Highlighting and explaining validation failures

You will need to check more than just one page on your web site, and this is a one-page-at-a-time affair; unfortunately, it's not possible to check an entire site at once using this validator. To ensure that your site is valid, you'll need to validate every page individually. However, the W3C validator is not the only online tool; the Web Design Group's HTML ValidatorWeb Design Group offers the ability to validate an entire site in one pass.

Validate Everything

Validation is not just about your XHTML—you can (and should) also validate your site's CSS using the W3C's CSS Validator.[21] You can even run an automated test to see if your page is accessible to people with disabilities.[22] I must point out, however, that automated tests can only really point out *possible* problems—rather than confirm that your web page is *truly* accessible. Once again, if you find that the results are

---

[21] http://jigsaw.w3.org/css-validator/

[22] The most popular accessibility validator is Cynthia Says [http://www.contentquality.com/].

too detailed to make sense of (it's a common complaint), try seeking clarification in an online forum. SitePoint's CSS forum[23] members will be able to explain most CSS validation failures; for answers to web accessibility problems, you should register an account at the Accessify Forum[24] and post your question there.

What Are All These Errors?

An automated validation service has no feelings. If you were to ask it, "How's my hair looking?", it might bluntly reply, "Well, it's not right—it's uneven at the back, there are tangles here, here, and *here*, and the color's all wrong." My point is, an automated service of this type won't go easy on you—all errors will be reported in a matter-of-fact way.

Don't let this get you down: it happens to all web designers and programmers. And don't be annoyed with yourself if you don't understand everything you're being told—it really can be a case of information overload.

The trick is to fix the obvious faults—those that you can easily identify—first. Then, when you've uploaded the amended pages, try validating again. You may find that fixing some simple problems also resolves some others that you didn't quite understand. One simple dilemma is often the cause of many other problems.

If you still can't quite make your web page to pass validation, make your way over to the SitePoint forums, specifically the HTML and XHTML forum,[25] and post your question there. Tell the people you're a newbie after some advice, and you should receive that more caring, tactful approach that the validator so sorely lacks!

Promoting Your Web Site

If you've confirmed that your web pages are using valid XHTML and CSS, and you're confident that they're widely accessible and look good on different browsers, you should now think about how you'll promote your web site.

Promoting your site can be a project in its own right. SitePoint offers kits for those with a marketing budget, including *The Search Engine Marketing Kit*[26] and *The*

---

[23] http://www.sitepoint.com/launch/cssforum/
[24] http://www.accessifyforum.com/
[25] http://www.sitepoint.com/launch/htmlforum/
[26] http://www.sitepoint.com/books/sem1/

Web Design Business Kit.[27] As a newcomer to the world of web design, though, these are probably too ambitious for the time being; I mention them to merely indicate how big this topic is in its own right (not to give you the big sales pitch!). So, what promotions can you undertake that won't cost you an arm and a leg?

Submit Your Web Site to Search Engines

An extremely high percentage of visitors to my personal web sites arrive through searches on Google, MSN, and Yahoo! (in that order), and the same will probably be true for your web site. However, a search engine will not know that your web site is there, unless either:

- there is a link to your web site from another web site that the search engine knows about (this is how search engines crawl the web—by finding links in pages that it knows about, and adding these pages to its database of pages)

- you fill in a form on the search engine to instruct it to visit and index the content of your web site (Google,[28] MSN,[29] and Yahoo![30] offer such pages)

Another good place to start is the Open Directory Project,[31] which aims to become a comprehensive directory of the Internet. This site is structured hierarchically, so you'll need to work out where your site fits in the hierarchy before you submit it.

These are just a few tips to help you start. For further advice about search engine submissions, pay a visit to SitePoint's Promotion Techniques forum.[32]

Cleaner Markup, Better Search Results

It's worth noting that web pages that conform to standards, and are lightweight and accessible, attract better search engine results. Without going into too much detail, search engines find it easier to retrieve search terms from a simple, well-structured web page than one that doesn't adhere web standards. You can learn more about how and why this is the case from the forum mentioned above.

---

[27] http://www.sitepoint.com/books/freelance1/
[28] http://www.google.com/addurl/
[29] http://search.msn.com/docs/submit.aspx
[30] http://search.yahoo.com/info/submit.html
[31] http://dmoz.org/add.html
[32] http://www.sitepoint.com/launch/promoforum/

Tell Your Friends and Colleagues

Well, it seems like an obvious idea, but it's worth mentioning. Your friends and colleagues could be your biggest fans—even if they've never seen your web site. And if you give them your web site address on a handy-to-keep card or similar, you never know how many times they might visit or who they might mention it to.

Craft an Email Signature with Your Web Site Details

Consider creating a default signature that's applied to every email message you compose. It's a simple marketing technique that's basically a no-brainer. A simple line or two at the end of each email you send, as shown below, can generate a surprising number of visits to your web site.

```
Hi Dad,

What time should we should expect you for dinner on Tuesday? Also,
have you had a chance to check out the new web site? Pretty
spiffy, eh?


--
Bob Dobalina
President of Bubble Under -- the diving club for the south-west UK
Visit our web site at http://www.bubbleunder.com/
```

Once you've added it to your signature, there's no real ongoing maintenance required, and every message you send could attract a new visitor to your web site!

Post on a Related Forum

Similarly, you can usually add a signature to posts you make in discussion forums that are related to your web site's topic. It could even include a clickable link to your web site. The advantage here is that the others who post and read these forum messages will be interested in the same thing. So, rather than the signature being a hit-and-miss affair, suddenly it's being presented to those most inclined to take a look.

Of course, this means that you'll need to be more prolific with posting on such sites, but that shouldn't be a great hardship if it's a topic of interest to you.

Link Exchange

Finally, I'd recommend that you look into swapping links with similar web sites. Be mindful of taking the right approach; emailing a site with "Hey, can you link to my web site—it's really good!" isn't considered the best etiquette. However, if you've already included a link to a site, and you approach them nicely with this fact, asking whether they would they be willing to link back, you may have more luck.

Link exchange programs that automate the process are available, but I don't recommend you use them. You can't be sure of the quality of links that'll appear automatically on your web site, nor the quality of sites that link to you, through these services. Also, link exchange programs often require you to display ugly banner ads or badges that can make your web site look unprofessional. It's better to remain a little choosy and stay in control of your site.

Summary

In this chapter, we've focused on the process of placing your web site files online, from the initial choices about where to host your web site, to the nuts and bolts of putting your files up on to the live server. I've explained how you can use free online services to check whether your web pages are in good shape, and suggested some ways that you can begin to promote your new online venture.

It may have been fun building your site. Perhaps at times you've found things difficult, yet you've battled on and seen your way through to the end result. But is this the end of your web site's development? Probably not—shortly after making your files live, you'll no doubt think of new additions. There are only so many hours in the day, though—how can you continually add new content to your web site as well as manage all the other things you have to juggle in your busy schedule?

One way of ensuring fresh content is to add a weblog (or just blog) to your site. In the next chapter, I'll explain what a blog is, what it can do for your web site, and how you can set one up and continue to manage it. Let's find out about blogging!

Adding a Blog to Your Web Site

Building web sites provides many of us with a lot of enjoyment, just as some people enjoy knitting sweaters or carving sculptures from old tree trunks. So updating our web site may actually be good fun—rather than be seen as a chore. However, if you update the content regularly, you'll need to go back to your computer files, alter them, and upload them using FTP each and every time you want to make a change. In short, content updates require you to have everything at the ready, which is a little complicated if all you want to do is make some simple text changes.

For instance, what happens if you feel like updating the web site when you're on holiday? This could well be the case with our diving project site—you might want to write a report on a dive trip while the events are still fresh in your mind. Even if you have your project files set up on a laptop, will you be able to connect at a local Internet café? What if other committee members want to add updates? Can you really let them come to your house and amend the web site on your computer every time there's an update to post? Indeed, would you want to?

One solution to these problems is to add a **blog** to your site. Hang on, though! What exactly is a blog?

What is a Blog?

Blogs started off life being known as weblogs—evolving from the words *web* and *log*. As the name implies, they started off as online logs or diaries that individuals published on the Web. These days, though, it's increasingly common to find pages on organizations' web sites that could readily be described as blogs.

Blogs often feature a comments facility that permits two-way communication between bloggers (those who post to blogs) and their readers—and among the readers themselves. This is often one of the main reasons why companies publish blogs rather than static web pages: suddenly, a faceless organization has a personality!

A key feature of blogs is that they allow bloggers to log into a central location from anywhere in the world—you don't need to manage the web site from your own computer. This is what makes blogging so accessible to people who, in the past, might not have been able to publish a web site.

A word of caution: although the word *blog* is becoming more prevalent, there are still a lot of people who have never heard the term before, so you might need to explain it when discussing the topic with others.

Where to Set up a Blog

There are numerous services that you can use to set up and manage a blog. Each has its advantages and disadvantages, the fine details of which I won't go into here. Suffice to say that if you are looking to set up a blog as quickly and painlessly as possible, any one of the following services would be suitable:

Blogger[1]

This was one of the first services to appear, and truly popularized the whole blogging format. Blogger is easy to set up and can be configured to integrate closely with your web site's look and feel. This is the service I'll be using in this chapter as we add a blog to our project site.

---

[1] http://www.blogger.com/

WordPress.com[2]

WordPress is a very popular blogging system, which is available as a hosted service (from WordPress.com) or as a self-hosted solution (from WordPress.org).

LiveJournal[3]

Another service that's been around a while (since 1999), LiveJournal was set up by Brad Fitzpatrick as a way of keeping school friends up to date with activities, but is now a fully-featured blogging service.

Windows Live Spaces[4]

Windows Live Spaces (formerly MSN Spaces) is Microsoft's offering to the world of free blogging tools. Don't be confused by the word *Windows* though—as an online browser-based service, you don't have to be running Windows to use this.

 ## Self-hosted Blogging Services

In addition to the blogging services above, there are several tools that you can set up on your own web site to host all the mechanics of the blog yourself; this would include a control panel of some kind, as well as a database. The advantage of this option is that you can tweak a self-hosted system more to your own liking, to make it work specifically for you. The applications we've described below use **plug-ins** to modify or extend their functionality. However, the downside is that with a self-hosted service, you must do all the work of setting the system up; also, the correct functioning of your blog relies on your web host being able to support certain technologies (which differ for each system). If you feel confident enough to try such a system out, here are a few worth investigating:

WordPress[5]

WordPress has powerful administration features that allow almost total control over how pages are published and organized. WordPress is incredibly popular and has an avid community associated with its development, so should you have difficulties, there are plenty of people who can help you through the issues.

---

[2] http://www.wordpress.com/
[3] http://www.livejournal.com/
[4] http://home.services.spaces.live.com/
[5] http://www.wordpress.org/

Movable Type[6]

An erstwhile favorite amongst the blogging community, Movable Type is a very powerful tool.

Textpattern[7]

Like the others mentioned, Textpattern allows you to create multiple templates for the same site. It's a great service for team environments and lets users customize blogs extensively to suit their web sites.

Personally, I opt for WordPress (self-hosted) because it offers more in the way of customization. I migrated all my personal sites from Blogger some time ago, and there's nothing stopping you from doing the same at a later date once you're more comfortable with the concepts involved with blogging.

For reasons of simplicity and speed, I'm going to show you how to set up an account and start publishing with Blogger. I've chosen to demonstrate Blogger because it's fairly simple to use, yet offers some handy customization options for those who want to dig below the surface. A great feature of Blogger that we'll take advantage of, is that it will allow your pages to appear on your own server.

By the end of this chapter, you'll have set up a system that will allow you to write and publish new content on your home page, making it look similar to Figure 9.1:

---

[6] http://www.movabletype.org/

[7] http://textpattern.com/

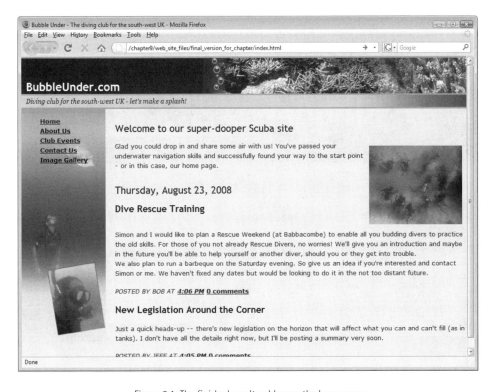

Figure 9.1. The finished result: a blog on the home page

Signing up for Blogger

Setting up a blog on your web site won't take long at all. And the time you have to take at the beginning of the process will easily be offset by the ease and speed of publishing content to your web site in the future. To start with Blogger, head over to Blogger's home page[8] and look for the **CREATE YOUR BLOG NOW** link as shown in Figure 9.2.

---

[8] http://www.blogger.com/

Figure 9.2. Blogger's home page

On the next page, you'll be asked to set up a Google account (Google owns Blogger and uses Google's authentication process, in case you were wondering). You may already have a Google account if you use their other services, like Gmail (Google Mail). If so, click the **sign in first** link in the first paragraph. Otherwise, you'll need to enter the usual details: a username, password, email address, and a display name, which will appear as the blog author's name. You'll also be asked to accept Blogger's terms of service. Complete this form, as shown in Figure 9.3, then click **CONTINUE**.

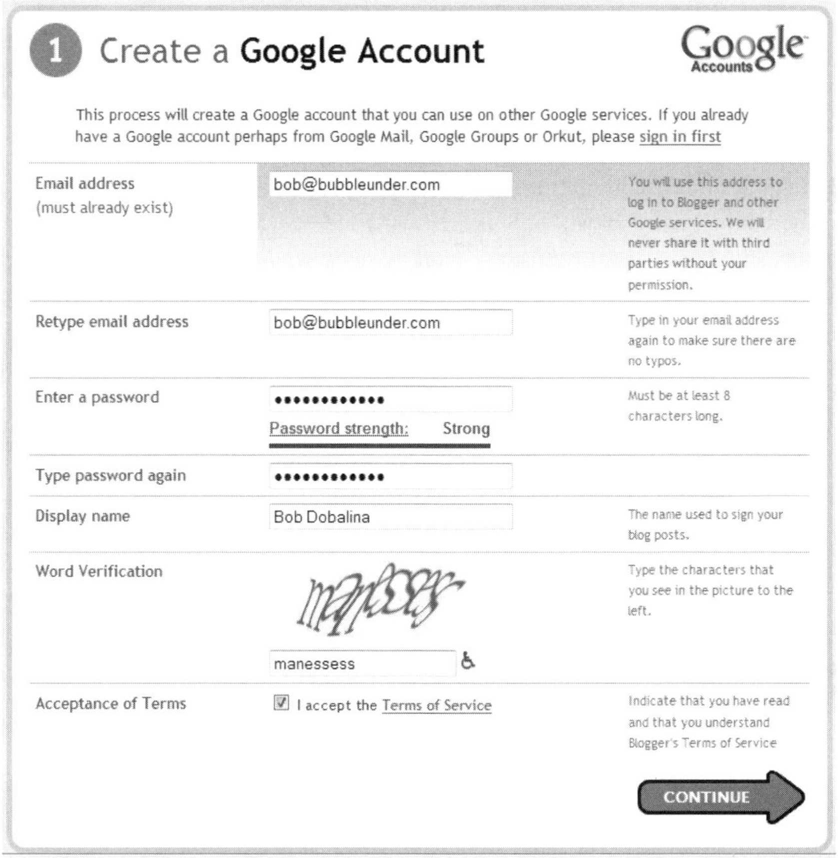

Figure 9.3. Establishing a Google account in order to use Blogger

The next page, **Name Your Blog**, provides the simplest possible setup procedure for your blog. It assumes that Blogger will provide the hosting for your blog, using an address like http://bubbleunder.blogspot.com/. We're going to skip this easy setup procedure and go for a more advanced option, so click the **Advanced Blog Setup** link.

Easy versus Advanced Setup

Most users who sign up for Blogger avoid the Advanced Setup options, but just what is the difference between a basic and an advanced setup?

Using the simple method (the one that Blogger normally guides you toward), you can quickly create a blog that looks the part, and to which you can post quickly and easily. There's very little configuration for you to do, as Blogger does it all for you. The procedure is made easier because Blogger publishes your blog pages to its own servers—all you need to do is choose your address in the format *yourname*.blogspot.com. Any files hosted by Blogger will have this blogspot.com address.

In the advanced setup procedure, you're given a choice about where you want to host your blog. Instead of publishing to Blogger's servers, you can publish to your own server—a good choice if you want total control of your blog's presentation.

Note that most people who sign up for Blogger don't choose the advanced route (it's no coincidence that Blogger doesn't promote that route very obviously to new users!). However, I'm guiding you down that path so that you can integrate your blog right into your home page, giving it a much more professional look.

The advanced setup page, shown in Figure 9.4, requests information about where you want to have your blog published. Many of these details you'll already know from when you set up your FTP service to upload files to your web site.

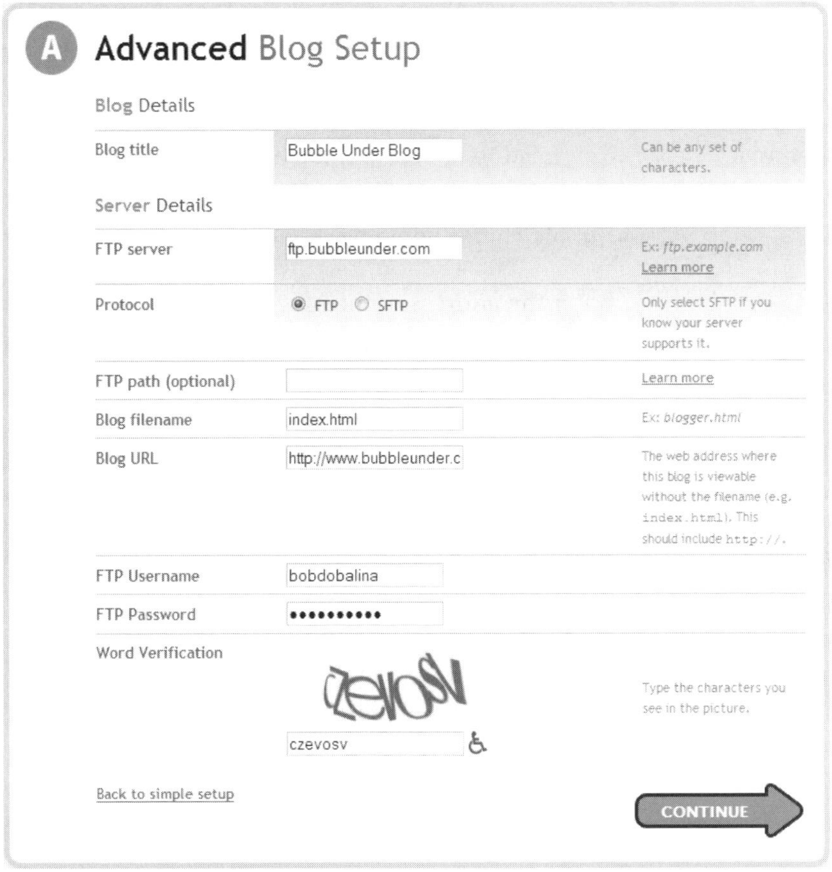

Figure 9.4. The advanced setup page

This is the information that you'll need:

Blog Title   The title can be anything you like. We'll call ours the
                        "Bubble Under Blog."

FTP Server   Use the address that you used in Chapter 8, for example:
                        ftp.bubbleunder.com.

FTP/SFTP   Here, specify whether your host supports Secure FTP
                        (SFTP). Unless your host has specified otherwise, select
                        FTP here.

FTP Path	Once again, refer to the settings that you used in the last chapter to fill in this item. For the Bubble Under web site, I've used the path of **web**.
Blog Filename	You need to choose a file where you want Blogger to save your blog. Since we want Blogger to save the blog to the Bubble Under home page, we'll enter **index.html** here.
Blog URL	Enter the address of the blog page. On the project site, the blog is going to be on our home page, so I've entered our home page's address.
FTP Username	You guessed it, it's another one of those 'refer to the FTP settings you set up in the previous chapter' responses.
FTP Password	And yes, same again! That's it for FTP now, though. Assuming the details you've entered here are correct, you shouldn't need to type in your FTP details again.
Word Verification	In this final step, enter the characters that appear in the image. You've probably come across this on other sites, used to deter automated spam-bots from abusing the Blogger service.

When you've entered all the details above, click **Continue**. Unless you've mistyped or left an item on this page blank (the word verification part often trips me up), you should be presented with the Choose a Template page, depicted in Figure 9.5.

These templates are actually well designed by people who really know their stuff. However, we're not really interested in these designs, as good as they are, because we're going to change the template later to fit in with the look and feel of our site. By all means, investigate to see what's on offer, but don't obsess on these choices. I chose Minima, but only because it was the first template in the list. Follow the **CONTINUE** link.

Figure 9.5. The template page for Blogger

If all is well, you should receive notification like that shown in Figure 9.6, to tell you that your blog is being created.

Figure 9.6. An encouraging sign

The service is actually uploading the various files that you'll need for your blog (images, CSS, and so on) to your server. There'll be another message, like the one shown in Figure 9.7, once the process has finished.

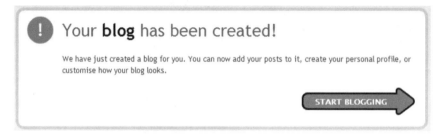

Figure 9.7. A blog is born—yours!

Follow the link that says **START BLOGGING**, and create a test post for your blog. On the next page, enter some test text in the title and body of your post, as illustrated in Figure 9.8, then click the **Publish Post** button.

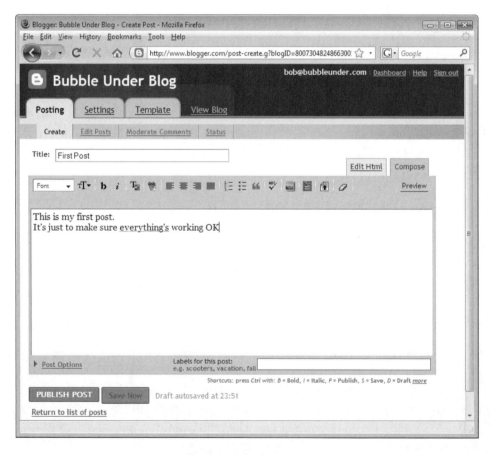

Figure 9.8. A simple test post

This is the point where the magic happens! You should now have notification, like that shown in Figure 9.9, to say that your blog entry was published successfully.

Your blog published successfully.

View Blog(in a new window)

/files/2008/08/first-post.html
/files/rss.xml
/files/atom.xml
/files/2008_08_01_archive.html
/files/index.html

Need to change it? **Edit post** | **Create a new post**

REPUBLISH INDEX ONLY   **REPUBLISH ENTIRE BLOG** Republishing your index will only republish the main page of your blog. Republishing the entire blog will republish the main page, feeds, archives and post pages. Learn more

Figure 9.9. Success! The blog entry published with no errors

You should see a link that reads: **View Blog**. Try it out. Can you see a page like Figure 9.10? And is it at the right location?

Figure 9.10. A successful blog creation revealing the first post

Having Trouble Publishing?

You may find that your host only allows one FTP connection to your server at a time. If you have trouble publishing your blog, try closing your FTP program (FileZilla or Cyberduck) if it's still open.

Don't Panic!

At this point, you may be worrying where your homepage has gone. By choosing to publish the blog to the same location as your homepage, Blogger has overwritten your homepage file. But there's no need to panic—you still have the local copy (the one stored on your hard drive). What we've done here is confirm that the process for publishing from Blogger to your web hosting service is working properly. The fact that it looks so different from the rest of your web site is not a problem—this is just a temporary stage in the process.

How Blogger Creates a Web Page

For many people, this is where the process of creating a blog ends. The off-the-shelf designs are fine—they do the job, and look attractive. But, as I mentioned before, you and I will go further afield. You now have in place the basic mechanics for publishing blog entries to your site. Next, I'm going to show you how to customize the Blogger template so that it complements your web site.

At this point, it's worth taking a step back to learn how Blogger publishes your web pages. The basic process, illustrated in Figure 9.11, is this:

- Take a standard document written in good old XHTML.

- Introduce a set of Blogger-specific tags. Some of these look like XHTML elements (for example, there's a `<BlogItemTitle>` opening tag and a `</BlogItemTitle>` closing tag), but other Blogger tags look nothing like XHTML (`<<$BlogItemTitle$>>`, for example). Regardless, none of these tags are XHTML; they're meaningless to the browser, but they're applied in the template that Blogger uses.

- Save the document as a template in Blogger.

■ When you save or publish your post on the Blogger web site, it's saved to their database. If you save the post (by clicking on the **Save as Draft** button), it won't be displayed to the public.

■ When you publish a post, Blogger takes your template, finds the Blogger-specific tags, and replaces them with the related entry for that page in the database. The end result is a complete web page in which all of the Blogger-specific tags have been replaced.

■ Blogger then sends this new XHTML page to your web server (using the details that you provided during the sign-up procedure).

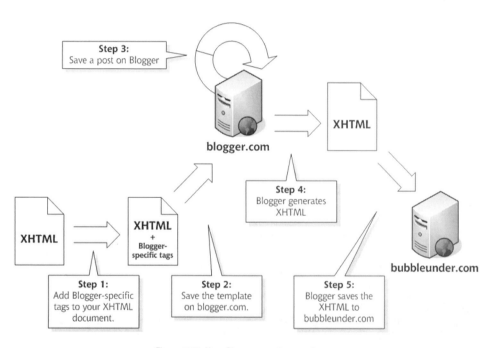

Figure 9.11. How Blogger creates a web page

We're going to see how this works in practice with the project web site now. First, you need to write your Blogger template.

Customizing Your Blogger Template

What's wonderful about about publishing systems like Blogger, is that they can give you a considerable amount of freedom to customize the display of your content. If you're familiar with blogs, you may have noticed that some blogs have comments, while others don't. Those that do may display the comments directly beneath the post, or they might display comments in a side panel. However, if you want to customize your blog to such a level, you'll have to get your hands dirty, so to speak, with those Blogger template tags we touched on earlier. This can be quite a confusing task for blogging newcomers, so my advice is simple: just take one of the existing Blogger templates, note the parts that contain the Blogger-specific tags, and leave them as they are for the time being. We'll do a little tweaking now, just to build a bit of confidence—but you're encouraged to fiddle with your Blogger template to your heart's content. If you mess it up, you can always reset the original template and start again.

Go to the templates section by signing on to Blogger from the homepage, filling in the **Username** and **Password** text boxes. (This assumes that you've signed off between setting up the account and this point; otherwise, select the **Back to Dashboard** link.) Figure 9.12 shows this step.

Figure 9.12. The Blogger sign-in box

When you reach the Dashboard, select the **Settings** link, as seen in Figure 9.13.

Figure 9.13. Changing the settings of your blog

Figure 9.14. The markup for your template is in the large text area

On the next page, click on the **Template** tab. You'll be presented with the template editor shown in Figure 9.14. Here you can see the markup for the Minima template, including the Blogger-specific tags that instruct Blogger how to use the template. Note that indenting the markup is a little haphazard, but this doesn't affect the display on the screen; we indent our markup only so that it's easier for humans to read.

On the Blogger template page, select all of the markup that begins with a `<Blogger>` tag and ends with a `</Blogger>` tag, as shown in the example below, and copy it by selecting **Edit > Copy**. Don't analyze the markup at this stage—it might make your head hurt! We don't need to understand all of the Blogger tags now—we just need to copy them:

Markup for the Blogger Minima Template (excerpt)

```
<Blogger>

    <BlogDateHeader>
  <h2 class="date-header"><$BlogDateHeaderDate$></h2>
  </BlogDateHeader>



  <!-- Begin .post -->
  <div class="post"><a name="<$BlogItemNumber$>"></a>
        <BlogItemTitle>
    <h3 class="post-title">
<BlogItemUrl><a href="<$BlogItemUrl$>" title="external
    link"></BlogItemUrl>
<$BlogItemTitle$>
<BlogItemUrl></a></BlogItemUrl>
    </h3>
    </BlogItemTitle>

        <div class="post-body">
<div>
    <$BlogItemBody$>
    </div>
    </div>

    <p class="post-footer">
      <em>posted by <$BlogItemAuthorNickname$> at <a
        href="<$BlogItemPermalinkUrl$>" title="permanent
```

```
         link"><$BlogItemDateTime$></a></em>
      <MainOrArchivePage><BlogItemCommentsEnabled>

      <a class="comment-link" href="<$BlogItemCommentCreate$>"<$B
logItemCommentFormOnclick$>><$BlogItemCommentCount$> comments</a>

      </BlogItemCommentsEnabled><BlogItemBacklinksEnabled>
<a class="comment-link" href="<$BlogItemPermalinkUrl$>#links"
   >links to this post</a>
</BlogItemBacklinksEnabled>
</MainOrArchivePage>  <$BlogItemControl$>
    </p>

  </div>
  <!-- End .post -->


  <!-- Begin #comments -->
 <ItemPage>
  <div id="comments">

<BlogItemCommentsEnabled><a name="comments"></a>
      <h4><$BlogItemCommentCount$> Comments:</h4>
      <dl id="comments-block">
    <BlogItemComments>
    <dt class="comment-poster" id="c<$BlogCommentNumber$>"><a
name="c<$BlogCommentNumber$>"></a>
      <$BlogCommentAuthor$> said...
    </dt>
    <dd class="comment-body">

      <p><$BlogCommentBody$></p>
    </dd>
    <dd class="comment-timestamp"><a href="#<$BlogCommentNumber$
>" title="comment permalink"><$BlogCommentDateTime$></a>
  <$BlogCommentDeleteIcon$>
  </dd>
    </BlogItemComments>
    </dl>
<p class="comment-timestamp">

    <$BlogItemCreate$>
    </p>
    </BlogItemCommentsEnabled>
```

```
    <BlogItemBacklinksEnabled>
    <a name="links"></a><h4>Links to this post:</h4>
    <dl id="comments-block">
    <BlogItemBacklinks>
        <dt class="comment-title">
        <$BlogBacklinkControl$>
        <a href="<$BlogBacklinkURL$>" rel="nofollow"><$BlogBacklin
kTitle$></a> <$BlogBacklinkDeleteIcon$>
        </dt>
        <dd class="comment-body"><$BlogBacklinkSnippet$>
        <br/>
        <span class="comment-poster">
        <em>posted by <$BlogBacklinkAuthor$> @ <$BlogBacklinkDateT
ime$></em>
        </span>
        </dd>
    </BlogItemBacklinks>
    </dl>
    <p class="comment-timestamp"><$BlogItemBacklinkCreate$></p>
    </BlogItemBacklinksEnabled>


<p class="comment-timestamp">
<a href="<$BlogURL$>">&lt;&lt; Home</a>
    </p>
    </div>

</ItemPage>

  <!-- End #comments -->

</Blogger>
```

Merging the Blogger Code with Your Existing Web Page

What we need to do now is take the markup above and insert it into a sensible location in one of our existing pages. Below is the current homepage of the Bubble Under web site—I've marked in bold where the Blogger template tags need to go:

index.html *(excerpt)*

```
<body>
  <div id="header">
    <div id="sitebranding">
      <h1>BubbleUnder.com</h1>
    </div>
    <div id="tagline">
      <p>Diving club for the south-west UK - let's make a
         splash!</p>
    </div>
  </div> <!-- end of header div -->
  <div id="navigation">
    <ul>
      <li><a href="index.html">Home</a></li>
      <li><a href="about.html">About Us</a></li>
      <li><a href="events.html">Club Events</a></li>
      <li><a href="contact.html">Contact Us</a></li>
      <li><a href="gallery.html">Image Gallery</a></li>
    </ul>
  </div> <!-- end of navigation div -->
  <div id="bodycontent">
    <h2>Welcome to our super-dooper Scuba site</h2>
    <p><img src="divers-circle.jpg" alt="A circle of divers
       practice their skills" width="200" height="162"/></p>
    <p>Glad you could drop in and share some air with us! You've
       passed your underwater navigation skills and successfully
       found your way to the start point - or in this case, our
       home page.</p>
    <!-- Insert Blogger code template tags here -->
  </div> <!-- end of bodycontent div -->
</body>
```

Open **index.html**, and just prior to end of the bodycontent `div`, paste the Blogger template markup by selecting **Edit** > **Paste**. Here's the page once the Blogger markup is inserted (I've formatted the Blogger markup in bold so it's easier to identify):

index.html *(excerpt)*

```
<div id="bodycontent">
  <h2>Welcome to our super-dooper Scuba site</h2>
  <p><img src="divers-circle.jpg" alt="A circle of divers practice
     their skills" width="200" height="162"/></p>
  <p>Glad you could drop in and share some air with us! You've
```

```
    passed your underwater navigation skills and successfully
    found your way to the start point - or in this case, our
    home page.</p>
<Blogger>
  <BlogDateHeader>
    <h2 class="date-header"><$BlogDateHeaderDate$></h2>
  </BlogDateHeader>
  <!-- Begin .post -->
  <div class="post">
    <a name="<$BlogItemNumber$>"></a>
    <BlogItemTitle>
      <h3 class="post-title">
        <BlogItemUrl><a href="<$BlogItemUrl$>"
            title="external link"></BlogItemUrl>
          <$BlogItemTitle$>
          <BlogItemUrl></a></BlogItemUrl>
      </h3>
    </BlogItemTitle>
    <div class="post-body">
      <div>
        <$BlogItemBody$>
      </div>
    </div>
    <p class="post-footer">
      <em>posted by <$BlogItemAuthorNickname$> at
          <a href="<$BlogItemPermalinkUrl$>"
          title="permanent link"><$BlogItemDateTime$></a></em>
      <MainOrArchivePage>
        <BlogItemCommentsEnabled>
          <a class="comment-link"
              href="<$BlogItemCommentCreate$>"
              <$BlogItemCommentFormOnclick$>>
              <$BlogItemCommentCount$> comments</a>
        </BlogItemCommentsEnabled>
        <BlogItemBacklinksEnabled>
          <a class="comment-link"
              href="<$BlogItemPermalinkUrl$>#links">links to
                  this post</a>
        </BlogItemBacklinksEnabled>
      </MainOrArchivePage>
      <$BlogItemControl$>
    </p>
  </div>
  <!-- End .post -->
  <!-- Begin #comments -->
```

```
<ItemPage>
  <div id="comments">
    <BlogItemCommentsEnabled>
      <a name="comments"></a>
      <h4><$BlogItemCommentCount$> Comments:</h4>
      <dl id="comments-block">
        <BlogItemComments>
          <dt class="comment-poster"
              id="c<$BlogCommentNumber$>">
              <a name="c<$BlogCommentNumber$>"></a>
            <$BlogCommentAuthor$> said...
          </dt>
          <dd class="comment-body">
            <p><$BlogCommentBody$></p>
          </dd>
          <dd class="comment-timestamp">
            <a href="#<$BlogCommentNumber$>"
               title="comment permalink">
               <$BlogCommentDateTime$></a>
            <$BlogCommentDeleteIcon$>
          </dd>
        </BlogItemComments>
      </dl>
      <p class="comment-timestamp">
        <$BlogItemCreate$>
      </p>
    </BlogItemCommentsEnabled>
    <BlogItemBacklinksEnabled>
      <a name="links"></a>
      <h4>Links to this post:</h4>
      <dl id="comments-block">
        <BlogItemBacklinks>
          <dt class="comment-title">
            <$BlogBacklinkControl$>
            <a href="<$BlogBacklinkURL$>" rel="nofollow">
               <$BlogBacklinkTitle$></a>
            <$BlogBacklinkDeleteIcon$>
          </dt>
          <dd class="comment-body"><$BlogBacklinkSnippet$>
            <br/>
            <span class="comment-poster"><em>posted by
               <$BlogBacklinkAuthor$> @
               <$BlogBacklinkDateTime$></em></span>
          </dd>
        </BlogItemBacklinks>
```

```
            </dl>
            <p class="comment-timestamp"><$BlogItemBacklinkCreate$>
                </p>
        </BlogItemBacklinksEnabled>
        <p class="comment-timestamp">
            <a href="<$BlogURL$>">&lt;&lt; Home</a>
        </p>
    </div>
</ItemPage>
<!-- End #comments -->
</Blogger>
</div> <!-- end of bodycontent div -->
```

If you were to save these changes and open **index.html** in your browser now, it would look a bit of a mess (as you can see in Figure 9.15). It's still full of strange Blogger tags, and the browser's not too sure what to do with them. We need to put this page back into Blogger, so that it can make sense of those tags. Then we can give the browser language that it will understand.

In Blogger's template editor, delete all of the text from the template. (Most browsers have an **Edit > Select All** function; select this menu item and hit the **Delete** key to get rid of the existing template.) Now, paste in the contents of **index.html**, and select the **Save Template Changes** button.

Figure 9.15. The Bubble Under site with untranslated Blogger tags

The next page will tell you that your changes have been saved, and that you'll need to republish the blog for them to take effect. Click the **Republish** button on this page and Blogger will once again upload the necessary files to your web server. Assuming that there were no errors in the publishing process, you should receive a confirmation page like the one in Figure 9.16, which includes a **View Blog** link.

Your blog published successfully.

View Blog(in a new window)

/files/2008/08/first-post.html
/files/rss.xml
/files/atom.xml
/files/2008_08_01_archive.html
/files/index.html

Need to change it? Edit post | Create a new post

REPUBLISH INDEX ONLY | REPUBLISH ENTIRE BLOG | Republishing your index will only republish the main page of your blog. Republishing the entire blog will republish the main page, feeds, archives and post pages. Learn more

Figure 9.16. The Blogger confirmation page

Excellent! You've successfully set up a blog on your web site. Now, updating the content on that homepage is going to be easy—there's no need to lug a laptop around with you, and you'll be able to make updates using a desktop computer. As long as you're connected to the Internet, you can head over to Blogger, sign in, and update your site. However, we do have a couple more items to look at before we break out the champagne.

Tidying up the Blogger Template

Blog Comments

Enabling people to comment on your blog is easy. All they need to do is follow the link that says: 0 comments. This will take them to the Blogger web site, as shown in Figure 9.17, where anyone can leave a comment on your blog. Follow that link, add a comment, and you'll see the number of comments on your post increase by one.

 Anonymous Comments

To make a comment on your blog, your site visitors will need to sign up as users on the Blogger web site. You can allow anonymous comments, but that will leave you open to **comment spam**; this is a form of spam where spammers leave comments on your blog exalting the benefits of online poker, cheap pharmaceuticals, and bargain stocks. I'd recommend that you choose not to allow anonymous comments, lest your web site should become flooded with junk.

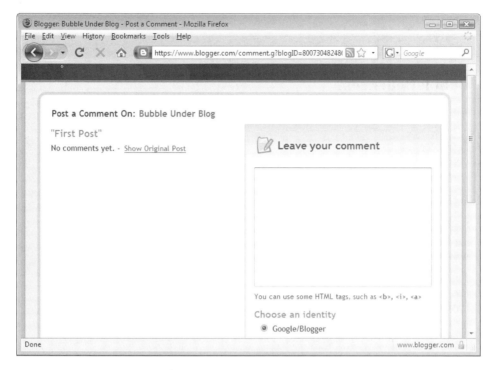

Figure 9.17. The Blogger comment form

In the background, Blogger will republish your home page so the number of comments stays up to date.

Viewing Comments

Blogger also publishes a separate page for each post where site visitors can view others' comments. Whenever a post is published or a comment is made, this page will be updated along with the homepage.

You can access this page by following the first link below your post (the link shows the time at which the post was first published). When you visit this page, you might receive a shock—all of your CSS style rules have disappeared! Figure 9.18 shows this sorry state of affairs. Don't worry, though: it's a cinch to fix.

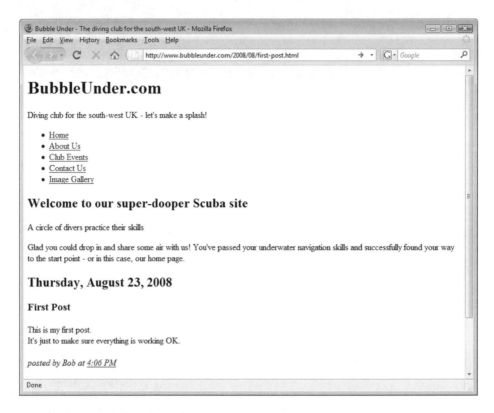

Figure 9.18. The comments page has lost its style

This problem arises because of the location to which Blogger writes our page: http://www.bubbleunder.com/2008/08/first-post.html. This isn't like the addresses of our other pages; they have addresses like http://www.bubbleunder.com/events.html and http://www.bubbleunder.com/contact.html. Blogger has put the **first-post.html** file inside another two folders that it has created—**2008** and **08**.[9]

Why does this matter? You may remember the `link` element that we used to include our style sheet:

first-post.html (excerpt)

```
<link href="style1.css" rel="stylesheet" type="text/css"/>
```

---

[9] These folder names relate to the date on which the post was published—it was posted in August, 2008.

This tells the browser to load the CSS file **style1.css** from the *current* directory. This works when all the files are in the same directory, but fails when the CSS file is in a different directory from the pages to which it applies. What we need to do is make these Blogger pages look for the style sheet file in its correct location—http://www.bubbleunder.com/style1.css—regardless of where the page calls it from.

Open up Blogger's Template Editor, locate the `link` element, and change it to the full address of the CSS file, as shown here:

Blogger Template (excerpt)

```
<link href="http://www.bubbleunder.com/style1.css"
    rel="stylesheet" type="text/css"/>
```

Before you save your changes, there's another element whose location also needs to be updated—the image that shows the circle of divers. Modify the `src` attribute of the `<img>` tag as follows:

Blogger Template (excerpt)

```
<h2>Welcome to our super-dooper Scuba site</h2>
<p><img src="http://www.bubbleunder.com/divers-circle.jpg" alt="A
    circle of divers practice their skills" width="200"
    height="162"/></p>
<p>Glad you could drop in and share some air with us! You've
    passed your underwater navigation skills and successfully
    found your way to the start point - or in this case, our
    home page.</p>
```

Finally, the same prefix needs to be added to our menu items. The navigation menu should look like this in your template:

Blogger Template (excerpt)

```
<div id="navigation">
  <ul>
    <li><a href="http://www.bubbleunder.com/index.html">Home</a>
        </li>
    <li><a href="http://www.bubbleunder.com/about.html"
        >About Us</a></li>
    <li><a href="http://www.bubbleunder.com/events.html"
```

```
            >Club Events</a></li>
      <li><a href="http://www.bubbleunder.com/contact.html"
          >Contact Us</a></li>
      <li><a href="http://www.bubbleunder.com/gallery.html"
          >Image Gallery</a></li>
    </ul>
  </div> <!-- end of navigation div -->
```

Save the changes to the template in Blogger, republish your blog, and reload the page to see it in its fully styled glory. Does your page look like the one in Figure 9.19?

Figure 9.19. Each post's comments page now has style!

That's it! You've set up a blog on your site, configured it so that visitors can leave comments, and the entire site is composed of valid, well-structured XHTML, so it's accessible to any browser ... or is it?

Validating Your Blog

If you now run your homepage through the W3C Markup Validator[10] that we saw in Chapter 8, you'll find that a couple of errors have been introduced, as Figure 9.20 reveals. These errors may cause problems for some browsers.

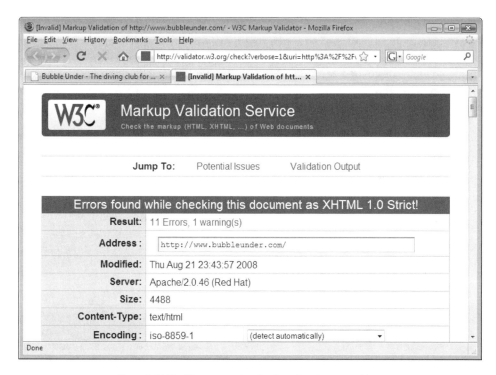

Figure 9.20. The Blogger template has introduced some problems

Here, the validator is complaining that there's no attribute called `location.href`, which is true. Thankfully, we're able to hunt down this invalid attribute and remove it from our Blogger template.

Take a look at the markup of the page that Blogger has created: load the homepage in your browser, and select **View** > **Source** (or **View** > **Page Source**). You'll see that all of the Blogger-specific tags have been replaced with the *almost* valid XHTML generated by Blogger. It's in this markup that you'll find the offending `location.href` attribute, which I've highlighted below (again, the markup has been formatted for readability—this won't affect how it's displayed in the browser):

---

[10] http://validator.w3.org/

```
<div id="bodycontent">
  <h2>Welcome to our super-dooper Scuba site</h2>
  <p><img src="divers-circle.jpg" alt="A circle of divers practice
      their skills" width="200" height="162"/></p>
  <p>Glad you could drop in and share some air with us! You've
      passed your underwater navigation skills and successfully
      found your way to the start point - or in this case, our
      home page.</p>
  <h2 class="date-header">Thursday, January 20, 2006</h2>
  <!-- Begin .post -->
  <div class="post">
    <a name="113469375771659009"></a>
    <h3 class="post-title">First Post</h3>
    <div class="post-body">
      <div>
        <div style="clear:both;"></div>
        This is my first post.<br/>
        It's just to make sure everything's working OK.
        <div style="clear:both; padding-bottom: 0.25em;"></div>
      </div>
    </div>
    <p class="post-footer">
      <em>posted by Bob Dobalina at <a
          href="http://www.bubbleunder.com/2006/01/first-post.html"
          title="permanent link">4:12 PM</a></em>
      <a class="comment-link" href="http://www.blogger.com/comment
.g?blogID=19907525&amp;postID=113469375771659009" location.href=ht
tp://www.blogger.com/comment.g?blogID=19907525&amp;postID=11346937
5771659009;>
          0 comments</a>
      <span class="item-control admin-594974497 pid-2135550719">
        <a style="border:none;" href="http://www.blogger.com/post-
edit.g?blogID=19907525&amp;postID=113469375771659009&amp;quickEdi
t=true" title="Edit Post">
          <span class="quick-edit-icon"> </span>
        </a>
      </span>
    </p>
  </div>
  <!-- End .post -->
  <!-- Begin #comments -->
  <!-- End #comments -->
</div> <!-- end of bodycontent div -->
```

We can locate the corresponding markup in the template by looking for the `<a>` tag with the `class="comment-link"` attribute, highlighted in the following code:

Blogger Template (excerpt)

```
<p class="post-footer">
  <em>posted by <$BlogItemAuthorNickname$> at
      <a href="<$BlogItemPermalinkUrl$>"
      title="permanent link"><$BlogItemDateTime$></a></em>
  <MainOrArchivePage>
    <BlogItemCommentsEnabled>
    <a class="comment-link"
        href="<$BlogItemCommentCreate$>"
        <$BlogItemCommentFormOnclick$>>
        <$BlogItemCommentCount$> comments</a>
    </BlogItemCommentsEnabled>
    <BlogItemBacklinksEnabled>
      <a class="comment-link"
        href="<$BlogItemPermalinkUrl$>#links">links to this
        post</a>
    </BlogItemBacklinksEnabled>
  </MainOrArchivePage>
  <$BlogItemControl$>
</p>
```

Comparing the two versions of the markup side-by-side, we can see that the `<$BlogItemAuthorNickname$>` tag has been replaced with the author's name, `<$BlogItemCommentCount$>` has been replaced with the number of comments that have been left on this blog post, and so on.

But what's introducing this mysterious `location.href` attribute? It looks like it's been slotted in just after the normal `href` attribute, so I'd bet my last dollar on the `<<$BlogItemCommentFormOnclick$>` tag being the one at fault. Let's delete that tag from our Blogger template (as shown below), click the **Save Template Changes** button and republish our blog. The page should now validate, as Figure 9.21 indicates:

index.html (excerpt)

```
<a class="comment-link"href="<$BlogItemCommentCreate$>">
  <$BlogItemCommentCount$> comments
</a>
```

After doing this, try the W3C Markup Validator again.

Figure 9.21. Success! The home page generated by Blogger is valid XHTML Strict

Now, updating the content on our web site using Blogger will produce valid markup, worthwhile for all those reasons we discussed in the section called "Validating Your Web Pages" in Chapter 8. And, thanks to Blogger, our web site's readers can now interact with the site and leave comments on any post's page. So what's next? It's time to put some real content into our blog!

Managing Your Blogger Posts

Let's add a more realistic post to the site, and delete our test post, too. In Blogger, click on the **Posting** tab—you should find yourself at the **Create Post** page shown in Figure 9.22. Type a message into the area provided, then click the **Publish Post** button.

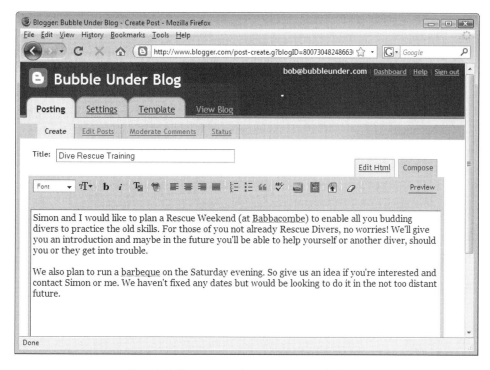

Figure 9.22. The text area where you type posts in Blogger

Again, Blogger will automatically update the necessary files on your web server. Now to delete our test post, go back to the Blogger dashboard and, under the **Postings** tab, select **Edit Posts** to access the list of all of your blog posts. Locate the test post and click **Delete**. The next page will ask if you really want to delete the post; click the **Delete It** button to eradicate it for good.

Now, at last, you can go and admire the web page on your live site. Finally, the site looks great, the markup validates,[11] and adding new content from any computer is a piece of cake. Give yourself a pat on the back!

---

[11] Unfortunately, our markup may not pass W3C validation once we start to receive comments on our blog. As of February 2006, Blogger's comments engine introduced invalid characters (uppercase tags and unencoded ampersands) that prevented pages from validating. There isn't much we can do about this, unfortunately. Having greater control over our markup is one advantage of using a self-hosted blogging solution.

Blogging with `class`

If you want to change the style of certain elements of the Blogger-generated markup, such as the post title or comments link, you can. You may have noticed that many of these elements have `class` attributes with reasonably intuitive names, such as `post-title` or `comments-link`. Simply add a rule for these classes to your style sheet, and by applying the CSS you've learned in this book, you'll have complete control over how they're displayed. Unfortunately, Blogger doesn't wrap the paragraphs typed in a post with `<p>` tags, the way it really should. To have this text display the same as other paragraphs throughout our site, expand the rule for p elements in our style sheet to read as follows:

```
.post-body div, p {
  font-size: small;
  color: navy;
}
```

Encouraging Others to Contribute to Your Blog

Arguably, one of the best features of managing and updating your site content via a blog is that it enables others to contribute. If you want to take some time off, a colleague can continue to update the web site easily. Even if you're not holidaying, it's great to have other people pitching in with their own writing styles and contributions. In this section, I'll show you how easy it is to add another author to your blog.

Click the **Settings** tab in Blogger, then click the **Permissions** link (not a particularly obvious place to look, is it?). You'll arrive at a page showing a list of the current "members" (or authors) of your blog which should, at this time, be a list of just one person—you! Click the **Add Authors** button, as shown in Figure 9.23.

Figure 9.23. The permissions page, where you can grant others the necessary rights to post on your blog

A text area should dynamically appear in the panel, and the **Add Authors** button re-placed by two new buttons: **Invite** and **Cancel**. This is shown in Figure 9.24. Enter the email addresses of those you want to invite to contribute, then press the **Invite** button.

Figure 9.24. Entering the email addresses of the people you want to contribute to the blog

The invitee will receive an email that explains how to join the blog, just like the one shown here:

```
The Blogger user Bob Dobalina has invited you to contribute to the
blog: Bubble Under.
```

```
To contribute to this blog, visit:
http://www.blogger.com/i.g?inviteID=833878766858320&blogID=11846504

You'll need to sign in with a Google Account to confirm the
invitation and start posting to this blog. If you don't have a
Google Account yet, we'll show you how to get one in minutes.

To learn more about Blogger and starting your own free blog visit
http://www.blogger.com.
```

Now, it's all set for your budding team of writers to do their stuff!

Summary

In this chapter, I've told you a little bit about what blogging is, and how it can help you keep your web site content fresh. I freely admit to limiting my discussion to the Blogger hosting service—this really makes it easy to get a blog up and running, and Blogger does not require any major technical knowledge beyond a bit of XHTML. You won't need to install and configure anything on your own server! However, if you find that Blogger is limiting you in any way, be sure to check out the other options available, and remember: if you get stuck with anything, you can always post a question on the SitePoint Forums.

If you've traveled this far, you should have a nicely rounded web site that's built to meet current standards, accessible to a wide audience, easy for search engines to index, quick to download, and an absolute cinch to update. To refer to my analogy of building a car in the early chapters of this book, your job is basically complete—you've built yourself a great car! But, no matter how cool your shiny new ride is, few motor heads can resist adding the odd feature here and there—dare I say it, adding a touch of bling! In the next chapter, I'll introduce you to some of the add-ons that you might consider clipping onto your web site to finish it off nicely. Bring on the chrome!

Chapter 10

Pimp My Site: Cool Stuff You Can Add for Free

Your web site looks great, everything seems to be going tickety-boo, and maybe you even have regular news updates happening, thanks to a group of budding bloggers who contribute regularly. Your work's done, right? Well, no. There's always something else to do!

When you first set up your web site, you probably had a good idea of the audience you were building it for, and you may well have catered admirably to that audience. But within weeks of launching your site and promoting it to the world (using some of the suggestions I made in Chapter 8), you started receiving emails from strangers asking questions about the site that you hadn't expected:

> "Can you tell me who can service my air regulators in North Devon?"

> "I can't find details of your training courses—do you offer any?"

> "My name is Abdul Akinbobola and I am the son of the recently deposed president of Burkina Faso and …"

Okay, so that last message has nothing to do with your web site, but trust me, you'll certainly receive emails like this! The point is, no matter what sort of planning you've undertaken, people beyond your expected audience will find your web site, and you'll likely need to be able to cater to them, too. This is where you should consider some add-ons to your site—extras that will:

- enable you to *discover how people are arriving at your web site* (e.g., through a Google search, or via another web site's link where you've promoted your own site)

- reveal *which search terms people used* to reach your web site, and provide some statistics about the most common ones

- let the visitor *search the contents of your web site* (rather than click around the navigation in the hope of finding what they need)

- allow the visitor to *search a group of related web sites* from the comfort of your web site

- provide a way for you to *manage a list of your favorite web sites* related to the topic in your own web site, and provide them as a links resource for others

- let your visitors become part of your web site community by *providing a discussion forum*

All of these goals can be achieved using free services, and in this chapter, I'm going to provide step-by-step instructions to help you add these services and truly pimp your site![1]

Getting the Low-down on Your Visitors

How can you be absolutely sure that what's on your web site is the right content for your audience? Well, the truth is that you can't—everyone's different, after all, and each person's needs are unique. However, you can be given some indication

---

[1] For those who don't understand the reference, Pimp My Site is my little pun based on the MTV show Pimp My Ride [http://www.mtv.com/ontv/dyn/pimp_my_ride/series.jhtml] in which old, neglected cars are renovated (or "pimped") for their owners. That's not to say that your web site is old or neglected, though!

about whether your web site is serving the audience's needs through some simple statistics

Some hosting companies will provide statistics software as part of your package, so be sure to check. If your package includes a statistics service, you might wish to skip this next section and just use the tools your host has provided. Most free hosting services—and many of the cheaper hosting plans—will not provide statistics for you. And even if your hosts *do* provide such services for you, they're not usually all that great. So it's up to us to make sure we receive the best information that we can.

Choosing a Statistics Service

As with a number of services I've mentioned elsewhere in this book, there are two ways that you could introduce a statistics service to your site:

- You could install and configure a statistics service on the web server that hosts your site. The web server keeps detailed records of every visit to your web site: it records the time of the visit, which pages were viewed, which browsers were used, how visitors found the site, and much, much more. There are many programs you can install onto your web server that will produce easy-to-read graphs based on this data. Installing this software is no easy feat, though, and I wouldn't recommend it for beginners.

- Thankfully, the second option is much easier—you can sign up for a third-party solution that collects and stores the data on your behalf. All you're required to do is add a link to an image or script file (hosted by the service provider) into your web pages.

Many third-party statistics services are available, but to narrow it down, I advise you to look for one that offers the following features:

list of referring web sites (recent referrers and totals)
  This information will tell you how your visitors found your web site.

number of visitors
  You should be able to view a count of the numbers of visitors your site receives each day and each month, as well as the total number of visitors who have stopped by since the site launched.

information about your visitors' computer setups

> This data will tell you whether your visitors are using PCs or Macs, which browsers they're using, and so on.

Any information beyond that is probably overkill for a small-scale web site (too many statistics can end up muddying the waters—there's a lot to be said for simplicity). There are a number of free hosted stats services you might want to consider using, including StatCounter,[2] Extreme Tracking,[3] and AddFreeStats.[4] However, for my money the best solution you could opt for is Google Analytics.[5]

In the past, I used a number of the free services mentioned, but have since switched all of them across to Google Analytics. The service is free but doesn't *appear* to be cheap—in short, you're receiving a whole lot more than what you paid for! In addition, it's so easy to set up and then analyse the data that it captures. Let's start by signing up for an account.

Registering a Google Account

Make your way over to http://www.google.com/analytics/. It doesn't take long to have Google Analytics up and running. If you already have a Google account—highly probably given the number of services they already offer, notably Gmail (Google Mail)—then you can simply log in and then sign up for Analytics. For now, though, I'll assume that you don't yet have a Google account.

▓ Click on the **Sign Up Now** link, as shown in Figure 10.1.

---

[2] http://www.statcounter.com/
[3] http://www.extreme-dm.com/tracking/
[4] http://www.addfreestats.com/
[5] http://www.google.com/analytics/

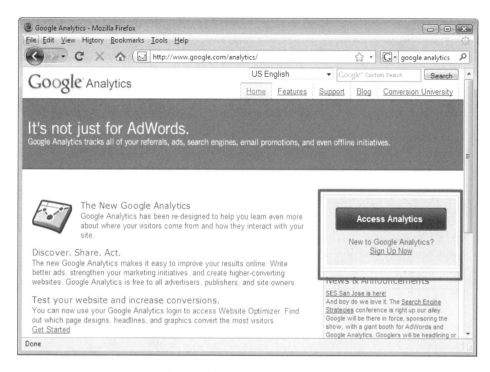

Figure 10.1. Google Analytics home page

This will take you to a login screen, as shown in Figure 10.2 (unless you're already logged in to your Google account). If you already have an account, you would use the login panel on the right, but let's assume you've never set up a Google Account. Click the **Sign Up Now** link (and yes, this does seem a bit like déja vu, doesn't it? Sign up now! Sign up now!).

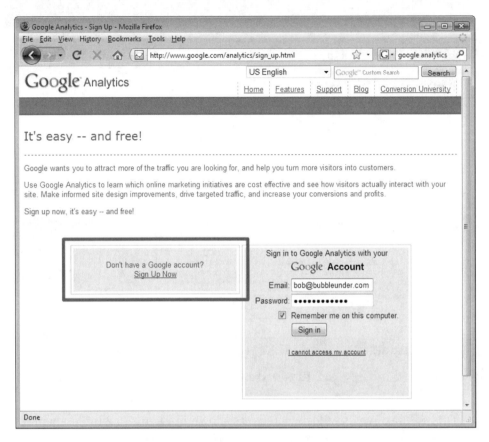

Figure 10.2. Google Analytics log in/sign up page

■ There are just a handful of details to input on this page—as seen in Figure 10.3. Just enter your email address, pick a sensible password, and then attempt to read the almost indecipherable characters in the word verification box (good luck—it usually takes me a few tries!). Press the button that says **I accept. Create my account**.

Figure 10.3. Creating the Google Account

- Having sent the form, Google will send an email to you to confirm your account is a genuine request. You do this by clicking on the link in the email, and you're now a step closer.

- You now have a Google account, but you do not, as yet, have a Google Analytics account set up. Log in to your Google account (using the http://www.google.com/analytics/ address from earlier). On the next page you'll see some more blurb about Analytics. Don't read it all (plenty of time for that later), instead just head straight for the panel with the button that says **Sign Up**, as shown in Figure 10.4

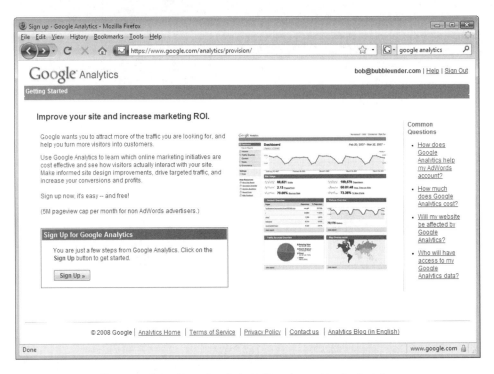

Figure 10.4. Logged in to Google, but still need to register for Analytics

There's nothing too taxing here at all (see Figure 10.5)—Google just needs to know a few details about your web site, where you are in the world (for the time zone), and some contact information. You're also asked to tick a box confirming that you've read the lengthy list of terms and conditions; should you comply, this would probably make you the second person in history after Google's lawyer to *actually* have done this (read it, not tick the box, that is!).

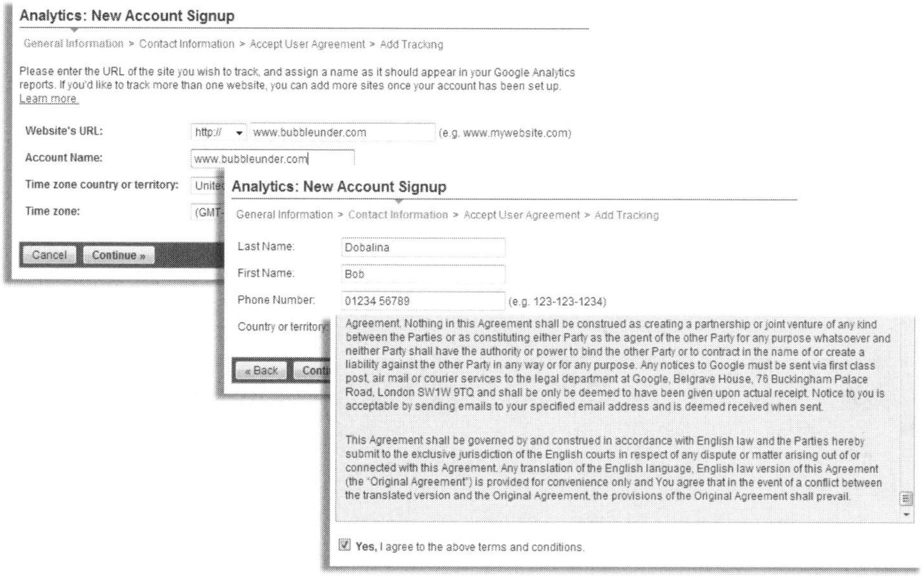

Figure 10.5. Some of the sign-up steps (and the beast of a Terms and Conditions page!)

In the final step of signing up, Google presents you with some code to copy and paste into your web pages. There are two options to choose from; select the first tab (which is displayed by default and titled **New Tracking Code**), then highlight and copy the markup provided in the text area (see Figure 10.6).

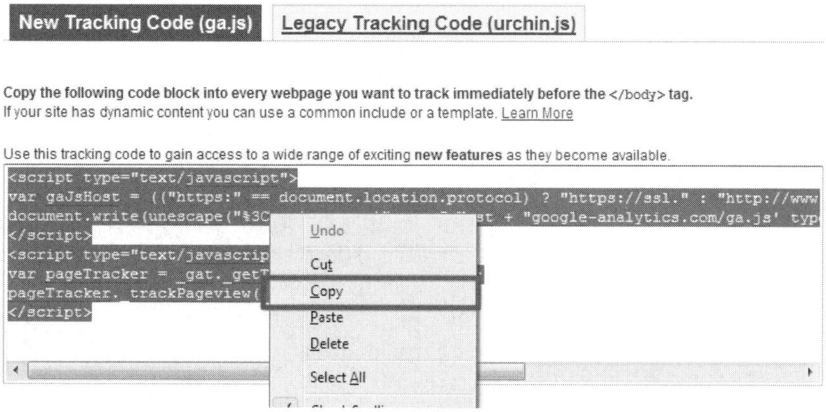

Figure 10.6. Copy the markup that Google Analytics provides

That's it for the sign-up process. Now all you need to do is put the generated markup—just a few lines of it—into your web pages.

Adding the Statistics Code to Your Web Pages

Your statistics code should look like this (though specific details relating to your account will differ):

```
<script type="text/javascript">
var gaJsHost = (("https:" == document.location.protocol) ?
➥"https://ssl." : "http://www.");
document.write(unescape("%3Cscript src='" + gaJsHost +
➥"google-analytics.com/ga.js'
➥type='text/javascript'%3E%3C/script%3E"));
</script>
<script type="text/javascript">
var pageTracker = _gat._getTracker("UA-1234567-1");
pageTracker._initData();
pageTracker._trackPageview();
</script>
```

To start, simply paste this code in your web page *just before* the closing `</body>` tag. It's good practice to place it here, as it's the last item loaded on your web page; that way, if Google takes a while to send the data requested, it will not hold up your web page loading. Here's how it looks in the context of the *About* page (which I've truncated to a degree):

```
                                                      about.html (excerpt)

    <p>
      Or as our man Bob Dobalina would put it:</p>
      <blockquote>
        <p class="fun">"Happiness is a dip in the ocean followed
            by a pint or two of Old Speckled Hen. You can quote
            me on that!"</p>
      </blockquote>
    </div> <!-- end of bodycontent div -->
      <script type="text/javascript">
var gaJsHost = (("https:" == document.location.protocol) ?
➥"https://ssl." : "http://www.");
document.write(unescape("%3Cscript src='" + gaJsHost +
➥"google-analytics.com/ga.js'
➥type='text/javascript'%3E%3C/script%3E"));
```

```
</script>
<script type="text/javascript">
var pageTracker = _gat._getTracker("UA-1234567-1");
pageTracker._initData();
pageTracker._trackPageview();
</script>
  </body>
</html>
```

This is just the *About* page taken care of, so you'll also need to add the code to the other pages in your web site, and save them all. If you've created a Blogger template, you'll also need to update that template with the statistics code. You can do this by logging into Blogger and adding the same code in the same location before the closing body tag, and then republishing your blog).

But what now? What have we done here? And what can we do with it from this point on?

Once you've added the tracking markup as described above, you'll need to upload the amended pages to your server by FTP (as described in Chapter 8). From now on, every user visit to your web site will also place a request to Google's files that you inserted at the end of the page—what Google does is track these requests to build up a picture of your web site usage. You can access these reports (click on **View Reports**) from the Google Analytics Settings page (always the first page after logging in—no hunting around required!), which is shown in Figure 10.7.

Figure 10.7. Google Analytics Settings page

Because we're only using a dummy site in this book with no real users, it's a bit difficult to demonstrate real, lifelike stats—so here's the Dashboard page from one of my own web sites, Accessify.com with a few examples. It's been around for quite a while and has enough traffic to produce some statistics, as Figure 10.8 shows.

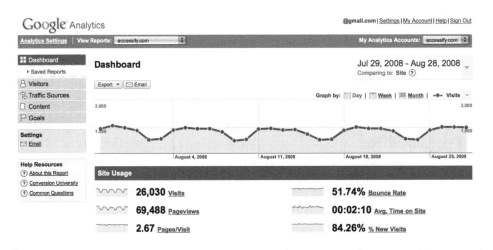

Figure 10.8. The Dashboard—showing an overview of visitor statistics

There are many other useful statistics here—too many to go into in more detail, in fact. My advice is to sign up, apply the statistics code, and upload your amended pages to your web server. Then, simply leave it for a few days—or weeks, even—before logging back in to check the statistics. By that time you might have enough data to see some patterns beginning to form (unless of course you've not told anyone about your site and not had anyone link to the site, in which case the usage statistics will point to just one user—you! New web sites can take time).

An example of the range of information Google Analytics can provide is shown in Figure 10.9, which is a montage of the main site navigation with various features. Google Analytics is the veritable Swiss Army Knife of free statistics, but like the famed knife, you'll probably not use 80% of the tools on offer!

Figure 10.9. Examples of the Google Analytics navigation menu options

What to Look for—a Summary

The most revealing statistics that you'll probably need will be on the front page (aka the Dashboard), and these are:

Visitors: How many people are using the site … and do they stay long?

It's great to know information about how many visitors your site receives, and see how that changes over time, too. But when they reach the site, do they stick around for long? Or do they just hit the back button on the browser and go elsewhere? The **Visitors** information tells you all of that and more.

Traffic Sources: Through which web pages do visitors arrive at your site?

If another site has linked to your web site, and a user follows that link to your web site, that information will be recorded in **Traffic Sources**. It's good to be aware of other web sites that have linked to you (if for no other reason than to give you an ego boost!), and why they've linked to you—it's easy enough to take a look at the *referring site* from these reports. In most cases, your key referrers will be search engines (and you can even find out what phrases people entered that led them to your web site).[6]

Browser Capabilities: What tools do people use to access your web site?

Knowledge is power. If you learn that 99% of your visitors are using one kind of web browser, you might not spend quite so much time worrying about display issues for the other 1% of users. This kind of information helps you prioritize any bugs you might need to fix.

A Search Tool for Your Site

This one's a cinch! We'll have you set up in minutes. And guess what? It's those people at Google that we have to thank, again. It could barely be any easier.

Here's the basic markup you'll need to have (this is so that Google can provide search results based on the content of your web site only):

```
<!-- SiteSearch Google -->
<form method="get" action="http://www.google.com/search">
<label for="q">Search:</label>
<input id="q" name="q" size="20" maxlength="255" value=""
    type="text"/>
<input name="domains" value="http://www.bubbleunder.com/"
    type="hidden"/>
<input name="sitesearch" value="http://www.bubbleunder.com/"
    checked="checked" id="mysite" type="radio"/>
<label for="mysite">Just this site</label>
<input name="sitesearch" value="" id="www" type="radio"/>
<label for="www">WWW</label>
<input name="btnG" value="Go" type="submit"/>
</form>
<!-- SiteSearch Google -->
```

All you need to do is change the bolded text to match your web site's address. It's so easy!

Here's that same code implementing the Bubble Under web site (at least, on a portion of the events page):

---

[6] Sometimes, web site managers talk about "checking their referrer logs." This is what that term means—looking through the lists of sites who have sent traffic to your web site, including search engines (and reviewing the search phrases users entered into search engines to find your site).

```
<!DOCTYPE html PUBLIC "-//W3C//DTD XHTML 1.0 Strict//EN"
    "http://www.w3.org/TR/xhtml1/DTD/xhtml1-strict.dtd">
<html xmlns="http://www.w3.org/1999/xhtml">
<head>
<title>Forthcoming club diving events and trips with Bubble
    Under</title>
<meta http-equiv="Content-Type"
    content="text/html; charset=utf-8"/>
<link href="style1.css" rel="stylesheet" type="text/css"
    media="screen"/>
</head>
<body>
<div id="header">
  <div id="sitebranding">
    <h1>BubbleUnder.com</h1>
  </div>
  <div id="tagline">
    <p>Diving club for the south-west UK - let's make a
        splash!</p>
  </div>
<!-- SiteSearch Google -->
<form method="get" action="http://www.google.com/search">
<div id="search">
<label for="q">Search:</label>
<input id="q" name="q" size="20" maxlength="255" value=""
    type="text"/>
<input name="domains" value="http://www.bubbleunder.com/"
    type="hidden"/>
<input name="sitesearch" value="http://www.bubbleunder.com/"
    checked="checked" id="mysite" type="radio"/>
<label for="mysite">Just this site</label>
<input name="sitesearch" value="" id="www" type="radio"/>
<label for="www">WWW</label>
<input name="btnG" value="Go" type="submit"/>
</div>
</form>
<!-- SiteSearch Google -->
</div>
<!-- end of header div -->
    ⋮
```

Note that we need to position the search form in an appropriate location, as well as format the text a bit. I've used CSS to achieve this, using absolute positioning to place the search box in the top, right-hand corner of the page. To do so, I wrapped a `div` around the form elements and gave it an `id` attribute. That way, I can reference the form in the CSS, as shown below:

```
#search {
  position: absolute;
  top: 77px;
  right: 10px;
  font-size: x-small;
  font-weight: bold;
}
```

Figure 10.10 shows how the search box looks on the page itself.

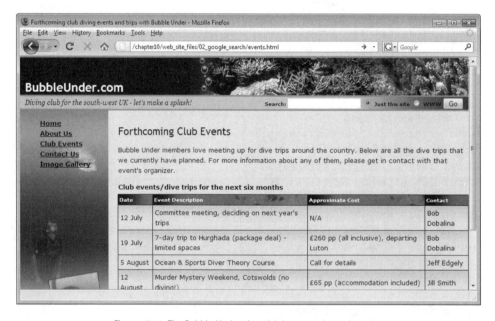

Figure 10.10. The Bubble Under site with integrated search option

Google Search Limitations

Using Google's service in this way is certainly easy, but you should be aware of its limitations:

- Google will only show search results if it *knows* about your web site—and it will only know about it if you've submitted your web site's address[7] to Google in the past (and Google has indexed it), or Google has found your web site by following a link from another site.

- The search results may not be completely up to date. If you make changes to your site, then upload those changes, Google may not recognize that a change has been made for days or even weeks—it really depends on when the search engine re-indexes your site.

- The search results cannot be customized. The results page will look like a standard Google-search results page, but the linked search results will all be pages from your web site (aside from sponsored links). However, people are familiar with Google, so this has its benefits.

Searching by Genre

If adding a Google search tool doesn't appeal, you might like to try another service called Rollyo, a *roll-your-own* search engine. Rollyo allows you to create a custom search interface: one that lets you pick and choose which web sites you want to search—so that the search results are more focused and closely related to your own web site's content.

- Click on the **Register** link in the top right-hand corner and complete the scant details requested of you by the registration page, shown in Figure 10.11.

---

[7] You can notify Google of your web site's existence at http://www.google.com/addurl/.

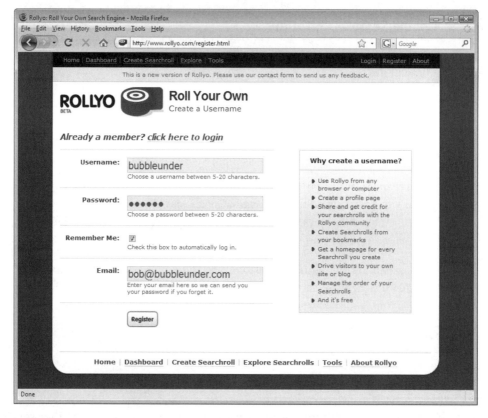

Figure 10.11. The Rollyo registration screen

■ Next, you'll be asked for profile information, and you'll see a big red arrow with the words, **Skip this for now**. You know what to do!

■ On the following page, select the **Create a custom searchroll** link, as illustrated in Figure 10.12.

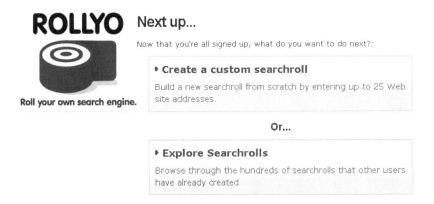

Figure 10.12. Choose **Create a custom searchroll**

In the page shown in Figure 10.13, you're asked to provide names for your
Searchroll—a list of web sites that you want to include—and identify any *tags*
(keywords that describe your search facility's purpose) that you'd like to assign
to your searchroll.

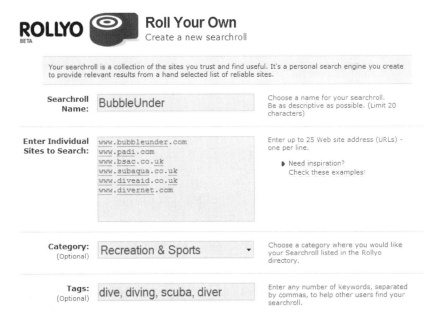

Figure 10.13. Adding sites that you want to search

With that done, you can create your searchroll. At the time of writing, Rollyo was yet to provide a simple method for grabbing the source code required to place search functionality on your web site. However, it's possible to view the source of a web page, take what you need, then adapt it slightly. I've done just that to show how Rollyo could be used on any web site. Here's the source code for the Rollyo search I created for Bubble Under:

```
<!-- SiteSearch Rollyo -->
<form id="searchform" name="searchform"
    action="http://www.rollyo.com/search.html" method="get">
  <div id="search">
  <input type="text" name="q" value="" id="search-box"/> in
    <select id="searchmenu" name="sid">
      <option value="6170">Bubble Under</option>
      <option value="web">The web</option>
    </select>
    <input type="submit" value="Search"/>
  </div>
</form>
<!-- SiteSearch Rollyo -->
```

Figure 10.14 shows how the search interface displays on the web page. (I placed everything inside the form in the absolutely positioned div—in the same position as the Google search box in the earlier example.)

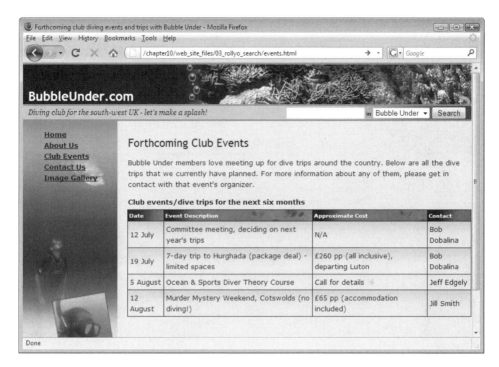

Figure 10.14. Adding a Rollyo search to the Bubble Under web site

Because the Rollyo search results are syndicated from Yahoo, the next step is to submit your site to Yahoo for indexing,[8] if you haven't already. As with most search engines, it may take days or weeks before Yahoo visits your site and adds your pages to its database. Your Rollyo searchroll will still work during this time, it just won't include your site in the results it displays.

Finally, Figure 10.15 depicts the search results displayed on the Rollyo web site.

---

[8] http://search.yahoo.com/info/submit.html

Figure 10.15. Displaying the search results on Rollyo

This is a novel way of adding search functionality to your site—but it's one that could potentially send people in another direction! However, if your web site is more of a fun venture, than focused on making cold hard cash, this could be the ethical way to go. Believe me when I say it'll be good for your karma—you'll see!

Caution: Contents May Have Shifted in Transit

Rollyo was new at the time of writing the first edition of this book. Some two years later, when I was putting this second edition together, it appeared to have had just the *tiniest* of changes—and was still showing as a **beta** version (a software term used to denote a work-in-progress, although these days, it's used more as a liability waver!). Like a volcano that's not erupted for a while, my gut feeling is that it may be overdue for a change or two. Or perhaps everything's working so well they will keep it as is—for another two or so years. Who knows? Certainly not me! So please bear in mind that it might change after this edition goes to print, and if that transpires you may need to adapt some of the steps.

Adding a Blogroll to Your Web Site

What's a **Blogroll**? A Blogroll[9] is a list of links that's included on your web site (or blog), and which is easily updated from a central point. A Blogroll is often a better option than creating a specific page on your site just for links—which can easily turn stale—and provides an easy route to fresh content on other web sites.

A range of tools are available for this purpose, but perhaps the simplest one to try is BlogRolling. Here's the process for setting up a Blogroll (once again, I've used the Bubble Under web site as an example).

Signing up for a Blogroll

- Go to the BlogRolling[10] web site.

- Follow the link to Create Account—you'll be asked for an email address and password, as Figure 10.16 shows.

Figure 10.16. Setting up a BlogRolling account

Once you've submitted the form, BlogRolling will send you an email. Open it and click on the activation link.

- Once you've activated your account, you can create a new Blogroll—in fact, you can create several Blogrolls with just one account. Look for the link on the left that says **New BlogRoll**. Then, simply enter a name and the web address of the page on which you'll be displaying the links, as shown in Figure 10.17.

---

[9] http://en.wikipedia.org/wiki/Blogroll

[10] http://www.blogrolling.com/

Figure 10.17. Creating a new BlogRoll

Most of the tools you'll need to manage your BlogRoll links are available from the **Home** option on BlogRoll's navigation menu. Figure 10.18 shows the BlogRolling control panel for BubbleUnder.

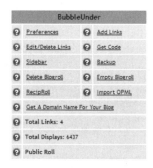

Figure 10.18. All your BlogRolling options are available here

Select **Add Links**. You'll be presented with a small form that looks like the one in Figure 10.19.

Figure 10.19. Adding a link to your Blogroll

You can keep on adding links until you run out of interesting web site addresses. Bear in mind though, that if you add too many links, your web page may resemble Yahoo gone mad.

■ Once you've added links to your favorite web sites, you have one final task to perform: determine the order of how the links will display on your web site. Select **Preferences** and scroll down to the section that says **Sorting your links**, as illustrated in Figure 10.20.

Figure 10.20. Setting the order in which your links appear on the page

■ Now all you need to do is access the code required for this feature to function on your web site. Go back to the Control Panel's homepage and click on the **Get Code** link. It will look like this:

```
<script language="javascript" type="text/javascript"
    src="http://rpc.blogrolling.com/display.php?r=ad7cab20d092c
2ee809d009e26ffcc11"></script>
```

Integrating the Blogroll with Your Web Site

Usually, people add Blogrolls to their sites' homepages, tucked away to one side. I'm going to do the same with the Bubble Under Blogroll.

As with the other sections on your web site, it's a good idea to wrap the Blogroll in a div element with an id attribute. This approach will allow you to reference the div in a style sheet, and makes it easy to find the Blogroll when you look through the markup at a later date. Here's the markup for the Bubble Under homepage (**index.html**), once the Blogroll has been added (for your Blogroll, you'd have a different value for the script's src attribute):

index.html *(excerpt)*

```
<div id="navigation">
<ul>
  <li><a href="index.html">Home</a></li>
  <li><a href="about.html">About Us</a></li>
  <li><a href="events.html">Club Events</a></li>
  <li><a href="contact.html">Contact Us</a></li>
  <li><a href="gallery.html">Image Gallery</a></li>
  </ul>
</div>
<div id="bodycontent">
<div id="blogroll">
<h2>Recently updated Diving Sites</h2>
<script language="javascript" type="text/javascript"
    src="http://rpc.blogrolling.com/display.php?r=ad7cab20d092c2
ee809d009e26ffcc11"></script>
</div>
<h2>Welcome to our super-dooper Scuba site</h2>
<p><img src="divers-circle.jpg" alt="A circle of divers practice
    their skills" width="200" height="162"/></p>
<p>Glad you could drop in and share some air with us! You've
    passed your underwater navigation skills and successfully
    found your way to the start point - or in this case, our
    home page. </p>
```

Without any further intervention, your list may look a little on the dull side. Let's suppose you wanted to style your Blogroll. This code will do the trick:

```css
#blogroll {
    float: right;
    margin-top: 55px;
    margin-left: 10px;
    margin-bottom: 10px;
    margin-right: 10px;
    width: 130px;
    border: 1px solid #006;
    font-size: x-small;
}

#blogroll h2 {
    font-size: x-small;
    background: #006;
    color: #fff;
    padding: 5px;
    margin: 0;
}

#blogroll div {
    padding: 5px;
}
```

Note that I've used contextual selectors (remember them from Chapter 3 and Chapter 4?) to style the heading as well as the links themselves. Although you can't see it from the code extract that BlogRolling provided (all that's visible is a link to a JavaScript file), each link that we add is wrapped in a `div`. I've added a little padding to each `div` inside the `blogroll` container, like so:

```css
#blogroll div {
    padding: 5px;
}
```

Also note that I've floated the `blogroll div`, and given it a specific width. This will place the list on the right-hand side of the screen (to the right of the previously floated feature image). Figure 10.21 shows how all this fits together on the page.

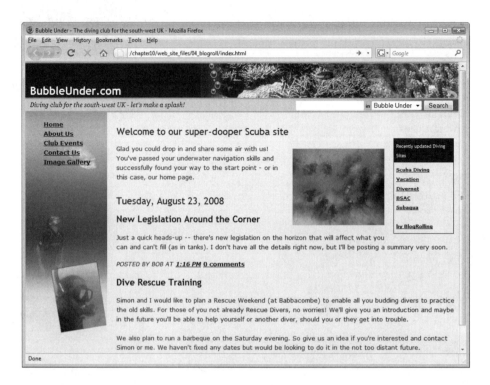

Figure 10.21. The blogroll in place

We've added a Blogroll! Now, any time you add a good web site to your book-marks—and it's related to your own web site's theme—you might consider adding it to your Blogroll, too. All you need to do is head over to the BlogRolling site, log in, and add a link as we did above.

Discussion Forums

Arguably, one of the best ways to create a virtual community around your web site—and to ensure that people come back time and time again—is to provide a chat forum. There is one small problem, though—forums aren't particularly straightfor-ward to set up. Furthermore, once you start to have regular posts appearing, you'll face the issue of moderating the forum's content. Will you moderate it yourself? Will you just let the forum discussions take their own course?[11] Will you empower regular visitors to moderate the forums?

---

[11] The short answer to that is: no! If you give people the freedom to run wild, they may well do just that—which could even place you in hot water, legally speaking. For example, a forum member could

Most of the fully featured (and free) forum software products that you could use have some prerequisites that basically rule out my covering them in this book. For example, many packages require your hosting company to support PHP (a scripting language) and to make a MySQL database available to you. At this stage, you probably find these quite foreign concepts.

A simple solution for creating a community is to use Yahoo Groups.[12] Signing up for the service is as simple as registering for an email account with Yahoo. Then, you can invite people to take part by registering for the discussion group themselves.

The beauty of using Yahoo Groups is that many people will already be familiar with Yahoo services—possibly having sign-in details they can use from their Yahoo mail accounts. Also, the service is provided by a company that you know and can trust and, as such, it's unlikely to disappear overnight—taking your new virtual community with it.

The downside of using Yahoo Groups is that this option takes users away from your web site. The best that you can do is to provide a link from your web site to the group that you set up. From that point forward, your community is entirely in the hands of Yahoo (capable though they are), but could present problems if you ever wanted to move the forum to another location.

Summary

In this chapter I've shown that no matter how much work you put into building a web site, there's always more you can do. I've focused on some add-ons that, I believe, really do improve a web site and encourage you—as well as others visiting the site—to use it more. However, I would like to sound one note of warning at this point, and it is this:

Know when to stop!

There are many web sites still kicking around today that were built in the mid-to-late 90s, when the motto seemed to be: the more flashing/spinning/bouncing widgets on the page, the better the web site. Thankfully, as the art of web design has matured,

---

slander another user on your forum, or link to copyrighted material for others to download, and you as the web site owner could be responsible for those people's actions. Moderation is a *great* idea.

[12] http://groups.yahoo.com/

people have come to realize that *less is more*. Please bear this in mind when adding features. Otherwise, before you know it, the bells and whistles will have taken over completely!

Don't Be too Reliant on Third-party Services

There's one other reason not to go overboard adding third-party features to your web site. If that third party's web server is slow for some reason, and your web page is trying to access that provider's server, your web page may appear to load slowly. Also, you need to be careful about *putting all your eggs into one basket*. If the service you use is free, be prepared that one day, the owners may decide to close the service down, or charge for it. Would your web site be able to function properly if this happened?

At this point, your web site should have all the features that it needs. If you've followed the advice I've given in this book, you'll have a well-formed, standards-based web site that you can be proud of. If you've enjoyed designing and building your web pages, you might want to improve your skills even further. Instead of me leaving you to fend for yourself at this point, I'm going to make some suggestions about where you can acquire the skills you need; frankly, there are an awful lot of bad web sites and books out there, and you could easily pick one up by mistake. I'd hate for you to undo any of the good work you've done so far! So, let's continue on to the final chapter, in which we'll explore the possibilities that now lie before you.

Chapter 11

Where to Now? What You Could Learn Next

In the course of this book I've given you a foundation for building web sites that will set you in good stead for many years to come. The methods described here are not workarounds—they don't try to use HTML or CSS to cobble together effects never intended to be created using these technologies. The techniques we've used are based on well-established standards to which any new web browsers should conform. In short, by following the advice of this book, rather than another beginner's manual that could teach you numerous bad practices, you now have a good base from which to further develop your skills.[1]

But what exactly can you do from this point forward? What are your options for developing your skills even more, without erring from the path of high-quality,

---

[1] Actually, you can afford to smile at this point. Although some of the concepts in this book are, on the face of it, quite simple—for example, using CSS to control the page layout—there are a large number of people out there who would consider them advanced. That's because those people have learned the old (wrong) methods, and re-wiring their brains to another way of thinking is not easy. You won't need to do that, though!

standards-based web design? These questions are precisely what this short chapter is all about—it's a road map to ensure that you get to learn from the best material out there.

I'm going to break the various options into four areas:

- XHTML/HTML: looking beyond the basics
- CSS: discovering just how far your designs can go with some clever CSS
- JavaScript: adding a little interactivity to your web site
- Programming: opening up the possibilities with scripting languages and databases

Let's start with our web page building blocks: XHTML.

Improving Your XHTML

First, let's have another pat-yourself-on-the-back moment. You've already grabbed a head start by learning the more picky (where syntax is concerned) XHTML rather than HTML. And because of that you've been putting into practice such techniques as:

- declaring a doctype at the beginning of the document (an essential aspect of XHTML)
- ensuring that all attributes are quoted properly (e.g. `<div id="sitebranding">`)
- writing your markup entirely in lowercase
- closing all tags correctly (e.g. `<p>This is a paragraph</p>`)—and that includes empty elements (e.g. `<input type="input" name="q" value="" id="search-box"/>`)

You've learned some of these techniques by copying, though perhaps you haven't always understood *why* some aspects of XHTML are achieved as they are. To refer this to the car analogy (once again), when you first learn to drive, you know almost nothing about why you have to perform certain actions, but you follow the instructor's advice nonetheless. After you've been driving for a while, you stop thinking about *why* you do it a certain way: you just do it and know that's how it should be done. But for some people, driving the car well isn't enough—they want to know how their car works, and to understand how the engine, wheels, gearbox, and electrical system all fit together. If they can understand that, maybe they can make the car drive more smoothly, and look better—they can really make it their own.

And this is the point we're at with XHTML: now's the time to find out more about the nuts and bolts of what you've learned to date.

It's worth just emphasizing at this point that there's *still* nothing wrong with using HTML 4.01 rather than XHTML. Both are acceptable, and should you choose to use the slightly less demanding HTML syntax (which will allow you to drop closing tags and so on), then that's perfectly okay—as long as you stick to the rules of the language's syntax. For this book, XHTML was chosen because it encourages better practices: it's arguably better to learn the *extended* version and then discard what you decide you don't need or want than to do it the other way around. Although this was mentioned in an earlier chapter, it's prudent to remind you of the differences between HTML and XHTML[2] again, particularly as you now have a greater understanding than you did when you started!

The Official Documentation

Perhaps that heading should read *Recommendations*, which is what the World Wide Web Consortium (W3C) likes to call them. If our web site was a car, the W3C recommendations would be the car's technical service manuals, complete with all the electrical wiring diagrams. In short, the recommendations don't make for light reading! However, in the search to truly understand how and why XHTML works the way it does, you can't find a more complete or technically accurate document than the W3C's own XHTML 1.0 recommendation at http://www.w3.or/TR/xhtml1/.

 Making W3C Specs a Little More Understandable

Because your first read of a W3C document will likely be a less-than-fun event (I'm being diplomatic here), it might be an idea to take a look at J. David Eisenberg's article How to Read W3C Specs.[3] This author does a great job of explaining some of the terminology and structures that you'll encounter on the many and varied W3C documents. It won't make reading the documentation as enjoyable as, say, an adventure novel, but you will at least be able to glean the information you need with less head-scratching.

---

[2] http://reference.sitepoint.com/html/html-vs-xhtml/
[3] http://www.alistapart.com/articles/readspec/

Other Useful XHTML Resources

If the official documentation is simply too much for you to take on board right now, park it for the time being—you can always go back when you come across a problem or want clarification on a specific issue. There are other sources of information that you may find a lot easier to take in, some of which I've listed below.

The Ultimate HTML Reference

Perhaps it should come as no surprise that I mention this one first here—this is the complete HTML reference that I wrote after writing the first edition of *this* book, and it fills in absolutely all the gaps that are present in this book. That's not to say that this book is lacking—I certainly hope that you agree, having worked your way through to this point—but as a beginner's book there were some omissions. These were all deliberate: sometimes because the chance of needing to use a certain HTML element was slim, and sometimes because the HTML elements concerned may be out of favor and can potentially harm your web site. In *The Ultimate HTML Reference*, everything's covered—all the elements, all the attributes, examples of how to use them, how the popular browsers cope with them, the lot!

The Ultimate HTML Reference is available as a hardback book from SitePoint (see http://www.sitepoint.com/books/htmlref1/). It massively expands the scope of the reference, which initially appeared as a 60-page appendix in the first edition of this book. And if you're not sure about buying the complete reference just yet, you can still check your facts online. You may already have been, actually; many of the references to HTML elements in this book point to the online reference—known as the SitePoint HTML Reference and found at http://reference.sitepoint.com/html/—as shown in Figure 11.1,

.

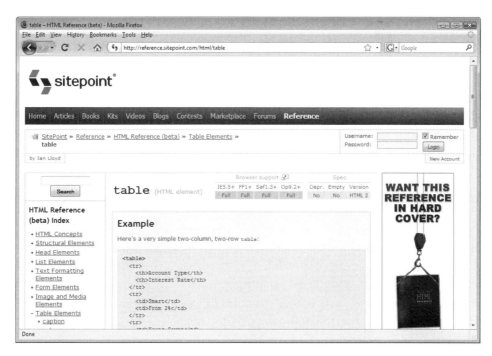

Figure 11.1. The SitePoint HTML Reference with the entry for 'table'

HTML Dog

While slightly older than SitePoint's *The Ultimate HTML Reference*, Patrick Griffiths' site, HTML Dog (http://www.htmldog.com/guides/) is still a great choice for furthering your skills. The site breaks HTML[4] and CSS into three levels: Beginner, Intermediate, and Advanced. The sections are short enough to learn in small bursts, and clearly marked examples illustrate each topic.

With the knowledge you've gained from reading this book, you can probably skip the Beginner and Intermediate sections; head straight to the Advanced information http://www.htmldog.com/guides/htmladvanced/, where you can learn a new set of XHTML elements that we didn't cover in the earlier chapters.

A List Apart

A List Apart (ALA) is an old favorite among the web design community. Unlike the other web sites I mentioned above, this one does not teach in modules; instead it takes more of a magazine-like approach—each feature is written as a complete piece

---

[4] Patrick refers to HTML, but all the examples shown are XHTML-compliant.

that either tackles a known problem or explains a creative idea to inspire others. The web site sorts its various articles (of which there are many) into categories: look for *HTML and XHTML* at http://alistapart.com/topics/code/htmlxhtml/.

You'll find links to a number of useful articles on that page. Some of the material will cross over into other technologies that you may not fully understand at this point (some of the articles on ALA focus on cutting-edge techniques), but you will almost certainly find inspiration from the articles on A List Apart.

Advancing Your CSS Knowledge

At this point, I think I'm obliged by web design convention simply to blurt out the following web address for CSS Zen Garden: http://csszengarden.com/.

More than anything, this web site demonstrates what CSS can do when it's placed in the right hands. I had intended to structure this section so that the official documentation was referred to first, followed by other examples. However, like the many thousands who've tried to promote greater use of CSS on web sites, I can't help but turn to this site first.

Canadian web designer Dave Shea created CSS Zen Garden back in 2003 because he felt, at that time, that the examples of CSS-based designs were less than encouraging. Boxy, boring, and generally unsexy. In short, the people who understood the CSS language were technical people first, and designers second (or even third or fourth). Dave approached CSS primarily as a designer, and a coder second. He launched CSS Zen Garden with a handful of his own designs—any one of them much more inspiring than contemporary offerings—then encouraged others to contribute designs based on the same document. Many years later, the site's archives contain literally hundreds of designs that prove that when you separate the presentation of a document from its structural foundation, you have a very powerful tool at your disposal. Figure 11.2 shows just a few examples of designs from CSS Zen Garden. Dave Shea's first version—which kicked it all off—appears top left.

Figure 11.2. A selection of styles from CSS Zen Garden

The key point to remember is that all the designs above use *the same underlying document*. All that changes between each design is the linked style sheet (which will refer to a different set of typographic styles, color palettes, and background images).

The CSS Zen Garden was intended to provide inspiration, and it really does its job well! If you see a design on the site that you like and want to look more closely under the hood to learn how it was done, just click on the link that reads **View This Design's CSS**.

The Official Documentation

We're back on track again with the official information. If you've taken a look at some of the work submitted to CSS Zen Garden, you might have spotted some fairly advanced CSS that you're eager to understand. As with XHTML, no source of information is more complete than that maintained by the W3C in its Cascading Style Sheets (CSS) Specification, at http://www.w3.org/TR/CSS21/.[5]

---

[5] This link refers to CSS level 2, revision 1. There are different versions of the CSS recommendations, as there are versions of other W3C documents. At the time of writing, the CSS2.1 documentation was

As with the XHTML document I mentioned earlier, the W3C CSS Specification is another highly detailed piece of documentation that's an involved read. It's very useful as a reference for those moments when you come unstuck with CSS. But where could you go for some information that's a little easier on the old brain-box? You know where this is going, don't you?

The Ultimate CSS Reference

Just as SitePoint offers a complete HTML reference for your reading pleasure, it also offers a complete—I'm sorry, I mean *Ultimate*—CSS reference. This is also available as a hardback book from SitePoint (see http://www.sitepoint.com/books/cssref1/, so you can keep it open as you work to check anything that's bugging you.

Figure 11.3. The SitePoint CSS Reference

It's also available as an online reference—known as the SitePoint CSS Reference and found at http://reference.sitepoint.com/css/—as shown in Figure 11.3. You can

---

labeled a *Candidate Recommendation*, which translates as "almost 100% approved." In other words, it's safe to use these as your benchmark.

use the thoughtfully organized navigation menus or type some text into the search field and see what it finds for you.

HTML Dog

HTML Dog also has a CSS section. You'll know some of the CSS tricks in the intermediate tutorial (found at http://www.htmldog.com/guides/cssintermediate/), but it contains other useful tips that you should pick up before moving onto the advanced section.

CSS Discussion Lists

You can learn a great deal from web site tutorials like those I've mentioned, but what happens if you have a question about specific issue? In previous chapters, I've suggested that you raise issues on SitePoint's CSS forum.[6] If you explain that you're a newbie, you should find that forum members will make a real effort to assist you, providing very clear instructions to help solve your problem. You'll probably find that this forum (along with the other SitePoint forums) has so many experts ready to respond to your questions that you likely won't need to venture much further afield for help.

There are other discussion lists that you could join if you want to further your CSS skills. The two that I'd recommend are:

- CSS-Discuss, at http://www.css-discuss.org/
- Web Design-L, at http://webdesign-l.com/

These lists tend to go more heavily into the nitty-gritty of CSS issues, and uninitiated observers can, at times, feel as if they've gate-crashed a rocket scientists' convention. These people really do know their stuff, but they're not always so easygoing on the beginners. So my advice is:

- Register first, then lurk (watch the discussions that come through, and see what goes on before contributing) for a while.

- When you decide to ask a question, be sure to prefix it with "I'm a newbie."

---

[6] http://www.sitepoint.com/launch/cssforum/

■ When you reply to comments, take care with your quoting style. The preferred style (which most email programs don't do for you automatically, unfortunately) is to use top-down quoting.[7]

 Discussion Lists versus Forums

Just what is the difference between a discussion list and a forum? A discussion list is a group that operates via email, and subscribers receive either separate emails for each post that's made by a group member, or a digest of the communications daily, weekly, or monthly. A forum, on the other hand, is a web-based service. That is, you use a web browser to log in to the forum, then pick and choose from the categories to read whichever posts take your fancy.

Which is better? Well, that depends on the way you like to learn. Some people prefer discussion lists because they can store the emails they receive, then search through archived messages to find specific solutions as the need arises. Others prefer to be able to dip into forums as they please, and avoid having their inboxes clogged up with messages.

The best advice I can give you is to try out a discussion list and see how it goes. If you find the amount of messages you receive too overwhelming, you could try sorting the mail into dedicated folders (check your mail client for rules that let you divert mail based on certain criteria). If that doesn't work out, you could try a digest, or even unsubscribe altogether. But you won't know if discussion lists suit you unless you give them a try, so be sure to give them a go!

Other CSS Resources

While most modern browsers do a very good job of understanding CSS and rendering the results on the screen,[8] there are some inconsistencies between browsers. One notable problem relates to early versions of Internet Explorer on Windows. Versions prior to IE6 calculated the widths of block elements incorrectly when a block contained padding or borders. Sometimes, the differences were slight; at other times (when large padding and border values were used), the different rendering caused

---

[7] Matt Haughey offers excellent advice in "How to Write Effective Mailing List Email" [http://www.digital-web.com/articles/how_to_write_effective_mailing_list_email], a piece written for *Digital Web magazine*. Look for point two: Top Down Formatting.

[8] And also on printouts—it's possible to target different CSS styles to different media types. See the SitePoint CSS Reference [http://reference.sitepoint.com/css/linkingcss/] for an easygoing introduction to the topic.

a page layout to break completely on IE, while rendering as expected on other, more standards-compliant browsers. You can learn more about this specific problem here in the discussion of the Box Model Hack at: http://css-discuss.incutio.com/?page=BoxModelHack.

The good news, though, is that the number of people using IE5.5 or earlier is extremely small now. If you think about it, it's a browser 2.5 versions behind the times! Many sites have either completely dropped support for these older IE versions or offer functional support only. This phrase may be understood a number of ways by different sites or companies, but basically means: if the site technically works but looks a bit of a mess, we can live with that. The numbers may be small, but there are still people out there using it, so it's good to at least have a heads-up on this old, lingering problem.

Enter the Hacks

One way to work around browser inconsistencies is to use CSS hacks. Essentially, these are purposely mangled pieces of CSS code that only some browsers are capable of interpreting. (Technically, this is known as **parsing** and refers to the browser's ability to understand the code and therefore render the display.) Meanwhile, other browsers won't be so tolerant when it comes to parsing that mangled CSS—they'll simply fail to apply that style and move onto the next CSS selector instead.

Designers have discovered many different types of hacks, each of which can be used to target specific browser issues. They generally look quite ugly in your CSS markup—though that's helpful as it makes them stand out more—and can be difficult to understand at first.

There's a good explanation of how to apply the many different kinds of hacks on the SitePoint CSS Reference: http://reference.sitepoint.com/css/workaroundsfiltershacks/.

The thorny topic of CSS hacks is also covered in Rachel Andrew's book, *The CSS Anthology: 101 Essential Tips, Tricks & Hacks.*[9]

---

[9] http://www.sitepoint.com/books/cssant2/

A Word of Warning regarding Hacks

Hacks should be your last resort to solving CSS dilemmas. A hack exploits a browser's shortcomings—its inability to work out a solution—and this is dangerous to rely on. As new browsers are released, the CSS programming behind those browsers can be changed or fixed—and when a hack is fixed, it ironically, *breaks* numerous web sites. Indeed, this was the case when IE7 was released, and that won't be the last time either.[10]

Here are a few simple rules to follow:

- Before resorting to hacks, you *must* verify that your CSS is valid.[11] A problem that appears in just one browser might be due to a typing error that doesn't cause problems in other browsers. The validator will pick up this kind of fault, removing the need to use a hack.

- You can write CSS in ways that prevent your needing to resort to hacks. Try some of these tips for avoiding hacks[12] before you use them.

- If you must use hacks, be careful about how you apply them. Molly Holzschlag provides a number of useful tips that you should take on board in her article, *Integrated Web Design: Strategies for Long-Term CSS Hack Management.*[13]

Are hacks a necessary evil? Well, not to the extent they were just a few years ago. Most browsers have moved on and the playing field is much more level. The usual culprit where CSS errors are concerned is Internet Explorer, although it's improved noticeably with each new version released. If you find that your web site looks great in all browsers installed on your machine (and I *do* recommend installing more than one for the purposes of testing) except IE, you are probably best to make use of IE-specific Conditional Comments[14].

The CSS Discuss List's Companion Site

The CSS Discuss list has a companion **wiki** (a page that can be edited or updated by anyone) that features an archive of best practices discovered in various email

---

[10] See the IEBlog's *Call to action: The demise of CSS hacks and broken pages* [http://blogs.msdn.com/ie/archive/2005/10/12/480242.aspx].

[11] Which you can do at http://jigsaw.w3.org/css-validator/.

[12] http://css-discuss.incutio.com/?page=AvoidingHacks

[13] http://www.informit.com/articles/article.asp?p=170511

[14] http://reference.sitepoint.com/css/conditionalcomments

discussions. Members of the mailing list frequently update the content displayed here. The information is not as ordered as it is in the sites I mentioned previously (at resources such as SitePoint and HTML Dog), but it will make sense once you've had a little more exposure to intermediate and advanced CSS. On the wiki's front page, at http://css-discuss.incutio.com, you'll find links to explanations of a number of good practices, and tips for improving your CSS to expert level.

I recommend you take a closer look at these sections:

Font Size great advice on how to size fonts consistently across a range of browsers

CSS Layouts methodologies and examples of various CSS layout techniques, such as two- and three-column layouts, and techniques to position footers that always align correctly

Media Types more tips on how to make the most of the different media types for which you can hone your CSS

Style Switching all the information and links you need in order to incorporate a *style switcher* into your web site (so that you can have more than one style sheet for users to choose from, according to their specific needs)

If you make web sites like these your regular haunts, you'll be well on your way to becoming a CSS guru. Perhaps I'll be reading one of your books on the topic one day?

Learning JavaScript

The next logical step after you learn XHTML and CSS is to take on a client-side scripting language. What's *client-side* all about? Client-side scripts are sets of instructions that are run on the client machine—that's the computer that displays the web page—rather than processing by the server. The most obvious choice here is a language called JavaScript.[15]

---

[15] It is possible to run a similar language called VBScript, but it's not widely supported as a client-side language, and I can't recommend it for use on a web site as some browsers do not provide built-in support for it. I mention it here so that you are, at least, aware of its existence.

Unusually, I'm going to recommend that you *don't* refer to any official documentation on this language because, frankly, I don't think it's the best way to learn JavaScript (it's the best way to be scared off, though). Once more, I find myself attracted to the modular, step-by-step approach that W3Schools takes in teaching JavaScript, at its Learn JavaScript[16] page. I wish that I'd been able to learn in such a nice way when I began to tinker with this language!

With JavaScript, the possibilities are limited only by your imagination. If you find yourself thinking, "I'd like that part of the web page to be moveable," or, "I want to be able to hide this part of the web page at the click of a button," JavaScript will let you do it.

Compared with HTML and CSS, though, JavaScript is quite complicated. This is partly because JavaScript is very unforgiving when it comes to typing errors—one missing semi-colon, and your whole script may break—and partly because no one can anticipate what tasks you're going to ask JavaScript to achieve on your site. Hence, teaching it can never be as focused or strictly defined as other topics.

To my mind, the budding JavaScripter would be best to do the following:

- Run through the W3Schools tutorial, and be sure to try out all the examples to have a feel for what the language can do.

- Think about a practical use for JavaScript on your own web site (having run through the tutorial, you should have a feel for how you might utilize this technology). Then, try putting it into action.

- Trawl through SitePoint's extensive back catalogue of JavaScript-related articles,[17] beginning with Kevin Yank's JavaScript 101.[18]

- Be sure to ask any questions you have about JavaScript at SitePoint's dedicated JavaScript forum.[19]

---

[16] http://www.w3schools.com/js/js_intro.asp
[17] All SitePoint's JavaScript articles are listed at http://www.sitepoint.com/subcat/javascript.
[18] http://www.sitepoint.com/article/javascript-101-1
[19] http://www.sitepoint.com/launch/javascriptforum/

▨ Naturally, SitePoint has a great book for you: Kevin Yank and Cameron Adams have compiled everything you need for learning JavaScript from scratch in *Simply JavaScript.*[20]

When you've spent some time playing around with JavaScript, and you're ready for more, look again to SitePoint. They have a book that will take you beyond the intermediate level, and into the realms of the expert! That book is titled *DHTML Utopia: Modern Web Design Using JavaScript & DOM.*[21]

Another option is to try a JavaScript library. In programming, a library is a set of ready-made functions and scripts that you reference on your web page (by linking to the library .js file); this enables you to write relatively simple scripts that leverage some hardcore JavaScript wizardry. It's beyond the scope of this book to cover these, but there's a quick run-down of the various merits of some of the libraries in the SitePoint article The JavaScript Library World Cup.[22] Personally, I have a real soft spot for a library called jQuery,[23] which makes it very easy to enhance a web page if you know a little bit of CSS (jQuery uses similar concepts for selecting elements on the page). All that said, though, it's better to learn some *real* JavaScript first before opting for a library (otherwise you'll never really gain a good understanding of how it all works and fits together).

Learning Server-side Programming

The final part of this road map to becoming an all-round web designer and developer involves server-side programming (or server-side scripting). While JavaScript is downloaded to the client computer and executed there, server-side scripts are executed on the server *before* the resulting web page is sent to the client. We use these types of scripting in different ways, but generally, you can assume the following:

▨ JavaScript is best used to change the display or behavior of elements on the screen in front of you. Depending on what the script does, even if you disconnected your Internet connection, the JavaScript may quite happily continue to function, as it's running locally on your computer within a page that's already downloaded to your hard drive.

---

[20] http://www.sitepoint.com/books/phpmysql1/
[21] http://www.sitepoint.com/books/dhtml1/
[22] http://www.sitepoint.com/article/javascript-library/
[23] http://jquery.com/

■ Server-side programming is best used to retrieve or update information stored in a database, and to generate a web page based on that information. With server-side programming, a site user's action might be intended to change a record in your database. Thus, a server-side language is essential for tasks such as checking stock levels on an ecommerce site, and adjusting them if an order is placed. JavaScript alone could not achieve this.

Of course you could use both, for example, in a web page that's generated dynamically based on certain search criteria. A search on an ecommerce web site—such as Amazon—that displayed a selection of toasters would use server-side scripting to build the search results page, which would be sent for display on the client computer. JavaScript could then be used on the client computer to manipulate that web page in some way, perhaps allowing the user to drag and drop items into a shopping cart.[24]

In fact, the lines between client-side and server-side scripting are being increasingly blurred, thanks largely to **Ajax**. No, it's not a cleaning product (well, it is, just not here) but a fancy buzzword for a collection of techniques that make use of the aforementioned scripting to create dynamic changes to the page. Using Ajax, it's possible to let JavaScript manipulate sections on a page and ask the server to process small parts of code, then update the page without forcing a complete page reload. It's difficult to explain, so at this point I usually refer to Google Maps. It may not surprise you to know that when you load Google Maps, it doesn't load all of the country's maps in one go! It loads the content for the current window and some surrounding areas; then, as you click and drag on the map, JavaScript sends a request to the server to fetch the next parts of the map before you need them, updating the page without you realizing. It's not necessary to reload the whole page. That's a great example of Ajax in action right there.

Scripting Languages in Brief

Your options for server-side programming are many. All the languages below could be used to create dynamic web pages and retrieve information from databases:

■ PHP

■ ASP/ASP.NET

---

[24] There's a great example of this kind of drag-and-drop behavior on Panic's web site [http://www.panic.com/].

- ColdFusion
- Perl
- Python
- Ruby/Ruby on Rails

There are many more in addition to this short list, believe me! Which one's right for you, though. This is where we start to veer into dangerous territory! The proponents of each language will swear blind that their language is the best tool for the job. In reality, each has its pros and cons, and some do a better job in certain circumstances than others. I can't list the strengths and weaknesses of all of them here—it would take far too long, and only confuse matters at this stage.

My advice would be to find out which languages your hosting company supports; that will refine your options quite quickly—there's little point in learning a scripting language only to find out that it won't work with your current hosting provider. If you're not sure which way to go next you can always post questions to SitePoint's Program Your Site forum[25]—explain your requirements and your level of expertise, and you can expect to receive sound advice on which language is best suited to your needs, and why.

Learning PHP

Of those languages listed above, I would recommend that you make PHP your first server-side language, because it's:

- intuitive and fairly easy to learn
- highly configurable and flexible
- a great companion language for MySQL (a free, fully-featured database software)
- very widely supported by hosting providers (cheap PHP hosting is easy to find)
- portable—PHP can be run on Windows, Mac OS, and Linux, so if you switch platforms it won't be an issue (unlike ASP/ASP.NET)

---

[25] Actually, this page is a collection of SitePoint's sub-forums [http://www.sitepoint.com/launch/programsiteforum/] that deal with specific languages—it's your best starting point for this kind of query.

Where Can You Learn PHP?

It's beyond the scope of this book for me to teach you how to create a site in PHP—or any other language, for that matter—but thankfully there are many books that do exactly that. Once again, SitePoint has covered this for you: Kevin Yank, an acknowledged PHP expert, is the author of *Build Your Own Database Driven Website Using PHP & MySQL*.[26] If you want to build on the knowledge you've gained in this book to create dynamic web sites, Kevin's book is the logical next step.

If, having done some research, you decide to build your site using Microsoft's .NET Framework,[27] SitePoint can help you with this, too: *Build Your Own ASP.NET 3.5 Website Using C# & VB.NET*,[28] by Zak Ruvalcaba, will tell you everything you need to know in order to build a dynamic web site using this technology.

Summary

In this chapter, I've provided some pointers as to how you can take your web skills to the next level. I've suggested resources that will help you refine your XHTML and CSS skills to perfection, highlighted JavaScript as a very practical addition to your virtual toolbox, and promoted scripting languages as a means to creating killer web sites. However, the path you choose from this point on is entirely up to you. All I hope is that you've enjoyed the steps you've taken to reach this point, and that I've set you up well for the journey ahead. Happy coding!

---

[26] http://www.sitepoint.com/books/phpmysql1/
[27] http://en.wikipedia.org/wiki/.NET
[28] http://www.sitepoint.com/books/aspnet3/

Index

Symbols

(number sign), 99

, (comma), 101

; (semicolon), 73

{} (curly braces), 76

"" (quotation marks), 84

A

a (anchor) element, 62–65

A List Apart web site, 411

absolute positioning

using, 151–161, 162–164

accessibility (*see* web accessibility)

action attribute, 253

addresses (*see* URLs)

alignment

tables, 230

alpha channel transparency, 185

alt attribute, 178

anchors (*see* links)

anonymous comments

blogs, 364

Apache web server, 319

assistive devices

about, 227

screen readers, 97

attributes

(*see also* specific)

defined, 26

sharing ids, 52

B

background images, 210–221

height and width, 216

for navigation area, 218–221

non-repeating images, 214

repeated patterns, 210

shorthand backgrounds, 216

for tables, 240

background-color property, 88, 92

bandwidth

defined, 309

web hosting, 317

best practices

warning about copying from other web
sites, 21

block-level elements, 118–135

borders, 128–135

IE width bug, 416

margins, 145

sizing, 124–128

versus inline elements, 118–124

blockquote element, 66

Blogger, 340, 343–374

Blogroll, 399–405

blogs, 339–376

Blogger, 343–374

Blogroll, 399–405

contributions to, 374

defined, 340

services for, 340

body element, 30, 82

bold border effects

block-level elements, 131

bookmarks

web forwarding services and, 312

border property

absolute positioning and, 152

borders
    block-level elements, 128–135
    padding, 142–145
    tables, 230
Box Model Hack, 417
box models
    block-level elements, 146
br (break) element, 69
browsers
    appearance of web pages in, 321
    block quotes, 68
    clearing history, 108
    CSS hacks and, 417
    Firefox, 7, 9
    hiding markup using comments, 38
    Internet Explorer, 4
    page loading, 227
    refreshing page view, 85
    Safari, 5
    title bar, 26
    web site statistics, 390
buttons (*see* radio buttons; submit buttons)

C

caching
    in browsers, 85
caption element, 193
captioning
    image galleries, 193–198
captions
    tables, 234
case sensitivity
    tags, 33
cells
    merging, 242
    spacing, 231

styling, 241
character sets
    defining with meta elements, 29
checkboxes
    forms, 259, 284
cite (citation) element, 68
class attributes, 374
class selectors
    about, 109–112
classes
    (*see also* pseudo-classes)
    contact class, 274
    limiting to specific elements, 111
    naming, 129
    span class, 113
    styling partial text using span element,
        113
    styling tables, 232
"Click here" links, 63
client-side scripting, 419–421
Client–Server Model, 307
codes
    for symbols, 39
color
    background-color property, 88
    borders, 135
    hexadecimal numbers for, 88
    for links in browsers, 104
    text, 241
colspan attribute, 243
column-based layouts, 419
comma (,), 101
commenting out
    XHTML, 38
comments
    blogs, 364
    XHTML, 36

compatibility
  HTML versions, 23
contact class, 274
contact pages
  building, 268–288
containing elements, 118
content
  inside div elements, 50
contextual selectors
  about, 100
controls
  forms, 255, 274
Crop, 200
CSS, 414
  current version, 413
  design examples, 412
  discussion lists, 415
  resources, 412–419
CSS (Cascading Style Sheets)
  defined, 72
  prior to CSS, 78
The CSS Anthology: 101 Essential Tips,
    Tricks & Hacks, 175
CSS floats, 168
CSS hacks, 417–418
CSS Zen Garden, 412
CSS-Discuss, 415, 418
Ctrl key, 264
curly braces ({}), 76
Cyberduck, 327

D

Dashboard, Blogger, 355
dashed borders
  block-level elements, 133
data
  (*see also* tables)

processing forms, 269, 289
databases
  scripting languages, 320
  web hosting, 319
declarations
  border styles, 134
  defined, 72
  examples of, 88
defaults
  emphasis and strong elements, 69
  form appearance in different browsers,
    266
deleting
  commenting out as an alternative to,
    38
directories (*see* folders)
discussion forums
  about, 404
  distinguished from lists, 416
  HTML and XHTML, 335
  posting on, 337
  SitePoint, 17
discussion lists, 415, 416
div element, 50, 275
div tag, 56
diving site example
  shaping and sizing, 136–148
Dock (Mac OS X)
  dragging applications to, 6
doctype (short for Document Type
    Definition), 23
doctype switching, 147
documentation
  image editors, 206
domain names
  defined, 309

dotted borders
   block-level elements, 132
double borders
   block-level elements, 133
downloads
   image editors, 10
   page layouts using tables, 227
   Picasa, 12
dynamic content, 424

E

editing
   (*see also* HTML editors; image editors;
      text editors)
   images, 198–206
elastic web design, 167
elements, 24–32, 62–70
   (*see also* XHTML elements)
   a (anchor) element, 62–65
   block-level versus inline, 118–124
   blockquote element, 66
   body element, 30, 82
   br (break) element, 69
   cite (citation) element, 68
   coding using editors, 30
   context of, 97–100
   div element, 50, 275
   em (emphasis) element, 68
   emphasis element, 38
   fieldset element, 254, 270
   form element, 250, 252, 270
   h1 (main header) element, 220
   head element, 26
   html element, 24
   img (image) element, 48, 178
   input element, 255–262
   label element, 255, 256, 278

legend element, 254, 272
li (unordered list) element, 34
limiting classes to specific elements,
   111
link element, 80
meta element, 28
nesting, 54–57
ol (ordered list) element, 34
p (paragraph) element, 34, 275
positioning, 148–161
pre element, 56
select element, 262, 280
strong element, 68
textarea element, 264, 282
title element, 27, 313
elements, XHTML
   HTML Dog and, 411
em (emphasis) element, 68
email
   clickable links, 48
   folders, 416
   in forms, 303
   preferred discussion list styles, 416
   signatures, 337
   web hosting, 318
embedded style sheets, 76–78
emphasis element, 38
emphasized text, 93
empty elements
   self-closing, 29
entities
   as replacement for symbols, 39
event table example, 235–241
examples
   background images, 210–221
   basic skeleton web page, 22
   basic web page with content, 31

block-level elements, 119

Blogger, 356–374

Blogroll, 402

body element in style sheet, 82

body elements, 30

borders for block-level elements, 129–
134

commenting out, 38

comments, 37

embedded styles, 76

external CSS file, 79

forms, 251–302

homepage, 41–57

image gallery, 187–198, 206

inline elements, 121–122

linking CSS to web pages, 80

linking web pages, 64

meta elements, 28

nesting div elements, 54

padding and margins, 136–148

positioning, 148–161, 162–173

Rollyo, 396

search tool, 390

sizing up blocks, 124–126

splitting up web pages, 60

statistics code, 386

style sheet styles, 86–114

symbols, 39

tables, 229–246

unordered lists, 35

welcoming new visitors, 43

extensions

files, 58

image files, 183

external style sheets, 78–81

creating, 79

linking to web pages, 80

Extreme Tracking service, 380

F

fade

tag lines, 219

fieldset element, 254, 270

file extensions

image files, 183

viewing, 58

filenames

for style sheets, 103

files

size of, 317

uploading files to, 321–330

FileZilla, 322

Firefox, 7, 9

forms, 266

Flickr, 209

floated positioning

using, 168–174

flow-on effects, 192

folders

My Documents folder, 14

Sites folder, 16

font sizing, 419

font-family property, 82, 92

fonts

viewing on-screen, 83

font-size property, 92

font-style property, 93

font-weight property, 93

footers, 419

form element, 250, 252, 270

formatting

image galleries, 191

forms, 249–306

about, 250

contact pages, 268–288

    sample code for, 289–305

    simple form example, 251

forums (*see* discussion forums)

forwarding (*see* web forwarding)

frames

    web forwarding, 312

FTP (File Transfer Protocol)

    defined, 309

    publishing blogs, 352

    settings for, 322

    web hosting, 314

G

galleries

    image galleries, 187–198

    thumbnail galleries, 208

genre

    searching by, 393–398

get method versus post method, 253

GIF image format, 184

Google accounts, 380

Google Analytics, 380, 388

Google Search, 253, 393

GraphicConverter, 12, 202

grouping

    styles, 101

H

h1 (main header) element, 220

hacks, CSS, 417–418

head element, 26

headings

    CSS, 84

    document hierarchy, 33

versus id attribute value of "header", 53

height

    background images, 216

    block-level elements, 125

height attribute, 178

help

    SitePoint forums, 17

hexadecimal numbers, 88

hidden inputs, 259

hierarchy

    headings in document, 33

history

    clearing in browser, 108

homepages

    about, 41–57

    nesting, 54–57

    paragraphs, 44

    splitting, 57–62

    structure, 50

    subheadings, 43

    title, 42

horizontal repeats

    background images, 211

hosting (*see* web hosting)

hover state

    defined, 105

href attribute, 62, 80

HTML

    (*see also* web pages; XHTML)

    compatibility, 23

    discussion forum, 335

HTML Dog, 411

HTML editors

    NoteTab, 7

html element, 24

HTML elements
  presentational, 97
HTML5 specification, 23
HTTPS
  security, 258

I

id attribute, 257
  sharing of, 52
  versus class attribute, 111
image editors, 9–13
  documentation, 206
  GraphicConverter, 12
  iPhoto, 13
  Picasa, 11
image galleries
  adding, 187–198
  thumbnail galleries, 208
images, 177–222
  (*see also* background images)
  captioning, 193–198
  editing, 198–206
  file formats, 183
  formatting, 191
  image galleries, 187–198, 206
  inline, 178–183
  sourcing, 209
  transparency, 184
IMAP, 318
img (image) element, 48, 178
indents
  in source markup, 56
inline elements
  versus block-level elements, 118–124
inline styles
  about, 72
  compare to embedded styles, 77

embedded style sheets, 76
input controls
  forms, 274
input element, 255–262
inset borders
  block-level elements, 130
Internet Explorer, 4
  block element rendering in Windows, 416
  clearing history, 108
  empty fieldset elements, 271
  forms, 266
Internet Explores
  box models, 147
iPhoto, 13
italics
  versus emphasis, 97

J

JavaScript, 419–421
JPEG image format, 184

L

label element, 255, 256, 278
languages
  (*see also* scripting languages)
layouts (*see* borders; height; padding; positioning; sizing; width)
legend element, 254, 272
li (unordered list) element, 34
linearization
  tables, 233
line-height property, 89
link element, 80
link exchanges, 338

links
    checking, 330
    email, 48
    external style sheets to web pages, 80
    link text, 62
    styling, 104–108
    web pages, 62–65
lists
    (*see also* discussion lists)
    styling, 174
    unordered, 34
LiveJournal, 341

M

Mac OS X
    Firefox, 9
    GraphicConverter, 12
    iPhoto, 13
    Safari, 5
    Sites folder, 16
    TextEdit, 5
    TextWrangler, 8
mailto: prefix, 48
margins
    block-level elements, 145
markup
    indents in, 56
maxlength attribute, 257
media types, 416, 419
merging
    table cells, 242
meta element, 28
meta tag, 22
method attribute, 252
Microsoft Windows (*see* Windows)
moderators
    discussion forums, 404

mouse
    submitting forms, 265
Movable Type, 342
My Documents folder, 14, 325

N

name attribute, 257
names
    (*see also* domain names)
    attributes, 26
naming
    classes, 129
navigation
    background images, 218–221
    image galleries, 187
navigation area
    location of, 162
    size of, 127
nesting
    elements, 54–57
    fieldset elements, 254
    inline elements, 121
non-repeating images
    background images, 214
Notepad, 3
NoteTab, 7
number sign (#), 99
numbers, hexadecimal, 88

O

ol (ordered list) element, 34
Open Directory Project, 336
options
    selecting, 262

OS X (*see* Mac OS X)

P

p (paragraph) element, 34, 275
padding
    borders, 142–145
padding property, 90
    removing for absolute positioning, 152
pages (*see* web pages)
paragraphs
    creating, 44–49
    p (paragraph) element, 34
password input control, 258
Photo Gallery, 11
photos (*see* images)
PHP language, 423
    (*see also* server-side scripting)
Picasa, 11, 199
pixels
    defined, 90
planning, 2
plug-ins
    blogging services, 341
PNG image format, 184
POP3, 318
positioning
    absolute, 151–161, 162–164
    elements, 148–161
    relative, 164–168
    types of, 162–174
post method versus get method, 253
pre element, 56
preselecting
    checkboxes, 260
    options, 263
    radio buttons, 262

presentational HTML elements
    emphasis versus italics, 97
print style sheets, 416
project planning, 2
promoting
    web sites, 335–338
properties
    defined, 73
pseudo-classes
    link states, 105
publishing
    blogs, 350

Q

quirks mode
    Internet Explorer, 147
quotation marks (""), 84
quotations
    discussion list replies, 416

R

radio buttons
    forms, 261, 284
refreshing
    page view in browsers, 85
relative positioning
    using, 164–168
repeated patterns
    background images, 210
resizing
    images, 198, 204
resources (*see* documentation; services)
    CSS, 412–419
    XHTML, 408–412
ridge borders
    block-level elements, 130

Rollyo, 393

rowspan attribute, 243

royalty-free images, 209

rules

    block-level and inline elements, 118

    defined, 76

S

Safari, 5

    forms, 268

sans-serif fonts

    viewing on-screen, 83

scope attribute, 244

screen readers, 181

    presentational HTML elements, 97

    summary attribute and, 234

scripting

    web hosting, 319

scripting languages

    client-side scripting, 419–421

    server-side scripting, 421–424

search engines

    presentational HTML elements, 97

    submitting web sites to, 336

    title element, 28

    web forwarding and framesets, 313

    for web sites, 390–398

Secure FTP, 314

security

    password input control, 258

select element, 262, 280

selectors

    class selectors, 109–112

    defined, 76

self-closing elements

    defined, 29

self-closing tags, 29

semicolon (;), 73

serif fonts

    viewing on-screen, 83

servers

    defined, 308

server-side scripting, 421–424

    client-side and, 421

    languages, 422

server-side scripting languages, 319

services

    for blogs, 340

shortcuts

    to Notepad, 3

sides

    block-level elements, 133

signatures

    email, 337

SitePoint forums, 17

    scripting languages, 420, 423

Sites folder, 16

size attribute, 257

sizing

    diving site example, 136–148

source

    indents in, 56

    viewing, 20

sourcing

    images, 209

spacing

    cells, 231

    tables, 230

spam

    blog comments, 364

span class, 113

span element, 74, 194

special effects

    images, 203

specificity
  class selectors, 112
splitting
  web pages, 57–62
src attribute, 178
SSIs (Server Side Includes)
  web hosting, 319
states
  links, 105
statistics
  web site visitors, 378–390
storage
  web hosting, 315
strong element, 68
structure
  web pages, 22, 50–53
style attribute, 72
style sheets, 81–114
  (*see also* external style sheets)
  adding styles, 86
  class selectors, 109–112
  elements in context, 97–100
  embedded, 76–78
  filenames for, 103
  grouping styles, 101
  headings, 84
  links, 104–108
  partial text, 113
  style declarations, 88–93
style switching, 419
styles
  (*see also* inline styles)
  adding, 86
  grouping, 101
subheadings
  creating, 43

submit buttons
  forms, 265, 286
submitting
  web sites to search engines, 336
summary attribute, 234
symbols
  XHTML, 39

T

tables, 223–247
  about, 224–230
  cells, 241–244
  styling, 230–233
  web accessibility, 233–241, 244
tag lines
  fade, 219
tags
  div tag, 56
  meta tag, 22
  symmetry of, 122
  XHTML elements, 24
templates
  Blogger, 354–372
testing (*see* validating)
text
  color, 241
  emphasized, 93
  input controls in forms, 274
  input in forms, 256
  link text, 62
  sizing, 91
  styling, 113
text boxes
  initial value, 258
text editors
  Notepad, 3
  NoteTab, 7

TextEdit, 5
TextWrangler, 8
textarea element, 264, 282
text-decoration property, 93
TextEdit, 5
Textpattern, 342
TextWrangler, 8
The Ultimate CSS Reference, 414
The Ultimate HTML Reference, 410
thickness
    borders, 135
thumbnail galleries, 208
title bar
    displaying in browser, 26
title element, 27, 313
titles
    setting, 42
tools, 3–13
    Firefox, 7, 9
    GraphicConverter, 12
    Internet Explorer, 4
    iPhoto, 13
    Mac OS X, 5–6, 8–9, 12–13, 16
    Notepad, 3
    NoteTab, 7
    Picasa, 11
    Safari, 5
    TextEdit, 5
    TextWrangler, 8
    web site search, 390–398
    Windows, 3–4, 7, 11–12, 14
top-down formatting, 416
traffic
    web site statistics, 389
transparency
    images, 184
type attribute, 257

U

unordered lists, 34
uploading
    files to web server, 321–330
URLs (Uniform Resource Locators)
    defined, 24
    from hosting service, 310
user folders (Windows Vista)
    displaying, 15
UTF-8
    importance of, 32

V

validating
    blogs, 369–372
    web pages, 331–335
validation
    CSS hacks and, 418
value attribute, 258
values
    attributes, 26
    defined, 73
vertical repeats
    background images, 214
viewport
    defined, 90
visitors
    web site statistics, 389
    to web sites, 378–390
Vista (see Windows)

W

W3C (World Wide Web Consortium)
    about, 24
    CSS Specification, 413
    XHTML recommendations, 409

W3C Markup Validation Service, 332
W3C's Link Checker, 330
W3Schools, 420
web accessibility
    images, 180–183
    tables, 233–241, 244
web browsers (*see* browsers)
Web Design-L, 415
web forwarding
    about, 311
    email, 318
web hosting, 309–320
    bandwidth, 317
    defined, 309
    email accounts, 318
    FTP access to server, 314
    jargon, 309
    paying for, 314
    scripting languages and databases, 319
    server space, 309
    SSIs, 319
    storage, 315
    web forwarding, 311
web pages
    about, 19
    appearance in different browsers, 321
    basic structure, 22
    creating with Blogger, 352
    image galleries, 188
    linking external style sheets to, 80
    links, 62–65
    loading, 227
    merging Blogger code with, 358–368
    nesting structure, 54–57
    refreshing in browsers, 85
    splitting, 57–62
    statistics code, 386

validating, 331–335
view source, 20
web sites, 307–338
    (*see also* URLs)
    blogs, 399–405
    checking links, 330
    Client–Server Model, 307
    homepages, 41–57
    hosting, 309–320
    promoting, 335–338
    storing, 14–16
    uploading files to server, 321–330
    visitor statistics, 378–390
web standards, 407
webmail, 318
width
    background images, 216
    block-level elements, 124
width attribute, 178
"wiki" pages, 419
Windows
    file extensions, 58
    Firefox, 7
    Internet Explorer, 4
    My Documents folder, 14
    Notepad, 3
    NoteTab, 7
    Picasa, 11
Windows Live Spaces, 341
WordPress, 341

X

XHTML, 19–40
    basic web page example, 31
    comments, 36
    discussion forum, 335
    doctype, 23

elements, 24–32

headings and document hierarchy, 33

lists, 34

paragraphs, 34

resources, 408–412

symbols, 39

validation and CSS, 332

viewing source, 20

web page requirements, 22

XHTML 1.0 recommendation, 409

XHTML 1.0 Strict doctype, 332

XHTML elements

using as intended, 51

Y

Yahoo Groups, 405